MW01229724

Contents

Instructor's Manual

Cost Control in the Hospitality Industry

Agnes L. DeFranco • *Pender B.M. Noriega*

PRENTICE HALL, Upper Saddle River, New Jersey 07458

© 2000 Prentice-Hall, Inc.
Upper Saddle River, NJ 07458

10 9 8 7 6 5 4 3 2 1

ISBN 0-13-756503-8
Printed in the United States of America

Acknowledgments

The authors would like to thank Alan T. Stutts, Dean of the Conrad N. Hilton College for his support and cooperation throughout the preparation of this text. Many thanks also go to Clinton L. Rappole, Douglas C. Keister, Cathleen Baird, Mary Wollin, and James Wortman for the materials and assistance into making this project a reality. Our gratitude also goes to Cheryl Adam, Barb Cassel, and Neil Marquardt at Prentice Hall for their invaluable and kind comments and suggestions in all phases of the text. Lastly, our sincere appreciation to our students, who challenge us on a daily basis; and our colleagues, who walk with us every step of the way in the education process.

Presentation of the Manual

This instructor's manual is designed to assist an instructor in delivering the material presented in the Cost Control in the Hospitality Industry textbook. The textbook is developed into four sections to provide students and instructors with a convenient means of covering and dealing with related topics of interest. With the common thread of understanding the importance of cost control throughout the text. The information in the manual is presented in the following manner:

1. Purpose of the chapter
2. Overview of the chapter
3. Learning objective
4. Definition of key terms
5. Teaching outline
6. Questions and answers

Placing the chapters into four sections and presenting the manual in this manner should provide instructors with and easy flow of information and presentation.

CHAPTER 1

MANAGING IN THE HOSPITALITY INDUSTRY

I. Purpose of the Chapter

This chapter is designed to provide readers with an overview of the hospitality industry and the demand for managing activities within this industry.

II. Overview of the Chapter

Taking into consideration why so many hospitality businesses fail, this text will attempt to provide managers with the pertinent information to prevent this from happening. By far, the most important element to the success of a business is to initially start with a sound business plan and try to stick to the plan once the business is in operation. There are four different major segments in the hospitality industry: food, tourism, lodging, and entertainment. All of these entities must undergo constant monitoring and control. Elements that are used to evaluate these operations are the income statement and the cost-volume relationship. The uniform systems of accounts are usually adopted by most facilities as they allow for easier comparison of national standards.

When comparing national standards, the items that are of the most concern are the prime cost items, which are food, beverage, and labor. The cost of these items and other controllable expenses must be constantly controlled if an operation is to survive.

By examining why some businesses fail while others are able to sustain themselves, managers and business owners can avoid some of the major pitfalls of business failure and become successful.

III. Learning Objectives

Those items that an instructor may wish to convey to the students are as follows:

1.   The six elements to evaluate productivity

     a. The Income Statement
     b. Uniform Systems of Accounts
     c. National Standards
     d. Cost-Volume-Profit Relationship
     e. Controllable and Non-Controllable expenses
     f. Operating Budget

2.   The three managerial attributes that are essential in managing the control function

     a. Professionalism
     b. Effective time management
     c. Accepting responsibility

3.   The four steps in the control cycle

     a. Establish controls or objectives
     b. Inform employees

   c. Evaluate performance
   d. Provide feedback and corrective action

4.   The ABCD classification for the security of products

   The ABCD classification is the placing of products into different categories for the recognition of security. Items placed into category A are those that require the most control and those in category D would require the least amount of control.

5.   The three major activities in sustaining a business operation

   a. Fulfilling a need
   b. Remaining competitive and
   c. Controlling cost

6.   The major reasons for business failure

   a. A lack of working capital
   b. Inexperienced managers
   c. The inability to control operational procedures
   d. The vast amount of competition
   e. Employee theft
   f. Wrong location
   g. Choosing the wrong concept
   h. Inadequate inventory control
   i. Poor credit practices
   j. Taking too much personal income
   k. Having the wrong attitude
   l. Not knowing yourself
   m. Unrealistic expectations
   n. Lack of planning

IV. Definition of Key Terms

ABCD classification – a method for prioritizing the importance for placing security and control methods on products.

Business failure – when revenues being generated by a business operation do not meet the expenses or the financial expectations of the owners which results in the closing or selling of the business.

Contingency planning – alternative plans that should be made available to deal with the fluctuations in business activities.

Control - the managerial function of ensuring that all operational procedures are in accordance with established standards.

Evaluation frequency – refers to how often business operational activities are being evaluated to compare operational activities against budgetary standards.

Four step control cycle – a four-step process in which control objectives are established, employees are made aware, operational procedures are then evaluated, and feedback is given and corrective action is taken if necessary.

Hidden costs – those incidental expenditures that were not given sufficient accountability in funding during budget development.

Life cycle curve – a means of illustrating how a business or products will normally go through the four stages of starting, growing, maturing, and declining.

National standards – are those percentages, especially in the area of prime costs, that are used by industry to gauge how efficient and successful are comparative operations.

Professionalism – conducting oneself in a manner that would be in keeping with organizational procedures and standards without jeopardizing, fraternizing, or compromising ones position and would set standards for employees to emulate.

Staying power – the ability to sustain business operations through the decline phase of the life cycle curve.

Uniform systems of accounts – standard account procedures that are used within a certain industry to allow for easy comparison of operational activities and allow for the smoother transition of managerial personnel throughout the industry.

V. Teaching Outline

A.   Segments of the Industry
B.   Importance of Accountability and Control
     1.   Income Statement
     2.   Uniform System of Accounts
     3.   National Standards
     4.   Cost-Volume-Profit Relationship
     5.   Controllable and Non-controllable Expenses
     6.   Operating Budget
C.   Managerial Attributes
D.   Definition of Controls
     1.   Establishing Controls or Objectives
     2.   Inform Employees
     3.   Evaluate Performance
     4.   Provide Feedback and Corrective Action
E.   What to Control?
F.   The ABCD Classification
     1.   Type of Operation
     2.   Location of Your Operation
     3.   Level of Usage
     4.   Convenience
     5.   Internal System
G.   Staying Power
     1.   Business Failure
     2.   Working Capital

3. Inexperienced Managers
4. The Inability to Control Operational Procedures
5. The Vast Amount of Competition
6. Employee Theft
7. Wrong Location
8. Choosing the Wrong Concept
9. Inventory Control
10. Poor Credit Practices
11. Taking Too Much Personal Income
12. Having the Wrong Attitude
13. Not Knowing Yourself
14. Unrealistic Expectations
15. Lack of Planning

VI. Questions and Answers

Review Exercises

1. For the purpose of control, financial reports in the hospitality industry should be made available for evaluation

    a. quarterly
    b. annually
    c. monthly
    d. as frequent as feasibly possible

2. Which of the following items can be used in an evaluation process?

    a. Uniform Systems of Accounts
    b. national standards
    c. cost-volume-profit relationship
    d. all of the above

3. Three important attributes in managing the control function in a hospitality operation that managers must understand are:

    a. motivation, professionalism, and measuring
    b. effective time management, professionalism, and accepting responsibility
    c. scheduling employees, effective time management, and motivation
    d. accepting responsibility, motivation, professionalism

4. Controllable expenses account for at least __ percent of the cost of managing the average hospitality operation.

    a. 20
    b. 30
    a. 40
    b. 50

5. If a manager practices time management on the job he would not do which of the following?

    a.   talk with guests
    b.   fraternize with employees
    c.   become involved with performance appraisals
    d.   waste time training employees

6. When should management provide feedback?

    a.   only when something goes wrong
    b.   if an employee is doing something correct
    c.   as soon after evaluation as possible
    d.   b and c

7. A lot of new managers will become disgruntled with the industry because of the following reason:

    a.   the pay is not sufficient
    b.   they do not want to relocate
    c.   they do not have enough responsibilities
    d.   they are unable to control their employees

8. The majority of all businesses fail due to the following:

    a.   having the wrong attitude
    b   a lack of planning
    c.   unrealistic expectations
    d.   poor credit practices

9. If a business is to sustain itself it should do which of the following?

    a.   fulfill a need
    b.   hold down cost
    c.   remain competitive
    d.   all of the above

10. The steps in the control cycle should include which of the following?

    a.   establish controls
    b.   inform employees
    c.   evaluate performance
    d.   all of the above

Review Exercises Answers

1.   d
2.   d
3.   b
4.   d
5.   b

6.   d
7.   d
8.   b
9.   d
10. d

11.   Describe why professionalism is so important in controlling an operation.

Professionalism means treating all parties with the appropriate respect and attention. It is important for a manager to be professional in controlling an operation because there is a fine line between professionalism and friendship. If managers become friends with their employees, they may have difficulty in counseling their "friends" as employees and thus compromise the standards of the operation.

12.   Describe the significance of the four-step control cycle.

The four-step control cycle of establishing controls, informing employees, evaluating performance, and providing feedback and corrective action is essential to thewell-being of a hospitality operation. In the first step, when control standards are established, and they are measurable, employees will be able to set the expectation levels. Once set, these control standards need to be communicated to the employees. Employees must be informed through training programs or other means so that they will know what is expected of them. Asking employees to demonstrate the correct procedures is one way to ensure that the expectations and control standards have been clearly communicated. The third step of evaluating the performance is significant in the control cycle since it is the step for validation of understanding. It is also the step where an employer can determine if corrective action is needed and to compile the feedback. This leads to the last step of providing feedback and corrective action. For any operation to continuously improve itself, employees must be able to receive feedback on their performance. Once performance is evaluated, either positive of constructive feedback must be given to the employees as soon as possible. This will reinforce the correct behavior and deter the incorrect behavior so that improvement can be made.

13.   Explain what activities can occur in the life cycle curve.

Four major types of activities can be found in the life cycle curve: formation (introduction), growth, maturity, and decline. The formation or introduction stage is when the operation is just starting up. The growth stage can begin as soon as the business starts, or in other instances, months later. This stage is usually signified by a huge increase in sales. The maturity stage is when an operation has growth to its maximum potential. Unless new ideas or new strategies are employed, sales normally remain constant, growth continues at a very slow rate or starts experiencing a bit of a decline. The last stage is when an operation has gone through the first three stages and has not capitalized on re-engineering or improving itself. Thus, sales will start to decrease.

14.   Explain why it is important to understand national standards.

National standards are essential because they provide a benchmark for comparison. By comparing the figures of an individual operation to the national standards, the effectiveness of this operation in relation to the industry can be determined. This data may then assist the particular operation to gauge its next strategical move.

Examination Type Problems

1.   List least five major reasons for business failure.

      The five major reasons for business failure are:
      i)   a lack of working capital
      ii)   inexperienced managers
      iii)   inability to control operational procedures
      iv)   vast amount of competition
      v)   employee theft

2.   List two major activities by which businesses can sustain themselves.

      The two major activities by which businesses can sustain themselves are (any two of the following):
      i)   fulfilling a need
      ii)   remaining competitive
      iii)   controlling costs

3.   List the three important attributes that a hospitality manager should have in managing the control function.

      The three important attributes that a hospitality manager should have in managing the control function are:
      i)   professionalism
      ii)   effective time management
      iii)   accepting responsibility

4.   What are the main segments of the hospitality industry?

      The main segments of the hospitality industry are:
      i)   food
      ii)   tourism
      iii)   lodging
      iv)   entertainment

Case Study

      The Case Study Hotel is a 700-room conference center in the downtown area of a major metropolitan city. Within Case Study Hotel are various dining outlets. The Model is a fine dining restaurant featuring continental cuisine with entrée prices ranging from $12.95 to $24.95. It is open for lunch and dinner, seven days a week. You have just been hired as the manager of Model and you report directly to the Food & Beverage Director. The revenue levels have been quite stable but the restaurant has been losing money. Your Food & Beverage Director has given you this position to see if you can turn the business around. You realize that there are two tasks you must

accomplish as soon as possible. These two tasks would be to evaluate the financial position of the

business and to have a meeting with the employees. Address the following two questions

pertaining to your actions concerning these two tasks:

a.   List five items that you would evaluate to determine the financialposition of the business.

b.   List six items that you would discuss with the employees.

Case Study Answers (answers may vary)

a. Any five of the following
    1. sales level
    2. sales mix
    3. cost of each menu item
    4. gross margin of each menu item
    5. net income
    6. food cost percentage
    7. labor cost
    8. labor scheduling
    9. labor cost percentage
    10. all controllable expenses

b. Any six of the following
    1. your management philosophy
    2. their general concerns
    3. customer service ratings
    4. training
    5. up-selling
    6. sales incentives
    7. work schedule
    8. menu mix
    9. menu prices
    10. specialty items

CHAPTER 2

THE CONTROL FUNCTION

I.   Purpose of the Chapter

The purpose of this chapter is to provide students with an understanding of the control function and how vulnerable businesses are if the planning and control processes are not well established.

II.   Overview of the Chapter

The control cycle is based on establishing standards, informing employees of those standards, evaluating performance to ascertain whether the standards are being met, and then providing feedback and taking corrective action if necessary. Performing an analysis of an operation can be an important process for a new manager. This would allow for establishing a general business plan to see if the goals and objectives are feasible, and will aid in satisfying the ideals of the mission statement. An operation should continuously develop a team concept and provide empowerment for employees. This will develop an organizational culture that will allow employees to have autonomy to achieve the organizational goals and objectives.

Managers must be made aware to anticipate factors in the market, competition, and economy that can have an affect on operational procedures. Shifts in one of these three activities can often present danger or opportunity to a business.

From menu selection to managing other costs, each activity in the control cycle will be addressed continuously throughout the book. It is within this control process where the manager has the greatest influence over profit generation and control.

III.   Learning Objectives

1.   The benefits of a business plan

The business plan forces the entrepreneur to evaluate as many aspects of the business as possible to develop strategies for the success of the business.

2.   The importance of market research

Market research can aid the entrepreneur in determining if the business will actually be able to fulfill a need in the market area and whether the business can be competitive and still acquire the required and expect revenues.

3.   The importance of differentiation

Unless the guest perceives that there is a difference in product, price, or service, it can be very difficult to obtain a competitive advantage.

4.   The importance of a mission statement to managers, employees, and guests

The mission statement tells managers, employees, and guests what type of business is being operated and therefore it provides a benchmark for managers, a common purpose for employees, and provides the guest with information concerning the values and culture of the organization.

5.   The importance of establishing goals and objectives

Goals and objectives must be written to support the business plan and the mission statement if controls are to be implemented and measured.

6.   The various steps of the control cycle

The control cycle begins with establishing objectives and standards, and the employees must be made aware of exactly what these standards are. Management must then evaluate performance to see if the standards are being met. If they are being met feedback must be given to employees for them to maintain this level of performance. If they are not being met corrective action must be taken and the cycle starts over again.

7.   The four major concerns of purchasing

Purchasing is when the business operation begins to spend money, and because resources are being utilized care must be taken. The four major areas of concern in the purchasing process are as follows:

a. Quality
b. Quantity
c. Time
d. Price

IV.   Definition of Key Terms

Business plan – provides information concerning the business mission, goals, objectives, and a method of strategies to reach the anticipated outcome.

Issuing – the process of passing and providing products to eligible individuals with proper documentation or authority to receive the products.

Marketing research – entails establishing the possible success of a business by defining whether the external environment is willing and able to support the possible success of the business.

Menu – a list of products or services provided by an organization and all business activities concerning the utilization of resources such as location, facilities, equipment, and personnel must be designed to support the menu.

Mission statement – informs as to what type of business the operation is conducting and may include the method in which the operation conducts business and the anticipated market.

Preparation and production – entails the process of preparing products for further production procedures or for direct service to the customer. It is during this process that internal controls must be implemented to ensure that quality is maintained.

Pricing – deals with the balancing of cost to the organization and the perception of value to the guest. An operation must spend a great deal of time in establishing price because of the perception of value and the difficulty in changing prices.

Purchasing – is the initial spending of resources to establish and operate a facility. Efforts must be made to ensure that quality and consistency are maintained at the most cost-effective price.

Receiving – is the process of accepting products that have been purchased by the organization and every effort must be made to insure that the required purchase specifications are met.

Sales and cash control – must be implemented to protect guest checks and cash, as cash is the most important resource that is generated by the business operation.

Service – provides an opportunity to satisfy or exceed customers expectations. If service is perceived to be unsatisfactory the facility can lose sales and customers.

Storing - entails the protection of products from deterioration and theft for future utilization.

V.   Teaching Outline

A.   Business Plan—An Analysis of the Operation
    1.   Mission Statement
    2.   Goals and Objectives
    3.   Empowerment, Involvement: A Team Concept
    4.   Organizational Structure
    5.   Supervision of Departments
B.   The Market, Competition, and Economics—An Analysis of the External Environment
    1.   The Market
    2.   Competition Awareness
    3.   Economics
C.   Setting Standards
D.   Menu Selection and Pricing
E.   Purchasing
    1.   Quality
    2.   Quantity
    3.   Time
    4.   Price
F.   Receiving
G.   Storing
H.   Issuing
I.   Production
J.   Service
K.   Sales and Cash Control Analysis
L.   Labor Cost
M.   Other Costs
N.   Mathematics in Control: Fractions, Decimals, Ratios and Percents

VI.   Questions and Answers

Review Exercises

1. The three contributions provided by the mission statement for managers, employees, and customers are as follows:

    a.   benchmark, common goals, and organizational values
    b.   organizational values, benchmark, and training
    c.   benchmark, common goals, and training
    d.   leadership, common goals, and organizational values

2. For a business to be successful it is essential for it to be _____.

    a.   feasible
    b.   realistic
    c.   as detailed as possible
    d.   adequate

3. In order to establish controls for an operation, one must first establish

    a.   what business one is in
    b.   the organizational goals
    c.   the organizational objectives
    d.   all of the above

4. Empowerment will lead to more involvement among employees in developing

    a.   a team concept
    b.   the accomplishment of goals and objectives
    c.   a work setting for less supervision
    d.   all of the above

5. Goals and objectives must be:

    a.   feasible and cost effective
    b.   ideal
    c.   imaginary
    d.   frequently changed

6. In most hospitality organizations, the organization structure is very _____.

    a.   flat
    b.   tall
    c.   large
    d.   small

7. A marketing audit should be completed

    a. the first couple of days that one is in business
    b. before one opens the business
    c. after the business has been established
    d. as part of the original planning process

8. The control cycle begins with

    a. setting standards
    b. receiving
    c. storing
    d. menu

9. When writing menus, this basic laws of economics must be considered:

    a. when supply is limited prices tend to rise
    b. when supply is abundant prices tend to rise
    c. people actually buy more when prices are higher
    d. the higher the price the greater the quantity demanded

10. The menu controls all of the following except _____ .

    a. equipment to be purchased
    b. the cost of labor
    c. managerial expertise
    d. site selection

Review Exercises Answers

1. a
2. a
3. d
4. d
5. a
6. a
7. c
8. d
9. a
10. c

As an entrepreneur of a 100-seat, fine dining, five-star restaurant, you are developing your new

business.

    The answers to questions 11-13 will vary according to the parameters that you, as the instructor, set for the class. In general, the following are the specific characteristics that you will like your students to include.

11. Develop your mission statement.

    Clear; concise; provide direction; values, norms and expectations.

12. Develop four goals for your restaurant.

    Support mission statement; feasible; cost effective; motivate, broad-based.

13. Develop four objectives for your restaurant.

    Similar to goals but more specific and outcome oriented.

14. Explain the value of environmental scanning of the competition.

    An environmental scanning of the competition will provide an operation information for it to stay abreast of the changes that happen in the marketplace and for the operation to remain aware of what its competitors are doing. Once there are noticeable changes among the competition, an operation should evaluate several scenarios for dealing with the anticipated activity. By contemplating different scenarios, the operation will be prepared to adapt to further anticipated changes.

Examination Type Problems

1.   List a factor that can affect market competition for a 300-seat family restaurant and

    explain how you would deal with it (answers may vary).

    Factor: The owner of a strong competitor sold his restaurant to a new entrepreneur and the service and business of this strong competitor have both declined.
    Strategies: This 300-seat family restaurant may wish to capitalize on this mismanagement of its competitor and increase advertisement to capture the guests of this previously strong competitor. First time discounts can also be given to increase loyalty. Better staffing may also be needed to handle the possible sales increase so that the quality of service will not be compromised.

2.   List four important factors associated with the storing of products (any four of the

    following):

        i)   store products as quickly as possible
        ii)   tag items where appropriate
        iii)   use first-in first-out storage procedures
        iv)   place cost, weight, count and other information on the tag
        v)   store products in specific location
        vi)   label shelves
        vii)   avoid storing expensive items close to the door
        viii)   allow only authorized personnel in the storage area
        ix)   avoid allowing delivery personnel to enter storeroom to store products

3.   What three factors must be taken into consideration while trying to obtain the lowest

price?

The three factors that must be taken into consideration while trying to obtain the lowest price are: quality of the product, quantity of the product, and the time when the ordered goods can be obtained.

4.   Explain why service should be included in the control cycle.

Service is an integral part of the control cycle because many issues can occur during service that will reduce the profit of the operation. From providing substandard service which may lead to guest dissatisfaction to providing superior service which may lead to repeat guests, service can enhance the guests' experience.

Case Study

The Case-Study Hotel is contemplating the opening of a medium priced 100-seat casual dining facility. Your hotel manager has just advised you that you will be the general manager of the new restaurant. You have full responsibility for establishing the theme and the type of business operation that will be implemented. Understanding the difficulty of the control function, establish a control cycle for this new restaurant. After the major steps in the cycle are determined, list two sub-items for each of these major steps and explain why you believe that these sub-items will help your new restaurant to become successful.

Case Study Answers (answers may vary)

Business Plan
i)   how funds are obtained
ii)   who are the target market segments
Market, Competition, Economics
i)   what are the themes of the competitors
ii)   what are the needs of the guests
Menu
i)   number and types of items
ii)   price range
Setting Standards
i)   standardized recipes
ii)   plate presentation
Purchasing
i)   quality of products
ii)   quantity needed

Receiving
i)   receiving time schedule
ii)   training of receiving personnel
Storing
i)   storeroom layout
ii)   storeroom cleaning procedures
Issuing
i)   issuing procedures and forms
ii)   issuing hours
Production
i)   equipment needed
ii)   preparation work
Service
i)   training of waitstaff
ii)   up-selling
Sales and Cash Control Analysis
i)   guest check control
ii)   credit card acceptance procedures
Labor Cost Control
i)   scheduling
ii)   pays scale and motivation
Other Goods
i)   linen costs
ii)   utility expense

CHAPTER 3

SETTING STANDARDS

I.   Purpose of the Chapter

This chapter provides students with an understanding of the importance of developing standards and assists them in understanding the importance of standards to a successful operation.

II.   Overview of the Chapter

Standards must be established in order to provide direction for employees and to establish a basis for control. The purpose for setting standards is to be able to control and measure the efficiency of production and the overall effectiveness of an organization. Setting standards in the hospitality industry involves determining the expected amount of income that can be derived from the utilization of a prescribed amount of resources. Establishing standards provides an operation with the ability to establish the amount of resources that will be utilized and the results that can be anticipated.

Standards must be established for all areas of an operation to include revenue centers and support centers. To be effective, standards must be measurable and attainable. Feedback must be provided to ensure that standards are working effectively, and it is pertinent to constantly determine if the standards can be improved.

When setting standards, an organization must take into consideration the operating expenses and required profit for that particular facility. Standards must aid an organization to cover all costs, both prime and hidden. It is essential to establish standards for all resources— food, beverage, labor, equipment and supplies.

If food, beverage, and labor standards are to be met, equipment and supplies must be located to maximize the efforts of time and motion. Additionally, proper equipment can enhance the products offered and help maintain the prime cost. For food and beverage areas, equipment can maintain portion sizes, taste, and aesthetic appeal; for other areas of the operation, proper equipment is essential in reducing repairs, maintenance and replacement costs.

After standards have been established they must be implemented, and routinely measured and compared so that necessary corrective action can be taken. An operation cannot function effectively without proper standards.

III.   Learning Objectives

1.   The concept of organizational standards and the purpose of establishing standards

The purpose for setting standards is to be able to control and measure the efficiency of production and the overall effectiveness of an organization. Setting standards in the hospitality industry involves determining the expected amount of sales income that can be derived from the utilization of a prescribed amount of resources. These resources in the hospitality field include the prime cost items such as food, beverage, and labor. In the case of casinos it also comprises of the utilization of equipment. The objective of standards is to provide employees with direction and to allow for efficient business decisions and employee performance evaluations.

2.   The are four major components in the overall process of developing standards. To be effective, standards must comply with the following four guidelines:

    a.   They must be measurable
    b.   If they cannot be attained, they should be re-evaluated
    c.   If they are attained, the organization must determine if they can be improved
    d.   Employees must be provided with feedback if the process is to work efficiently

3.   The eight major areas of concern when setting standards for food and beverage operations are as follows:

    a.   Establish standardized recipes
    b.   Establish servable portion and cost
    c.   Determine range of acceptable cost
    d.   Determine labor procedures and cost
    e.   Control quality
    f.   Set ideal number of menu items
    g.   Consider available resources
    h.   Set prices to generate profits

4.   Determine the as purchased (AP) and usable portion (UP) as they relate to standardized recipes and costs are very important.

Because of trimming that must occur with certain products and the amount of shrinkage that may occur during cooking. The as purchased (AP) price and the servable or usable portion (UP) price can be completely different; and this can change the overall costs to the operation. AP and UP become more important when dealing with high priced items such as meat.

5.   The importance of labor and equipment standards to the overall costs control process.

A product labor standard must be set for all services and products production, especially for the production or delivery of those activities that may consume a vast amount of time. Proper equipment should be available to enable employees to maintain standards.

6.   The five major steps in any action plan of cost control would include the following:

    a.   Implements Standards
    b.   Measurement of Standards—The Audit
    c.   Provide Feedback
    d.   Take Corrective Action
    e.   Continue Improvement

7.   A preliminary audit for measuring standards

The best way to measure is to perform an audit. An audit is simply a set of standards for the various areas of a business. If all the standards are arranged as items of an audit, then measuring standards will simply be completing a checklist with some simple analyses. The easier you make the procedures for others to use and follow, the more these procedures will be used and followed.

IV.   Definition of Key Terms

As purchased (AP) – describes how an item is purchased and delivered to the hospitality facility. Most products must undergo some type of additional preparation that may include trimming or cooking. Because of this process additional portions or weight may have to be purchased.

Attainable – standards must be attainable or managers and employees are apt to become discouraged and productivity and quality may decrease.

Compromise – can occur once a manager exposes himself/herself to suspicion or disrepute. Therefore, a manager must always conduct himself or herself in such away to avoid suspicious conduct.

Feedback – is the informing of employees and upper management concerning operational activities and procedures. Feedback is important if positive conduct is to be continued or if negative conduct is to be changed.

Hidden costs – those incidental expenditures that were not given sufficient accountability in funding during budget development.

Labor intensive – is a major problem for the hospitality industry, as machines have not been developed to provide the majority of work to replace employees.

Objectives – are the measurable standards that must be attained for an organization to reach its goals and mission.

Operational cost – is the cost involved in paying for the expenses to run the operational activities.

Prime costs – are those primary cost associated with hospitality operations which are labor, food, and beverage costs.

Revenue center – are those components of an operation that are actually in the business of generating revenue as opposed to providing support services.

Servable portion - or usable portion (UP) price can be completely different; and this can significantly change the overall costs to the operation.

Standardized recipe – is a formula that provides production personnel with the information and processes to prepare products.

Standards - is a model or method that serves as a basis for comparison.

Support centers – are those components of an operation that are not directly involved in generating income such as housekeeping in hotels.

Turnover – is referred to as the number of time a goods, customers or employees are rotated during a given period.

Usable portion (UP) – refers to that portion of a product that is actually of quality to sell to a customer.

V.   Teaching Outline

A.   Guidelines for Standards
    1.   Measurable
    2.   Attainable
    3.   Improvement
    4.   Feedback
B.   Standards Must Be Germane
C.   Setting Standards for Food and Beverage Operations
    1.   Establish Standardized Recipes
    2.   Establish Servable Portion and Cost
    3.   Determine Range of Acceptable Cost
    4.   Determine Labor Procedures and Cost
    5.   Control Quality
    6.   Set an Ideal Number of Menu Items
    7.   Consider Available Resources
    8.   Set Prices to Generate Profits
D.   Setting Standards for Labor
E.   Setting Standards for Equipment and Supplies
F.   Industry Standards
G.   The Action Plan
    1.   Implement Standards
    2.   Measurement of Standards—The Audit
    3.   Provide Feedback
    4.   Take Corrective Action
    5.   Continue Improvement

VI.   Questions and Answers

Review Exercises

1. All of the following are major components in developing standards except::

    a.   they must be measurable
    b.   they should be established by the employees
    c.   if they cannot be attained, they should be re-evaluated
    d.   if they are attained, the organization must determine if they can be improved

2. The purpose of establishing standards is to:

   a.   allow customers to know what is on the menu
   b.   to inform employees what is on the menu
   c.   to Inform employees how to prepare menu items
   d.   to give variety to the menu

3. The major benefits of using standards recipes:

   a.   quality and consistency
   b.   reduce the cost of menu items
   c.   will be able to use unskilled workers
   d.   items can be prepared from scratch

4. The importance of determining servable portions cost:

   a.   allows manager to know the exact cost of items
   b.   help in determining the selling cost of items
   c.   informs management on exactly how much to order
   d.   all of the above

5. Why is it so important to convert standard recipes correctly?

   a.   can save trip to the storage room
   b.   will reduce the cost of a product
   c.   cooks will not over prepare
   d.   c and d

6. If standards are not attainable owner/operators have a choice of trying to implement which of the following:

   a.   rise prices
   b.   reduce portion size
   c.   purchase lower quality
   d.   all of the above

7. Once standards are being met, management should implement the following practice:

   a.   give employees a raise for maintain and meeting standards
   b.   try to improve cost by raising the standards
   c.   try to provide better service by lowering the standards
   d.   ensure that each standard is cost effective

8. Why can the cost in two franchised facilities that are identical in size and menu be totally different?

   a.   one facility may have to implement additional security
   b.   because of location and the job market, the cost of labor
         can be significantly different

    c.   menus for two different facilities could be the same but because of the demographics of the area, the popularity of menu items could be completely different

    d.   all of the above

9. Standards must be established for the sole purpose of:

    a.   generating a profit
    b.   provide quality of products and service
    c.   trying to stay in business
    d.   b and c

10. Why must standards be established for the utilization of equipment?

    a.   management must know the capacity of their equipment
    b.   management can determine when to turn on equipment
    c.   equipment can be purchase before writing the menu
    d.   a and b

Review Exercises Answers

1. b
2. c
3. a
4. d
5. e
6. d
7. b
8. e
9. d
10. d

11. What is the purpose of establishing standards?

The purpose of setting standards is to be able to control and measure the efficiency of products and the overall effectiveness of an organization.

12. Describe the importance of standardized recipes.

Standardized recipes are important because they give the details in the production of a food item. The standardized recipe includes the name of the item, yield, ingredients needed, pre-preparation procedures, preparation method, and portion size. With a standardized recipe, consistency can be achieved and left-overs and overproduction can be minimized.

13. Explain how as purchased (AP) and usable portion (UP) relate to standardized recipes and

costs.

It is important to understand the difference between these two terms as they relate to standardized recipes and costs. AP is referred to as the purchase price of a product while UP is referred to as the servable or usable portion price of a product. For instance, if a standardized recipe calls for 1-pound of carrots as the servable or usable portion (UP), an operation will need to purchase 20 ounces (AP) of carrots rather than the 16 ounces required (1-pound). This is because there is waste and trim in carrots of about 20%. Thus, it is important to look at the AP for pricing rather than the UP. If the recipe is cost using the UP of 16 ounces, and not the AP of 20 ounces, the recipe will be cost lower and the actual food cost will be higher.

14. Describe the four major components in the overall process of developing standards.

The four major components in the overall process of developing standards are:
i)   standards must be measurable
ii)   if standards cannot be attained, they should be re-evaluated
iii)   if standards are attained, the operator must determine if they can be improved
iv)   employees must be provided with feedback if the process is to work efficiently

Examination Type Problems

1.   List the eight major areas when setting standards for food and beverage operations.

The eight major areas when setting standards for food and beverage operations are:
i.   Establish standardized recipes
ii.   Establish servable portion and cost
iii.   Determine range of acceptable cost
iv.   Determine labor procedures and cost
v.   Control quality
vi.   Set ideal number of menu items
vii.   Consider available resources
viii.   Set prices to generate profits

2.   List categories that a typical standardized recipe includes.

A typical standardized recipe includes:
i.   Name of recipe
ii.   Yield
iii.   Ingredients
iv.   Pre-preparation procedures
v.   Preparation method
vi.   Portion size

3.   Describe the significance of labor and equipment standards to the overall cost control

process.

Labor and equipment standards are significant to the overall cost control process. When
a labor standard is set for a particular service or product production, the estimated labor
cost can then be calculated. This can also consist of time management and labor
planning so that the right amount of labor can be scheduled and guests do not need to
wait for an unnecessary amount of time for a product to be produced.
Equipment standards include all equipment used in food service and production, both big
or small. Standards should be written as to which piece of equipment should be used for
cooking and serving each product. For instance, a slotted spoon is used to serve
marinated mushrooms, whereas a #10 scoop should be used to dish up mashed
potatoes. In doing so, there should be no miscommunication or waste in production and
serving.

4.   What are the five steps in action plan of costs control?

An action plan of costs control include these five steps:
i)   implement standards
ii)   measurement of standards – the audit
iii)   provide feedback
iv)   take corrective action
v)   continue improvement

Case Study

After setting a control cycle for Model and helping your friend in giving him advice on his

new restaurant, you are ready to set some standard measurements for Model. You fully

understand that standards will help you assess the efficiency of your restaurant.

As mentioned in the previous chapters in this text, standards for the receiving function can

include:

*   Are separate receiving records maintained?

*   Are all deliveries checked against the written purchase order/price/brands/size?

*   Are bottles checked for leakage or breakage—verify bottles count?

*   Who is the receiving agent?

*   Have all invoices been entered—items, price, units?

Given the situation of your restaurant within the Case-Study Hotel, there are various areas that warrant a separate section of an audit. For a start, your General Manager would like to concentrate on these six areas:

1.   food production
2.   food purchasing
3.   labor-waitstaff
4.   labor-kitchen
5.   labor-utility
6.   customer comment cards

Case Study Answers

Prepare three audit questions for each of the above audit areas.

1. Food production
    - i)   who is in charge of the production schedule?
    - ii)   are standardized recipes used?
    - iii)   is AP or UP used in the standardized recipe?
2. Food purchasing
    - i)   when is food purchased on a weekly basis?
    - ii)   is there a list of preferred or approved vendors?
    - iii)   who is responsible for the purchasing function?
3. Labor - waitstaff
    - i)   how many full-time or part-time employees are available?
    - ii)   what is the procedure if employees want to change shifts before a schedule is posted?
    - iii)   what is the procedure if employees want to change shifts after a schedule is posted?
4. Labor - kitchen staff
    - i)   how are the kitchen staff trained on safety procedures?
    - ii)   is there a person on staff who can train others in meat cutting?
    - iii)   is there a plan for continuing training for the kitchen staff?
5. Labor - utility
    - i)   how are they trained to operate the dishwasher?
    - ii)   are the procedures of mixing chemicals clearly posted?
    - iii)   do they have access to the storeroom for chemicals?
6. Customer comment cards
    - i)   do employees have input on the questions used on the cards?
    - ii)   how often are the results tabulated?
    - iii)   how are the results being used?

CHAPTER 4

THE MENU AS A COST CONTROL TOOL

I.   Purpose of the Chapter

This chapter is designed to provide students with an understanding of how the menu actually serves as the driving force of the hospitality operation.

II.   Overview of the Chapter

The menu acts as the blueprint for the hospitality operation. Because the document is so important to the survival of an operation, the procedures for maintaining the consistency of this document must be controlled.

Site selection, demographics, equipment, labor, and all other facets of the operation are dependent on the menu. The structure of the menu must be developed for marketing the operation and designed so that food products can be produced and served within the maximum possible quality. Each type of menu has its own unique set of circumstances that must be controlled. Managers have the task of selecting products for those menus that will be acceptable to the public and will generate the maximum amount of profit possible.

While generating sales and controlling costs, managers must ensure that nutritional and sanitary standards are maintained. A variety of products should be developed to complement the goals and objectives of the operation but sanitary conditions, quality, and service must not be allowed to decline in the process of generating a profit.

When developing menus and accepting orders from guests, concern must be given to the capacity of equipment, and the skills capability to serve the products. A manager must always have a concern for controlling quality and consistency throughout the production process.

Plans must be developed to anticipate changes in business events and computers should be used as a tracking device to ensure accountability through the operational process. Controlling menu procedures is one of the primary functions of hospitality managers. Any decline in quality of consistency can cause a reduction in sales.

III.   Learning Objectives

1.   The importance of the menu in site selection and demographics

Whether a product can be legally sold or prepared at a certain site or whether the product or service listed one the menu would be acceptable by the customer base must be investigated.

2.   The importance of the relationship between menu and equipment requirement

There must be equipment available to support the preparation of products and services listed on the menu and management must be well aware of the limitation and constraints of the equipment.

3.   The labor market, weather and major events can effect the determination of menu items

There must be sufficient skilled labor available in the labor market to prepare the menu items, and the weather must be conducive to the acceptance of the product. Additionally, major events that routinely occur can be used to increase sales or may have a negative effect on sales.

4.   The importance of variety and appeal when developing menus

Foods must be paired and placed together that will give good eye appeal and perception of value. Eye appeal can have a great deal to do with whether a meal is perceived to be outstanding or unacceptable.

5.   Factors involved in truth in advertising when establishing menus

When developing menus, it is a responsibility of management to ensure that items stated on the menu are in fact what they are advertised to be. To control the mistake of misspelling the names of products, names should be taken directly from the product labels themselves. Emphasis must also be given to correct specifications of content and correct origin.

IV.   Definition of Key Terms

A la carte – is being used when each item on the menu has a separate price

Cyclical – is a menu wherein regular items are repeated and is normally written for a week or more. There are several benefits, including control factors, which are associated with this type of menu.

Demographics – are the characteristics of the population segment for identifying the consumer market.

Labor skills – refer to the knowledge, skills, and ability of the available employees.

Limited menu – is more closely associated with the quick service industry and is used to reduce waste and target a specific market.

Major events – are events of such magnitude that they can have a major significance in increasing or decreasing sales.

Off-hour menu – is an excellent tool for increasing sales and for assisting managers in controlling the utilization of labor. Special menus and special prices during slow periods can be an excellent way to market to a different market segment. Off-hour menus could also provide managers with a means of utilizing leftovers from lunch and utilizing employees that must remain on duty.

Site selection - can often determine the success of a business operation. Management must ensure that products can be developed, prepared, and are acceptable to the demographics of the location. Since a return on investment in a business venture is usually based on an operation succeeding in the long run, it is important to discover if there are plans for rezoning or reconstructing the area in which the facility will be constructed. Accessibility, safety and security of employees and guests are of the utmost importance to the long-range success of an operation.

Table d'hote – a full-course meal served at a fixed price.

The magic number – refers to what should be the number of items on a menu. The magic number is the number of menu items that can be safely controlled and will still maximize the profit of the organization. Items should not be carried if they cannot be safely prepared, safely held and safely served. A manager will have to balance guest satisfaction, sanitation, labor skills, service required, and profit in determining the magic number.

Truth in advertising - is a responsibility of management to ensure that items stated on the menu are in fact what they are advertised to be. Control the mistake of misspelling and ensure that products are of the correct specifications and correct origin.

Variety and appeal – can be accomplished by pairing and placing foods together that will give good eye appeal and perception of value. Eye appeal can have a great deal to do with whether a meal is perceived to be outstanding or unacceptable.

V.   Teaching Outline

A.   Factors to Consider When Designing Menu
    1.   Site Selection
    2.   Demographics
    3.   Equipment
    4.   Prices
    5.   Food Products Availability
    6.   Labor Market
    7.   Major Events
    8.   Competitors
    9.   Number of Menu Items
B.   Structure of the Menu
    1.   Menu Item Placement
    2.   Appetizers and Soups
    2.   Entrees
    3.   Salads
    4.   Starches and Vegetables
    5.   Desserts and Breads
    6.   Beverages
C.   Types of Menus
    1.   A la Carte
    2.   Table d'hote
    3.   Limited Menu
    4.   Cyclical Menu
    5.   Off-hour Menu
D.   Other Considerations
    1.   Menu Index
    2.   Nutrition and Health

3. Meal Periods
4. Sanitation and Safety
5. Variety and Appeal
6. Truth in Advertising
7. Production Capabilities
8. Equipment Capacity
9. Space Usage and Allocation
10. Kitchen Layout and Design
11. Service Capabilities
12. Computers in Menu Planning
13. The Magic Number

VI.   Questions and Answers

Review Exercises

1. All of the following factors except _____ are major decisions that must be taken into consideration when writing the menu.

    a. labor market
    b. weather
    c. uniforms
    d. prices

2. A problem with the site selection process may include:

    a. rezoning
    b. construction
    c. licenses
    d. all of the above

3. The demographics of the area can be changed very quickly because of the following:

    a. weather changes
    b. a nearby corporation could move
    c. a school may open
    d. a and c

4. All of the following pertain to the purchasing of food service equipment except:

    a. non-commercial items are inexpensive and will save money over the long run
    b. purchasing equipment that is not required ties up capital
    c. the volume of business that must be anticipated
    d. purchases must be made to satisfy quality, quantity, and consistency

5. The following activities must be considered when establishing price:

    a.   cover all cost
    b.   the location of the establishment
    c.   unexpected repairs
    d.   all of the above

6. Which of the following is extremely important to establishing food products on the menu?

    a.   products should be available for a diverse market
    b.   products should be available for dieting
    c.   the changing of price of seasonal products should be accounted for
    d.   there should be some type of meat free dish on the menu

7. Labor is an important element in the construction of a menu because:

    a.   there are so many menu items
    b.   all restaurants require cooks that are highly trained
    c.   labor is a large portion of the costs
    d.   skilled labor must be available for the type of menu

8. The weather in an area can have an effect on the sale of certain products,

    a.   if it is too cold
    b.   if it is too hot
    c.   if it rains a lot
    d.   all of the above

9. Which of the following statements concerning a major event is true?

    a.   a major event will always cause a reduction in sales
    b.   a major event will always cause an increase in sales
    c.   major events can have a negative or positive effect on sales
    d.   all of the above

10. Which type of menu lends itself better for the planning of leftovers?

    a.   cyclical menu
    b.   off-hour menus
    c.   a la carte
    d.   all of the above

Review Exercises Answers

1. c
2. d
3. d
4. d
5. c

6. c
7. d
8. d
9. c
10. a

11.   From the different types of menu discussed in the chapter, choose two types and

develop a menu for each type. List three problems that could occur in trying to control

the production, holding, and serving of each menu.

A la Carte

Entrees
Filet Mignon
Spicy Jumbo Shrimp
Grilled Chicken Vista
Blackened Snapper
Old Fashioned Meatloaf

Starches
Saffron Rice
Fettuccini Alfredo
Fried Sweet Plantains
Red Beans
Baked Potato
Fried Yucca

Vegetables
Grilled Mixed Vegetables
Sweet Peas and Red Peppers
Broccoli and Cauliflower Florets
Tomato Provencale
Mushrooms in Sherry Sauce
Roasted Cherry Tomatoes

Concerns:
1. Too many side dishes to be prepared
2. More items have to be served and waitstaff must be well trained and knowledgeable
3. Labor costs can increase due to more intense preparation
4. Kitchen layout and design will need to accommodate all items
5. Waitstaff may need to assist guests to make the right choices to ensure that the dish
    will be eye appealing
6. Unsanitary conditions may occur

Table d'hôte

Appetizer
Spring Rolls

Soup	Salad
Hot and Sour Soup	Mixed Greens with peanut vinaigrette, topped with crispy fried noodles

Entrees
Beef with Sweet Peppers
Beef with assorted sweet peppers served with fried rice and snow peas.

Sichuan Chicken
Chicken marinated in a spicy sweet and sour sauce and lightly sautéed. Served with steamed rice and mixed vegetables.

Kung Poa Pork
Diced pork loin with peanuts and green onions served on a bed of fried rice with mixed vegetables.

Dessert
Fruit Cup

Concerns:
1. Increases the size of the window for theft
2. Too much food might be produced and lead to waste
3. Increases the temptation of theft when overproduction occurs
4. Increases temptation of theft when a large amount or number of the same products are produced
5. Management needs to monitor portion sizes carefully

Cyclical

Monday	Tuesday	Wednesday	Thursday	Friday
Southern Fried Chicken	Chopped Sirlion Steak	Club Sandwich	Hearty Hamburger	Salmon en croute with a Creamy Lobster Sauce
Mashed Potatoes, Coleslaw, or Seasoned French Fries	Mashed Potatoes or Rice Pilaf	Tangy Coleslaw. French Fries, or Potato Chips	Fruit Cup, French Fries, or Mixed Vegetables	Mushrooms, Green Beans, or Glazed Carrots
Choice of Beverage	Choice of Beverage	Choice of Beverage	Choice of Beverage	Choice of Beverage
Brownies	Ice-cream	Carrot Cake	Key Lime Pie	Chocolate Cake

Choice of beverage includes fruit juice, soft drinks, tea, or coffee.

Concerns:
1. Use of leftovers can be planned ahead
2. Over production may occur and may lead to more waste
3. Ensure variety for customer satisfaction
4. Plate presentation needs to be enhanced as the same items are served to all guests
5. Planning must be done carefully so items will not be repeated too often
6. Choices may not be offered to satisfy a larger number of guests

12. List five factors concerning the importance of demographics and site selection when

designing menus.

1. Age of residents
2. Type of business
3. Zoning rules
4. Access roads
5. Safety and security measures
6. Average household income
7. Major downsizing of neighborhood businesses

13. Develop a list of at least five food products that may vary in supply and demand during

certain times of the year.

1. Certain fish products
2. Shellfish such as oysters and lobsters
3. Strawberries/raspberries/blueberries
4. Increase in demand of chestnuts in the holiday season
5. Increase in demand of ham and turkey during the holiday season
6. Increase in demand for cranberries during the holiday season
7. Watermelon during the summer

14. List five major events that occur in your area and explain how any two of these events

may have a positive or negative effect on: 1) a full service hotel; 2) a limited service

hotel; 3) a full service restaurant; and 4) a fast food restaurant.

Answers may vary
Consult the local Chamber of Commerce or the Convention and Visitors Bureau for the
list of local events.
A. Arts and crafts festival in a downtown area:
   1. If the full service hotel is in downtown, this festival may provide a different venue for the guests to visit but may create traffic and parking problems around the area.
   2. Limited service hotel: some of the town vendors may stay in the limited service hotel as the price of these hotels tends to be more economical.
   3. Full service restaurants: may increase the business of such restaurants if the arts and crafts show has some high-end quality products.

4. Fast food restaurants: will most likely increase sales especially in snacks and drinks as spectators will stop in for a quick rest.

B. The Olympics

For an event of such magnitude, all four hospitality operations will most likely be affected positively in sales. Yet, management in the four operations need to be prepared for such increases so that guest satisfaction will not be reduced.

Examination Type Problems

1.   List five considerations and/or constraints that could be associated with the development

of a cyclical menu.

1.   Use of leftovers can be planned ahead
2.   Overproduction may occur and may lead to more waste
3.   Ensure variety for customer satisfaction
4.   Plate presentation needs to be enhanced as the same items are served to all guests
5.   Planning must be done carefully so items will not be repeated too often
6.   Choices may not be offered to satisfy a larger number of guests

2.   Explain the importance of developing a menu index.

A menu index can be used to evaluate and establish menu items that are most appealing to the guests. This can aid in future planning and can assist management in determining the items that should be deleted or added. This can also be used in controlling leftovers and help in costs.

3.   Name five concerns associated with selling, serving, and controlling beverages?

i)   serving alcohol with care so that guests can enjoy their stay with the operation without having negative experiences
ii)   be aware of the contribution margins of the drinks served
iii)   need to balance the perception of price value
iv)   waitstaff should always ask guests regarding refills before automatically refilling drinks
v)   Ensure that coffee and tea are made fresh

4.   Why are variety and appeal in menu design so important and what are some of the

activities a manager can control to ensuring that this occurs?

Variety and appeal are important as food must be paired and presented well. Dining is an entire experience. While the taste of the food is important, the plate presentation and choices that guests can have are also part of the dining experience.

Case Study

While you are effectively operating the Model Restaurant at Case-Study Hotel, your friend called you up for some advice. He is a manager of a small 150-room hotel in a business community that does not have a food service facility. He has just been contacted by his supervisor and advised that the hotel will purchase the lot next to the hotel property and build a freestanding restaurant for the hotel guests and the community. The facility will seat approximately 300 guests. He has been given the task of developing the menu for the facility, and he is seeking your general ideas and suggestions for the following activities:

1.   Type of menu and items: what and why?
2.   Hours of operation: what and why?
3.   Required kitchen equipment: when should they decide and why?
4.   Other questions that he may have for his boss.

Case Study Answers

As this restaurant will service both the hotel guests and the neighboring business community, breakfast and lunch will be the two main meal periods while dinner may be the slowest of the three. Thus, a breakfast, lunch, and dinner menu with a table d'hôte concept will probably be preferred.

Items on the menu should offer variety. The breakfast and lunch menus should consist of a majority of items that can be prepared very quickly since both the hotel guests and the business community may only have a limited amount of time for meals. Take-out items should also be advertised and offered to appeal to those who are on-the-go.

The hours of operation may be from 6:00am through 10:00pm with some extremely slow periods such as between 9:00am and 11:00am and between 3:00pm and 6:00pm. Off hour menus or a happy hour hors d'oeuvres menu can also be offered from 5:00pm to 6:00pm to increase possible business and the after work crowd. Depending on how the menu items are prepared, the appropriate equipment can then be decided.

A good list of questions can be developed for his boss and a preliminary plan:
1.   budget
2.   themes of restaurant
3.   preferred or approved vendors
4.   any market study on quest preferences
5.   any demographic data in detail, especially on their spending habits in food

CHAPTER 5

PRICING

I.   Purpose of the Chapter

This chapter is designed to inform students of the importance of pricing and to introduce them to different methods of pricing.

II.   Overview of the Chapter

Numerous activities can affect menu prices. A manager should be very conscientious in trying to develop the most cost-effective prices. A menu should be pre-costed and standard recipes should be developed to ensure consistency over the long run. If consistency in purchasing, receiving, storage, production, and serving is not maintained, established prices cannot be effective in producing a profit. Specialty and discount items can be priced to increase sales, to take advantage of seasonal items, and can help in preventing loss through possible waste and spoilage.

Non-food and beverage items and other profit centers must also be priced correctly. Room rates and membership dues can be positioned economically to enhance revenue. The price of rooms can be adjusted for special events and periods that will increase revenue. The amount of membership dues can often be adjusted to balance costs as long as the increase is on an occasional basis.

Actual cost should be as close to ideal cost as possible. The amount of tolerance from ideal cost should be minimized. Different approaches to pricing must be evaluated in order to account for an amount of tolerance and to maximize pricing efforts. Costs and pricing have to be thoroughly evaluated and balanced if profits are to be maximized.

Now that computerization and software are so affordable, management should use these products to save time and increase accuracy. Management must also be advised that computers do not eliminate the need for routinely taking a physical count of products and other resources. Figures may not relate what is actually occurring in the business in the short run. The evidence of a problem may only become visible through a reduction in guest count.

Developing prices takes time and must be viewed as one of the most essential elements to the success of an operation. Prices must be as accurate as possible in order to cover all costs. Hidden costs and unexpected costs can be major problems for new establishment.

III.   Learning Objectives

1.   The reasons for setting prices

    a.   Setting prices for volume to generate profit.
    b.   Setting prices to be comparable with the prices of competition.
    c.   Setting prices for quality and prestige.

2.   Factors that can affect menu prices

There are many factors that affect menu pricing. However, from a strict break-even analysis standpoint, prices must cover all costs and prices must generate a profit. The cost factors that need to be considered are as follows:

a.   Fixed costs, which remain constant despite increases or decreases in sales volume.
b.   Variable costs, which usually increase as sales volume increases and decrease as sales volume decreases.
c.   Total costs, which is fixed costs plus variable costs.

3.   The break-even point and the amount of profit or loss

Break-even is a relationship between profit and volume. When constructing break-even, all costs must be classified as either fixed costs or variable costs. When sales cover all variable costs and all fixed costs the amount remaining is profit or at the point wherein fixed costs are covered is break-even. Therefore, break-even is fixed cost over 1 minus the variable cost percent.

$$\text{Break-even} = \frac{\text{Fixed costs}}{(1 - VC\%)}$$

It is important to understand that once an operation reaches break-even, the additional sales do not result in a 100 percent profit. This mistake is often made when establishing the amount of profit or loss after the break-even point has been determined. Until an operation passes break-even, profit cannot be generated.

4.   Pre-cost menus to determine contribution margin

To evaluate the contribution margin it is accepted that each dollar of sales is divided into two portions. One portion must cover variable costs associated with the item sold and the other to cover fixed costs and to provide profit. With this interpretation, the dollar amount remaining after variable costs have been subtracted from the sales dollar is defined as the contribution margin.

5.   Cost and pricing of non-food and beverage products or services

Hotels and clubs will have prices for their non-food activities as well as their food and beverage operations. Items such as club dues and room sales must have prices established thatwill cost effective for the organization. A pricing method should still be used that will consider any physical resources used and labor resources.

6.   The use of ideal or standard cost

To effectively deal with the cost issue, operations need to develop an ideal or a standard cost. All efficient operations have a standard cost, which is the ideal cost of products or services. Standard cost is then compared with actual cost in order to determine operational effectiveness. For example, if all standards for a particular menu item are met during the control process of purchasing, receiving, storing, production, and service, then the cost that has been established for that item should be met. If for some reason a standard was not met during the control process, then the actual cost for that particular item may not meet the standard cost that has been established.

7.   The informal and formal approaches to pricing

The most informal approach to menu pricing is pricing to compete by garnering menus from competitors and price items accordingly. This is often done by individual businesses entering the industry for the first time. Needless to say, always trying to match the prices of competitors can be a major mistake. An establishment must be concerned with the prices of competitors but an establishment cannot allow the prices of competitors to dictate the prices for its own operation as expenses can be totally different.

Formal methods are far more successful as they attempt to account for all costs. The four methods described in the chapter are as follows:

    a.   Derived Food Cost Percentage
    b.   Pricing Factor or Multiplier
    c.   Combined Food and Labor Cost
    d.   Actual Cost Pricing

8.   Computerization in the hospitality industry and discuss its role in cost control

Computerization can provide managers with a fast and efficient means of comparing standards to determine if controls are being met. It is essential in the hospitality industry to be able to evaluate and compare standards in a timely manner. This is especially true for labor cost. Adjustments in labor must be made very quickly. By taking hourly cash register readings, a manager can often make cost saving adjustments. It is important to remember that computerization is not a substitute for management actually observing operational activities.

IV.   Definition of Key Terms

Break-even – occurs when sales cover all variable costs and all fixed costs the amount remaining is profit or at the point wherein fixed costs are covered is break-even. Therefore, break-even is fixed cost over 1 minus the variable cost percent.

$$\text{Break-even} = \frac{\text{Fixed costs}}{(1 - VC\%)}$$

Cost – is the price paid by the operation for products Cost represents the expense of operating a business and can be fixed, variable, total costs, or semi-variable.

Fixed costs – remain constant despite increases or decreases in sales volume.

Hidden costs – those incidental expenditures that were not given sufficient accountability in funding during budget development.

Markup - is often referred to as gross profit or margin, and is the difference between the cost of the products and the selling price. The percent of markup can be based on the cost percentage of selling price. The markup for products must be large enough to cover operating expenses and have an amount left over for net profit.

Menu mix – is the balancing of menu products and prices Considerations must be given to menu mix and guest demand to ensure that the price is the most effective one. The menu mix may allow you to try and spread cost around without having to establish prices that are unacceptable for certain products. Every attempt must be made to factor in all costs and develop an effective menu mix.

Net profit - is the amount of money that remains after operating expenses have been paid and the percent of net profit is based on the selling price.

Operating expenses – are expenditures such as rent and utilities and other types of expenses that are involved in the daily cost of running an operation.

Percent of markup – is the desired percentage that management would like to add to the selling price of an item. A desired percentage for marking-up items and the price for a product can be obtained by dividing the dollar cost of the product by the desired percent.

Profit - is the difference between costs, revenue, and sales that are generated after break-even is reached.

Total costs - is fixed cost plus variable costs

Variable costs – are costs that usually increase as sales volume increases and decrease as sales volume decreases.

V.   Teaching Outline

A.   Factors Affecting Menu Prices
     1.   Setting Prices: Volume for Profits, Competition, Prestige
     2.   Demographics and Type of Services
B.   Break-even Analysis
     1.   Classification of Costs
     2.   Formulas
     3.   Hidden Costs
C.   Pre-costing the Menu
     1.   Standardized Recipes
     2.   Specialty and Discount Items
D.   Costs in Non-food and Beverage Product or Services
     1.   Rooms
     2.   Membership Dues
E.   Ideal or Standard Cost
     1.   Ideal Cost Versus Actual Cost
     2.   Tolerance to the Variance
F.   Approaches to Pricing
     1.   BCG Matrix
     2.   Contribution Margin in Pricing
     3.   Informal Approaches
     4.   Formal Approaches
          a.   Derived Food Cost Percentage
          b.   Pricing Factor or Multiplier
          c.   Combined Food and Labor Cost
          d.   Actual Cost Pricing
     5.   Rounding and Print Size

G.   Costs, Pricing, and Profits
    1.   Correct Costing Provides Information for Pricing
    2.   Accurate Pricing Leads to High Sales Volume
    3.   Appropriate Controls Maximize Profits
H.   Computerization
    1.   Spreadsheets
    2.   Data Base
    3.   Proprietary Software

VI.   Questions and Answers

Review Exercises

1. The order of priority of customers used to be price, quality and service; it is now:

    a.   price only has to be reasonable
    b.   price is still the most important
    c.   quality is not the most important
    d.   price, quality, and brand name

2. The two main concerns when establishing menu prices are:

    a.   prices must be affordable and cheap
    b.   prices must not change during seasons or increase during the accounting period
    c.   prices must cover all costs and generate a profit
    d.   quality and availability

3. A menu must be pre-cost in order to obtain:

    a.   the amount of popularity of items
    b.   contribution margin
    c.   the quality of products necessary
    d.   when items will be available

4. Which pricing approaches do "Mom and Pop" restaurants most often use?

    a.   informal approach
    b.   formal approach
    c.   combined food and labor cost
    d.   actual cost pricing

5. One of the major problems associated with posting non-computerized spreadsheets is:

    a.   accounting for credit memos
    b.   comparing prices
    c.   double payments
    d.   inspecting quality

6. The formula for attaining the break-even point is:

    a.   fixed cost over one minus the variable cost percent
    b.   variable cost over one minus the fixed cost percent
    c.   fixed cost over sales
    d.   variable cost over one plus the fixed cost percent

7. One of the main reasons for using proprietary software is:

    a.   it can be purchased at any computer software facility
    b.   it is easy to learn
    c.   it is far less expensive than most software
    d.   it can be used to implement additional control

8. Some of the best methods for changing menu prices are as follows:

    a.   tape the new price over the old price
    b.   remove the item from the menu and bring it back at a higher price
    c.   use whiteout to cover old prices
    d.   only change the dollar amount

9. When establishing the break-even some items that may be identified as variable costs are:

    a.   labor
    b.   rent
    c.   interest
    d.   insurance

10. Specialty items can increase sales through:

    a.   differentiation
    b.   using cheap products and selling them at a higher price
    c.   using special servicing utensils
    d.   all of the above

Review Exercises Answers

1. a
2. c
3. b
4. a
5. a
6. d
7. b
8. a
9. e
10. d

11.   Discuss the three types of services that affect menu pricing.

There are basically three levels of service that are instrumental in determining prices. They are quick service and cafeteria style restaurants, basic table service style restaurants, and luxurious or elegant dining.

Quick service or volume intensive types of restaurants will normally price foods with a very small amount of markup. The intent is to generate revenue through volume and cost control. These types of facilities will have the lowest prices. They can keep prices low by using convenient types of prepared products and therefore they can reduce waste. Additionally, labor cost is normally lower because they can use unskilled employees with a minimum amount of training.

Basic table service or mid-level restaurants will have more full time employees and more choices of menu items. These operations may have several different price ranges and may adjust more to the demographics of their guests.

Luxurious or elegant service illustrates the fact that an operation can actually establish any price for food as long as the perception of value is acceptable. A fine dining restaurant has to be located in a city where there is a sufficient population base to support the prices that will be charged. It usually takes a large city to support these types of operations, as guests may visit an establishment for a special occasion. These facilities must deliver impeccable service in order to maintain their market share. At these facilities, the concern for service and quality far exceeds price.

12.   Explain the four formal approaches to pricing.

The four formal approaches to pricing are : (1) derived food cost percentage; (2) pricing factor, a multiplier or mark up; (3) combined food and labor cost; and (4) all or actual cost pricing.

In the derived food cost percentage method, management will determine a desired percentage for marking-up items and the price for a product is obtained by dividing the dollar cost of the product by the desired percent. If a product has a cost of $2.50 and the desired percent is 36 percent, the price would be established by dividing $2.50 by 0.36 which would ($2.50 divided by 0.36 = $6.94) establish a menu price of approximately $6.95. This method of pricing is probably used more than any other methods as it provides an easy means for quickly establishing prices for all menu items.

The pricing factor, markup or multiplier method is closely related to the derived food cost percentage. In this method, an operation would begin by establishing the food cost percentage and divide this percentage into 100 and come up with a factor. If an operation establishes that it would like to have a food cost of 40 percent they would come up with a factor of 2.50. An operation would simply multiply the raw food cost times the pricing factor to establish the sales price. With a factor of 2.5, an entree that costs $3.00 will have a selling price of $7.50.

This combined food and labor cost is also known as the prime cost. If an operation wants 36 percent food cost and a 28 percent labor cost, the combined food and labor cost would be 64 percent. If the cost of the food item is $2.50 and all labor costs are $1.50, the two costs would be combined and divided by the combined percentage ($2.50 + $1.50) divided by 0.64 = $6.15. This procedure works well for operations that want to include food and labor costs in their selling prices.

The fourth method is actual cost pricing. In this method, an operation would establish the food cost, the total labor cost, other variable costs, fixed costs, and profit. Once these costs have been determined an operation would add food, labor, operating cost, and the percent of required profit to arrive at the selling price. If food cost is $2.50, labor is $1.50, operating cost is $1.10 and the desired profit is 10%, then the selling price is calculate by adding all costs ($2.50 + 1.50 + 1.10

= $5.10) and divide the sum by 1 minus the profit percentage of 10% (100%- 10% = 90%) to obtain the selling price of $5.70 ($5.10 / 90%). The actual cost method will allow an operation to account for the profit that should be generated when establishing prices.

13.   What are some examples of hidden costs and why are they important in menu pricing?

        Hidden costs are costs that have not been identified by management as being additional costs. Hidden costs can exist because of numerous activities. Any activities that increase variable costs or unexpectedly reduce sales can result in a reduction in profit. For example, bad weather conditions can destroy a crop and the produce will increase in price. If an operation is highly dependent on lettuce for food products it could cut deeply into the profit. Hidden costs are important in that if they are not counted or allotted as a cost item, the cost of producing that product or services will be deflated. And if prices are set using such wrong information, then the operation will not obtain enough sales to pay the bills or generate a profit.

14.   The Food and Beverage Director of Hotel Premiere has estimated sales of $80,000 for the

        month of April. His estimated payroll is $30,000, overhead is $8,000 and a food cost of

        25%. What is the break-even point in dollars?

        Break-even   = $\dfrac{FC}{1 - VC\%}$ or $\dfrac{FC}{CM\%}$

        Fixed costs = $30,000 + $8,000 = $38,000

        Variable costs = 25%

        Break-even   = $\dfrac{\$38,000}{1 - 0.25}$

                      = $50,667

15.   According to question (4), if the average check is $25.00, how many guests does Hotel

        Premiere has to serve to break even? Also, what is the profit at the $80,000 sales level?

        Break-even level = $50,667

        If an average check is $25.00, the number of guests needed to break-even is:
                = $\dfrac{50.667}{25}$ = 2,026.68   or   2,027 guests

To obtain the profit at $80,000 sales, the first step is to calculate the contribution margin in dollars. Since 25% is the variable cost, then 75% (1-25%) has to been the contribution margin. Thus:

$80,000X.75 = 60,000 is the contribution margin

From there, all the other costs are deducted, including payroll of $30,000 and overhead of $8,000. Thus the profit is $22,000 ($60,000-$38,000).

16.   Identify four advantages of using standardized recipes.

Standard recipes are essential in developing the correct price for menu items. By using standardized recipes, an operation will know exactly how much it cost to prepare an item and how many individuals can be served from that particular recipe. The four major advantages in using standard recipes are:
    a.   consistency
    b.   controlled labor cost
    c.   effective scheduling
    d.   predetermined product cost

17.   Discuss the role of computerization in menu pricing, especially the use of spreadsheet,

database and proprietary software.

Computerization can provide managers with a fast and efficient means of comparing standards to determine if controls are being met. For multi-unit operations that may have to send financial information and other mathematical analyses to their corporate offices, using computerized spreadsheets can reduce the possibility of error. By using the full spectrum of spreadsheet programs, e-mail, and Internet, an operation can prevent mistakes. With the correct cost data, prices can be set correctly to reflect all costs and the desired profit.
    Data base software as a control activity is greatly under used. Historical data on products, prices, sales, employees, and guests can be an invaluable aid to an operation. The ability to index menu items and to see when and in what quantity of products were sold can assist in production planning. Production planning could prevent waste and reduce the possibility of stockout. All these activities can assist in reducing food cost and thus pricing.
    Proprietary software also plays an important role in pricing by tailoring information to fit the particular requirements of an operation. Various costs can be tracked and calculated. If the correct information can be obtained without filtering the extra information that is not needed, the process of pricing can be more accurate and efficient.

Examination Type Problems

1.   What are the informal and formal approaches to pricing? Name and define each of them.

The two informal approaches to menu pricing as discussed in this chapter are pricing to compete and pricing to the market. Pricing to the level of the competitors is to look at what the competition charges and the operation will charge similar prices. Charging to the market is exactly what it is: charge what the guests will pay. However, it is important to bear in mind that whether prices are reasonable depends on the type of operation, the menu, the service, the demographics, and the availability of competitors.

The four formal approaches to pricing are : (1) derived food cost percentage; (2) pricing factor, a multiplier or mark up; (3) combined food and labor cost; and (4) all or actual cost pricing. In the derived food cost percentage method, management will determine a desired percentage for marking-up items and the price for a product is obtained by dividing the dollar cost of the product by the desired percent.

The pricing factor, markup or multiplier method is closely related to the derived food cost percentage. In this method, an operation would begin by establishing the food cost percentage and divide this percentage into 100 and come up with a factor.

This combined food and labor cost is also known as the prime cost. To calculate the price, an operation will simply add the combined dollar cost and divide that by the combined percentage. This procedure works well for operations that want to include food and labor costs in their selling prices.

The fourth method is actual cost pricing. In this method, an operation would establish the food cost, the total labor cost, other variable costs, fixed costs, and profit percentage. Once these costs have been determined an operation would add all costs and divide by 1 minus the percent of required profit to arrive at the selling price. The actual cost method will allow an operation to account for the profit that should be generated when establishing prices.

2.   What are some demographic factors that affect menu pricing?

When establishing menu prices, the level of service, the demographics of the area, as well as the products being served, all have an important role in determining prices. These include, but are not limited to, population, household income, age, occupation, and the like.

3.   Define ideal cost and how would one use the concepts of ideal and actual costs to

ascertain the health and effectiveness of a hospitality operation.

Ideal cost is the same as standard cost. It is the cost that when all aspects of the production of that item are included, steps such as but not limited to purchasing, receiving, storing, production, and service, then the cost that has been established for that item should be met. To ascertain the health and effectiveness of a hospitality operation, the actual cost for that particular item will be compared to the standard cost that has been established.

Tolerance to the variance between the ideal or standard cost to the actual cost must be established so that management will know what and when to monitor and when to take action. Every organization will differ in the amount of cost fluctuations that can be tolerated. A small change within some organizations can be devastating if the reason for the change is not evaluated quickly enough.

4.   Give five examples of mixed costs and explain why they cannot be purely fixed or variable.

        Five examples of mixed costs can be labor, supplies, utilities, maintenance, and marketing. They cannot be regarded as purely fixed or variable since they both vary with the sales level and yet some part of such cost has to be incurred no matter what the sales level is. For instance, there has to be a minimum crew for a restaurant to open its door and yet when the guest count is up to a certain level, more labor has to be scheduled.

5.   If the average guest check is $12.00 and the variable costs are 25%, what is the number of guests that the bar and grill needs to serve to cover their annual fixed cost of $250,000?

Break-even   = $\dfrac{FC}{1 - VC\%}$ or $\dfrac{FC}{CM\%}$

Fixed costs = $250,000

Variable costs = 25%

Break-even   = $\dfrac{\$250,000}{1 - 0.25}$

              = $333,333

If average check is $12.00, the number of guests needed to break-even is:

= $\dfrac{\$333,333}{12}$ = 27,777,78   or   27,778 guests

6.   Fantasia Hotel has a monthly fixed cost of $100,000, average daily rate of $100.00 and an occupancy percentage of 65% with 80 rooms. What is the break-even point (in number of rooms) in March with 31 days if its variable cost is 30%?

Break-even   = $\dfrac{FC}{1 - VC\%}$ or $\dfrac{FC}{CM\%}$

Fixed costs = $100,000

Variable costs = 30%

Break-even   = $\dfrac{\$100,000}{1 - 0.30}$

              = $142,857

If average daily rate is $100.00, the number of rooms needed to break-even is:

$$= \frac{\$142,857}{100} \quad = 1,428.57 \quad \text{or} \quad 1,429 \text{ rooms}$$

The occupancy percentage, the number of rooms in the hotel, and days given are not important in the calculation at this point. However, they may be used to evaluate if the break-even point is attainable or in other calculations.

Case Study

To practice pricing correctly and to maximize profits, Case-Study Hotel notices that

weekends in the summer are normally not the high demand times. Therefore, it is planning to offer

weekend packages to their guests by serving a dinner on Friday, three meals and ateatime snack

on Saturday, and breakfast and lunch on Sunday. The target guests are mainly couples on their

retreat away from the kids and honeymooners. The owner would like to offer some wine to go with

lunch and dinner. He would like to see a food cost of 35% to 40% and a beverage cost not to

exceed 20%.

First, design the menu for the Friday night opening dinner. List an appetizer, soup or salad,

entrée, and dessert. Then, write up a standardized recipe for the entrée. After the standardized

recipe is established, research the costs to produce the entrée. Last but not least, if a 35% food

cost is desired, determine the selling price if the entrée is ordered asan a la carte item.

Case Study Answers

The answers to this case study can vary. This case is designed for students to be creative
and then use the principles of control and costing to see if a certain menu is chosen, and a 35%
food cost is desired, what might be the price range that the menu needs to be priced at. Additional
parameters can be added to make this case more or less challenging depending on the level of the
students and depending on the time allotted to the students to complete this case.

CHAPTER 6

THE PURCHASING FUNCTION

I.   Purpose of the Chapter

This chapter is designed to illustrate to students the importance of the purchasing function as it relates to control and the expenditure of funds.

II.   Overview of the Chapter

The purchasing function is very important to the bottom line. Any money that is saved during the purchasing process goes directly to the bottom line. Because of the importance of the purchasing activity, managerial training programs should place more emphasis on this aspect during training.

Before purchases can be made, an organization must establish the needs of the operation. Once the needs have been established, purchasing strategies should be established to provide guidelines for all individuals that will be involved in the purchasing process. During the establishment of strategies, concern should be given to the maximization of purchasing, the importance of comparing purveyors and brands, and the advantage of discounts. Additionally, unit pricing, the amount of inventory, labor saving devices, and considerations of financing must be reviewed and analyzed. The significance of ethical conduct must also be established. This becomes increasingly important when purchasing expensive equipment or when having equipment repaired.

Managers must also be made aware that there are several alternatives that will be presented any time a purchasing decision is to be made. These alternatives should be evaluated and managers should be informed not to purchase any products that are not necessary regardless of how inexpensive the price of product.

Managers will have to be trained to understand how closely related the purchasing function is to generating a profit. If money is wasted through purchases, it will take a vast amount of sales to offset the loss. Additionally, mangers must be aware that it is within the purchasing function that theft and collusion have the greatest possibility of occurring on a large scale.

III.   Learning Objectives

1.   The importance of establishing specifications

Because such a large percentage of the cost of operating a business is incurred during the purchasing process, controlling this process will often determine the success of a business. Purchasing specifications should be written for every item that the operation intends to purchase as a direct means of carrying out its day to day functions.

2.   You should try not to exceed your specified level of quality

When discussing the aspect of quality in the purchasing function, it must be pointed out that quality is relative. An operation should only purchase products at the level of quality for the specifications of the menu or that the operational plan requires. To exceed quality may increase cost while not increasing the quality of the final product.

3.   It is important to establish the needs of an organization

When establishing strategies for purchasing, an organization must first identify the needs of the organization. This is an essential element in the cost control process. For a manager to be able to control costs during the purchasing process a manager must know the exact needs of the organization in order to try and prevent any excessive purchases. Several managers will purchase "nice to have" items. If items are not necessary purchasing these items creates a loss. Therefore, needs must be specifically defined to prevent waste.

4.   Purchasing alternatives

Along with establishing strategies, cost control in purchasing will always involve the consideration of some basic alternatives. Every purchasing situation will usually have one or several of these possible alternatives. The alternatives will revolve around the following questions:

    a.   Is it possible to make the item instead of purchasing the item?
    b.   Is it necessary to purchase a particular brand?
    c.   Is it possible to delay the purchase?
    d.   Should the item be paid for in cash?
    e.   Who is the most reliable supplier when considering price, quality, consistency, and service?

5.   The importance of establishing purchasing strategies

To control costs as effectively as possible, managers and other purchasing agents must develop strategies to protect the hospitality organization. Strategies will allow all personnel who are performing the purchasing task at any level to know what is expected by the organization. Staying within the framework of the strategies will allow the hospitality organization to control cost and reduce costs. Not developing strategies can lead to wasted opportunities, overspending, and financial difficulties for the hospitality operation. Overspending can occur in business just as it may occur with personal spending. Certain strategies must be practiced so that the opportunity costs of making decisions can be maximized to the benefit of the organization.

Once the needs of the organization are defined an organization can establish purchasing strategies to control cost. Some of the strategies that can be used to help control cost during the purchasing function are as follows:

    a.   Maximize purchases
    b.   Compare purveyors
    c.   Compare brands
    d.   Compare yields
    e.   Take advantage of cost effective discounts
    f.   Use unit pricing to compare packages
    g.   Purchase only the safest amount of inventory
    h.   Purchase labor saving products whenever possible
    i.   Compare cash to credit
    j.   Compare interest rates
    k.   Read and understand all contracts

l.   Beware of "good deals"
m.   Deal with reputable sources in an ethical manner
n.   Negotiate

6.   How to determine the standard yield of a product

It is essential to know the standard yield that you will receive from particular items. Without having knowledge of the standard yield, you may be unaware as to whether your cooks are over purchasing products. The as purchased (AP) weight of products can be totally different from the usable portion (UP). The amount of production loss from trimming and/or cooking can increase the cost of servable portions. For example:

A 9-pound pork lion cost $4.85 per pound. A total of 15-ounces is lost in boning and trimming and an additional 1-pound 8-ounces is lost through shrinkage during the roasting period. How much should a 3-ounce serving cost?

    $4.85   Price per pound
    X   9   Pounds Purchased (AP)
    $43.65   Total cost

    Per ounce price AP = $4.85/16 = $0.3031
    3-ounce portion cost = $0.3031 X 3 = $0.9094 or $0.91

        16   Ounces in one pound
    X   9   Number of pounds purchased
       144   Ounces purchased

       144   Number of ounces purchased
     - 39   Ounces lost (15-ounces from boring and trimming and
                   24-ounces from shrinkage during roasting)
       105   Number of ounces as useable portions (UP)

    $ 43.65   Total cost
        105   UP ounce
    = 0.415   Cost of one ounce of cooked meat

    $ 0.415   Cost of one ounce
    X   3   Ounce serving portion
    $1.245   Cost of each 3 ounces of pork loin served

Thus, the real cost of 3 ounces should be $1.25 versus $0.91, a 37.36% difference.

7.   How to determine the cost per servable pound

The cost per servable pound would be the cost per ounce of the product once the real cost of the useable portion is determined.

8.   The need for comparing brands

When purchasing solely by brands, an operation can often waste a lot of money. Managers have to compare similar products to see if the product fits their needs and if it is providing the same quality and the utilization of purpose. If a product can fit the required purpose and give the desired quality, an operation may be able to go with a non-branded product. In many cases the products will have to be taste tested to determine which product would provide the most desired taste.

9.   The need for comparing purveyors

Purveyors need to be compared for standards besides prices and quantity discounts. If the purveyor does not practice good sanitation habits, you can get dry goods and other products that are close to deterioration or that may contain infestation from bugs or harmful levels of microorganisms. Is the transportation method of delivery going to allow for timely delivery and be able to maintain frozen products at a temperature to keep them frozen during the movement from delivery to storage? Managers must understand the significance of making comparisons, as there are many of these extenuating circumstances that can make price less of a factor. An operation can lose guests because of poor quality, stockout, and a lack of consistency. Managers must compare vendors; you cannot believe that because of state and federal regulations, all establishments will provide quality products or use ethical practices.

10.   The overall importance of the purchasing function to the bottom line

Managers of any business venture must understand the importance of controlling the purchasing function. Not understanding the impact of the old adage "it is not how much you make, it is how much you spend" has been the cause of numerous business failures. If your operation only nets about 5 percent profit, in theory you would be required to have about a $1,000 in sales to net $50. It is very difficult to generate the $1,000 in sales, not to mention all of the other hidden costs such as wear and tear on the facility that it takes to generate the $1,000 in sales. If you can save $50 during the purchasing process, then the savings can go straight to the bottom line. The difficulty of generating a profit is but one of the reasons why the purchasing function is so pertinent.

IV.   Definition of Key Terms

As purchased (AP) – describes how an item is purchased and delivered to the hospitality facility. Most products must undergo some type of additional preparation that may include trimming or cooking. Because of this process additional portions or weight may have to be purchased.

Commercial purchasing – can influence the price, the method of marketing, and the manufacturer chosen by the supplier's management. This is because the commercial purchases can be very large. The purchases of most hospitality operations are large in volume, and in many cases, very specialized. Due to such volume purchases, large sums of money are involved, and therefore commercial buyers may have more bargaining power than an individual, basic consumer may have.

Consumer purchasing - is on such a small scale that the consumer cannothave a great influence on price, method of marketing, or the manufacturer chosen by the supplier.

Price analysis - must be obtained whenever possible because we live in a world of over-choice and a particular item can have numerous different prices.

Purchasing cards - are credit cards that are issued to individuals within an organization that will be performing purchasing functions. Corporate purchasing cards are used to reduce the administrative costs for low-dollar direct items

Purchasing directs - present a problem for owners and managers of large facilities as these items are usually inexpensive and do not go into storage. Because directs do not go into storage the accountability for such items can become losses very quickly.

Purchasing strategies - will allow all personnel who are performing the purchasing task at any level to know what is expected by the organization. Staying within the framework of the strategies will allow the hospitality organization to control cost and reduce costs.

Specifications – are descriptions written for the purchasing of a particular product and they should be written for every item that the operation intends to purchase as a direct means of carrying out its day to day functions.

Standard yield – is the amount remaining after a product has gone through the production process. The as purchased (AP) weight of products can be totally different from the usable portion (UP).

Unethical conduct – is the practice of deviating from the principles, policies, and procedures of the organization and may or may not be for personal gain.

Unit pricing – is used when evaluating product brands. From one container to another, you may pay one or two cents more per ounce for the same product. The amount of daily utilization also plays a part in the decision making process. It is important to use a convenient size of a product even if it is more expensive. The amount of labor saved by using a convenient size can warrant the utilization of a more expensive product.

Usable portion (UP) – refers to that portion of a product that is actually of quality to sell to a customer.

V.   Teaching Outline

A.   The Importance of the Purchasing Function
      1.   Controlling the Purchasing Function
      2.   Specifications on Quality
      3.   Specifications on Quantity
      4.   Specifications on Time and Price

B.   Purchasing Strategies
      1.   Maximize Purchase
      2.   Compare Purveyors
      3.   Compare Brands
      4.   Compare Yields
      5.   Take Advantage of Cost Effective Discounts
      6.   Use Unit Pricing to Compare Packages
      7.   Purchase for Only the Safest Amount of Inventory
      8.   Purchase Labor Saving Products Whenever Possible
      9.   Compare Cash to Credit
     10.   Compare Interest Rates

        11.   Read and Understand All Contracts
        12.   Beware of "Good Deals"
        13.   Deal with Reputable Sources in an Ethical Manner

C.   Purchasing Systems
        1.   Purchasing Directs
        2.   Buying Methods

D.   Furniture, Fixtures, and Equipment

E.   Inexpensive Purchases

VI.   Questions and Answers

Review Exercises

1. When purchasing products, what methods can be used to reduce cost?

    a.   coop-buying
    b.   purchasing in volume
    c.   purchasing in large quantities
    d.   all of the above

2. What method of theft is more apt to take place during purchasing and is difficult to detect?

    a.   ordering the wrong size
    b.   ordering a lower quality
    c.   under purchasing
    d.   over purchasing

3. In a food service operation, who should be involved in deciding the specifications of the products?

    a.   chef, manager, and receiving clerks
    b.   cook, manager, and servers
    c.   chef, receiving clerks, and servers
    d.   manager, chef, and storeroom clerk

4. What documents should be used to retrieve items from the storeroom?

    a.   invoice
    b.   receiving report
    c.   requisition
    d.   credit memo

5. How many requests for bids should be given when purchasing large quantities of products?

    a.   it is not necessary
    b.   at least 1
    c.   at least 2
    d.   at least 3

6. When purchasing fresh fish, what is the utmost important concern?

    a.   size
    b.   quantity
    c.   quality
    d.   price

7. What are some of the added valued to the price of products?

    a.   transportation
    b.   time
    c.   brand names
    d.   all of the above

8. If a guest requests a bottle of alcohol that the restaurant has sold out, the manager should do one of the following except:

    a.   send an employee to a liquor store
    b.   contact the vendor
    c.   explain to the guest that they are out of stock
    d.   ask the guest if he or she will accept a substitute

9. Before using a convenience product, management must:

    a.   try the product out
    b.   ask vendors questions about the product
    c.   perform a value analysis
    d.   give away samples to guests

10. The UP price is usually _____ the AP price.

    a.   the same as
    b.   higher than
    c.   lower than
    d.   cannot be compared to

Review Exercises Answers

1. d
2. b
3. a
4. c
5. d
6. c
7. d
8. a
9. c
10. b

11. From the list of purchasing strategies discussed in the chapter, describe five of them and

discuss how you would go about ensuring that the purchasing process would be

accomplished using those five strategies.

(The list of purchasing strategies includes the following thirteen items. The student can choose any of the five to expand. This answer will discuss the first five strategies.)
1.   Maximize purchases
2.   Compare purveyors
3.   Compare brands
4.   Compare yields
5.   Take advantage of cost effective discounts
6.   Use unit pricing to compare packages
7.   Purchase for only the safest amount of inventory
8.   Purchase labor saving products whenever possible
9.   Compare cash to credit
10.   Compare interest rates
11.   Read and understand all contracts
12.   Beware of "good deals"
13.   Deal with reputable sources in an ethical manner

Maximize Purchases

Purchasing in large volumes will normally provide an operation with additional purchasing power and thus can lower cost. Purchasing in volume also prevents the purveyor from having to make several trips and anytime an operation can cut the costs of the vendor, the operation can improve its bargaining position. The operation would also want to seek vendors who carry special products or trade in large amounts since they may be able to obtain certain products at a much cheaper cost than others can.

Compare Purveyors

Services that are provided by the purveyors are also important to the purchasing practices of an operation. Purveyors who practice good sanitation habits will have products that are of good quality. Produce should be transported in refrigerated trucks and frozen products should be transported in the right temperature. Whether purveyors will provide "hot shot" or "will call" services is also an important consideration. Thus management must compare purveyors on all aspects.

Compare Brands

Brand recognition is important in marketing and most brand products command a higher price than generic products. In purchasing, however, a name brand may not have the highest quality. Thus, brands must also be compared and can-cutting, quality assessments and price analysis need to be performed. If a product can fit the required purpose and give the desired quality, an operation may be able to go with a non-branded product.

Compare Yields

It is essential to know the standard yield of a product so that the pricing can be done accurately. In fresh food items, the as purchased (AP) weight of products can be totally different from the usable portion (UP). The amount of production loss from trimming and/or cooking can increase the cost of servable portions. In canned food, the net weight is also important as it is the UP of the product. Thus if different prices are quoted, it is important to note that the APs are compared to the APs and the UPs to UPs respectively.

Take Advantage of Cost Effective Discounts

Purveyors may at times make available to their clients certain discounts. Management should take advantage of such offers when they are cost effective. Some discounts may not be cost effective because of the products or because of the volume that one is required to purchase in order to obtain the discount. When taking advantage of discounts, management needs to ensure that quality and consistency are maintained.

12.   Describe how cooking and trimming can increase the price of a product.

Pre-prepared or convenience products, as the names suggest, do not require much trimming or cooking. For the most part, re-heating or certain cooking methods are used and the products are ready to be served. However, most food service products come into an operation at the raw stage and need to be trimmed and cooked before they can be served. Produce and meat are the two main items. Because of the trimming and weight loss in cooking, a one pound product may only yield 80% or 90% of its raw weight. Therefore, if a 4 ounce portion is planned as usable portion (UP) or servable portion, more than 4 ounce of the raw products will need to be purchased as the as purchased (AP) quantity. The price of the menu should also be calculated using the AP portion rather than the UP.

13.   Make a list of five branded food items that you would use on a daily basis. Conduct a price analysis and blind taste tests of such branded items to generic brands in your class.

(This exercise is to heighten the students awareness of the price and quality of brand products. The choices of products and answers may vary).

14.   Consider apples used in fruit compote. List five specifications that could be required of

apples used in this recipe.

The five specifications can be:
1. Grade
2. Color (for example red or green to achieve the color mixture that is desired)
3. Origin
4. Price
5. Brand, if appropriate
       The size of the apples should not matter much in this case as they will be cut up into pieces when they are served.

15.   Define and explain five buying methods that are available to maximize the purchasing

function. Name one method of collusion that could be used between purveyors and

managers during the purchasing function.

There are six buying methods discussed in the chapter for the purchase function. Any

five of the following methods will be appropriate:
1. Cost-plus buying
2. Bid buying
3. Stockless purchasing
4. Standing orders
5. Co-op purchasing
6. One-stop shopping

Cost-plus buying is where the buyer pays products at an agreed upon percentage above what the supplier paid for the product. In bid buying the hospitality operation will publish a written notice of the desired product, including the specifications, amount required, and other specific details. Sellers will reply in writing stating their price and conditions of the sale. Bids are usually opened in public and the lowest bid may be awarded the contract. Stockless purchasing is often used to purchase large quantities of products. Delivery of the entire shipment is either taken or placed in storage and the supplier will deliver the requested amount as needed. This form of forward buying can be very convenient in overseas areas, or for operations that have their own commissaries. This form of buying can be used if a buyer anticipates that prices of a specific product are about to have a substantial increase or the product may become limited. Standing orders are where the delivery person will stop by the facility, take an inventory of products and bring the level of the product back to the agreed upon par stock. Co-op buying is when operations add their individual orders to place one big order with a vendor so as to achieve a better price. One-stop shopping, as the name implies, allow operators to buy everything from one vendor. By trying to have one vendor provide all of the products it reduces the cost of ordering and the amount of paper work that must be maintained.

There are many ways managers or the purchasing agent can collude with purveyors during the purchasing function. One example is the purchase of furniture, fixtures, and equipment where the old equipment is still usable but is sold to a friend at a very inexpensive price. Even worse, equipment in good condition might be intentionally broken or marred so that it can be disposed and new one can be purchased from a "friendly" purveyor.

Examination type problems

For the following examination questions, assume that you are the owner of a 150-seat full

service restaurant in a medium priced hotel.

1.   Make a list of five purchasing strategies that you would implement for your manager to

follow.

(The list of purchasing strategies includes the following thirteen items. The student can choose any of the five upon which to expand. Question 11 in the Review exercises discussed the first five points. This answer will discuss the next five strategies.)
1.   Maximize purchases
2.   Compare purveyors
3.   Compare brands
4.   Compare yields

5.   Take advantage of cost effective discounts
6.   Use unit pricing to compare packages
7.   Purchase only the safest amount of inventory
8.   Purchase labor saving products whenever possible
9.   Compare cash to credit
10.   Compare interest rates
11.   Read and understand all contracts
12.   Beware of "good deals"
13.   Deal with reputable sources in an ethical manner

Use Unit Pricing to Compare Packages

When evaluating brands or other products, unit price rather than stated price should be used. A product may have a lesser total price but its net weight may also be less. With 150 seats, and depending on the usage, there may be instances when the smaller or convenient size products are more beneficial to the operation, even if they might be more expensive. Nonetheless, the unit price should be used.

Purchase Only the Safest Amount of Inventory

Due to the limited amount of storage space in most hospitality operations and the amount of money that can be tied up in inventory, the amount of inventory is very important to the success of the operation. Since this restaurant has only 150 seats, the amount of inventory should not be much, especially if there might be a banquet or catering operation of the type where inventory can be shared among the different outlets. Therefore, the right amount of inventory needs to be carefully calculated and ordered to prevent overstocking or stockout and par stocks levels should be set.

Purchase Labor Saving Products Whenever Possible

Depending on the skills of employees, equipment and/or time limitations and other concerns, convenience or pre-prepared products that can save labor costs should be considered and a value analysis must be completed.

Compare Cash to Credit

Operations must bear in mind that a lack of working capital is one of the main reasons for business failure within the hospitality field. If credit is offered without additional costs or penalties, operations should take advantage of such. On the other hand, cash payments made on a timely basis is a good business practice.

Compare Interest Rates

The restaurant also needs to research and determine if it would be more advantageous to use the credit that is being offered by the purveyor, if interest is charged, or would it be cheaper to go to the bank and borrow the money. The length of credit terms must be evaluated. Since interests rates fluctuate, it is very important to evaluate the rates and the availability of money in the restaurant and the hotel.

2.   If you had a request submitted to you for the purchase of an automatic potato peeler,

what actions would you take before approving the request?

Before the request is approved, one should list all the functions that the automatic potato peeler would perform and assess if all or some of those functions are needed for the operation. Then, price quotes should also be gathered for all the potato products that this machine would do and are needed by the restaurant. The next step would be to calculate how much the same products would cost if they were produced with the labor in house. In short, a value analysis needs to be performed to ascertain the feasibility of the potato peeler.

3.   Name two aspects of purchasing that provide an opportunity for collusion.

Collusion can happen in many forms during the purchasing function. The vendor can give cash or product rebates to the buyer in return for placing a good order. The buyer can also sell "old" or "used" products or equipment as salvage to a vendor at a much discounted price in return for monetary or other favors. Lower quality products may also be substituted and the difference in prices might be shared between the two guilty parties.

4.   What action would you take before changing brands of a product that your kitchen uses

a large quantity of on a weekly basis?

A value analysis or "can-cutting" will need to be performed. The brand product and the new proposed substitutes should be used in the appropriate recipes to see if the quality of the end products have been compromised. The yield of the products will also need to be determined so that the unit costs of the brand and other products can be compared. If the quality of the end products is the same and the unit cost is less with the new brand, then the brand should be changed.

5.   What items entering the kitchen might be considered directs?

Directs are usually inexpensive items that do not go into storage and are immediately used by the operation. It can be anything from certain garnishes that are not purchased from the major vendors or specialty items that are purchased for a particular function. It can be any food item or a bottle of a particular liqueur for cooking.

6.   List three purchasing situations for which you may require a value analysis to be

completed before making the decision.

The three situations can be:
1. New product. A new product is one which the market and the vendor has given you to sample.
2. Product or brand substitution. A less expensive product is proposed by the vendor to replace the current name brand that the restaurant is using.
3. New equipment. A piece food processor that promises better productivity is available.

Case Study

The Case-Study Hotel has a lounge that sells alcoholic beverages to the guests. As the

Restaurant Manager, you are also responsible for the lounge. You have submitted a request for some new chairs for the lounge and would also like to offer free finger food for happy hour twice

a week. You believe that the present lounge chairs, though they are in good repair, are

uncomfortable, so guests do not stay very long. You also estimate that more people would drop

in after work on Monday and Thursday if they could have a drink and some snacks without

having to go home first.

You realize this is a simple request but you also realize how the purchasing function can

affect the bottom line.

1.   How would you go about securing the specifications for the lounge chairs and what

       would those specifications be?

       The manager should contact a few restaurant-furnishing vendors and obtain their
       catalogs. Once some models are chosen, the manager should also ask to see the
       materials and make of the chairs. It is best if the vendor can take you to or give you
       some references to some restaurants or lounges that are currently using such chairs.
       Then, the manager may want to interview the current or previous clients about their
       satisfaction level with the product. The specification of the chairs should include the
       materials that they are made from, normal wear and tear period, workmanship, price,
       origin (manufacturing), warranty, service contract for the material or upholstery (if
       applicable), delivery options including delivery time, and shipping price (negotiated to be
       absorbed by the vendor).

2.   Knowing that the finger foods are provided as "free" items, write a menu of finger foods

       for one day and determine the general quality specifications of such items.

       Since free items and finger foods are to be consumed with alcohol, the answer to
       this question may vary. However, there are a few points that need to be addressed.
       Although the food is advertised as free, it cannot be just one item and a cheap item.
       There needs to a variety and yet be economical to produce.
       Potato chips and dips
       Specifications: any potato chip is acceptable. Brand name is not a necessity as
       there is not much difference between brands. For dips, homemade dip at the lounge will
       be more economical then the prepared ones. Dips made from sour cream, chives, and
       other herbs are also easy to prepared without much labor costs.
       Party mix – this will include some mixed nuts with pretzels, cereal mix and the like.
       Specifications: a party mix will be better than a straight mixed nut mixture as this
       will help in the cost of the items while adding variety to the mixture at the same time.
       Again, brand name is not important in this case, as the lounge can also add in other
       items in the mix when appropriate. Goldfish crackers or mini crackers can also be mixed
       in or served separately to add to the variety.

Meatballs – this is one of the more economical items as an hors-d'oeuvre. The cost is less than chicken fingers or other meat items. It can be served with different sauces to make barbecue, Swedish, or even sweet and sour meatballs. Mini rolls can also be served to make the food more substantial. These can be frozen meatballs and they only need to be reheated in an oven. Thus, skilled labor is not need to produce this product.

3.   What purchase system or method would you use for the furniture and the finger food?

Explain.

A number of purchasing systems and methods are discussed in the text. Purchasing direct is not recommended for either furniture and finger food items, as it will not provide the accountability and controls that are needed. Furniture cannot be purchased direct as it needs to be capitalized as an asset. One-stop shopping may be notfeasible as there are not many food distributors who also engage in the furniture business.

For the furniture, since the purchase can be a considerable amount of money, cost-plus and bid buying would be the most appropriate as stockless purchasing or standing orders do not work well with furniture purchases.

For the finger food, since these items are only served one day a week and other items are served the other day, there may not be a volume to do stockless purchase. Standing orders can be used for the mini buns or even chips but normally not for meatballs and others. If there are other hotels or restaurants near by and there is a chance of quantity buying, perhaps co-op purchasing may work; otherwise, the small quantity that might be needed may not be enough to make the process beneficial.

CHAPTER 7

THE RECEIVING FUNCTION

I.   Purpose of the Chapter

This chapter describes how essential it is to control the receiving process because the hospitality operation is so vulnerable to theft and fraud during this process.

II.   Overview of the Chapter

Receiving involves checking deliveries for quality and quantity and comparing them against the purchase order. Important aspects of the receiving process are to ensure the quantity, quality, and price of products that are received with what the organization requested. Once it is established that these comparisons are satisfactory, products must be secured as quickly as possible to prevent deterioration and theft. Correct and appropriate records all need to be kept. The importance of having knowledgeable receiving personnel cannot be overstated. Even the best specifications will not be of use if receiving personnel do not know how to inspect products and understand the importance of inspecting products. For receiving to work as effectively and efficiently as possible, the layout of the area must be designed for speed and security.

Receiving personnel should have the necessary equipment to adequately and effectively perform their duties. Large and small operations should have specific procedures for the receiving process. The personnel should be familiar with all receiving documents and should know how to process credit memos.

Receiving personnel will have to be made aware of the importance of their responsibility in protecting and safe guarding products during the receiving process. This includes inspecting products form deterioration and theft. This can only be accomplished by scheduling receiving for those times where personnel are available to effectively perform their tasks.

The organization must operate as a team in order for all functions and processes to work efficiently. Receiving personnel are expected to be knowledgeable and use this knowledge to the benefit of the organization. Honesty is a primary attribute for receiving personnel and for those employees that have access to the receiving area. If any employee thinks that dishonesty has occurred he or she should be able to report this without fear of retribution. Employees may only report these activities if they are made to understand how theft affects the bottom line and the security of their employment.

III.   Learning Objectives

1.   The importance of the layout and location of a receiving area

The layout of the receiving area must be operational and designed for control, security, and speedy access to the storage areas. Because of the costs of products, receiving must be given a great deal of priority. It is essential that the hours of delivery be established for those times when receiving personnel actually have the time to inspect products that are being delivered. The receiving area should be located where there is easy access to the storage area. Frozen products and other perishable items should be checked first so that they can be placed into storage as quickly as possible. If operations are very large and products are received in large quantities, management may want to have surveillance cameras strategically located so that the security of the receiving area can be monitored. Receiving personnel have to be aware that all products should be treated the same as money since they actually represent an expenditure by the operation. The layout of the receiving area should always be established with a concern for security and the prevention of the deterioration of products.

2.   The importance of having trained personnel in the process of the receiving function.

        It is essential that receiving personnel be highly trained in the expectations and specifications of products received by a hospitality facility. It is a bad business practice that most hospitality operations do not understand the importance of having trained personnel involved in the purchasing and receiving functions. The industry spends a great deal of money on training programs to train managers in operational procedures. However, it has overlooked the training of managers on the basics of purchasing and receiving products. In hotel operations alone, about 40 percent of all income goes back into purchasing in the form of inventory and other direct operating expenses. Receiving personnel should be able to recognize products, the quality of products, and should be able to discern the different grades of products. If receiving personnel are not trained, then some delivery personnel, as well as vendors, will take advantage of these operations. The majority of all business personnel are honest individuals; however, mistakes do happen and receiving personnel must be able to protect the interest of the hospitality organization. Large operations will usually have qualified receiving personnel. Small operations will often allow anyone to sign for products when they are delivered. Even small operations should ensure that the individuals signing for products should have at least a basic knowledge of the products that the organization receives. Personnel must be trained to ask certain questions pertaining to the origin of products. Items such as shellfish and certain produce can have different levels of usefulness due to their origin and they can vary substantially in price because of their origin.

3.   Equipment that is a necessary part of the receiving process

        Receiving personnel must have the proper tools and equipment to perform their tasks. Such equipment should be secured and remain in the receiving area. Because of the need to store and secure products as quickly as possible, receiving personnel should not have to run back and forth to the kitchen and other areas to locate thermometers and other pieces of equipment. If personnel have to search for equipment there will be times when products will stay unsecured too long or will be allowed to deteriorate. At a minimum, receiving personnel should have the following equipment: thermometers, scales, rulers, knives, chippers, and chipboards.

4.   An example of the procedures that should be used during the receiving process

        A lot of care must be taken during the receiving process as prices can vary among certain products from shipment to shipment. Fresh produce presents a constant issue because the market changes very rapidly in supply, price, and quality. Additionally, market practices in packing can differ throughout the country and items can actually fall below their grade by the time they are delivered. For this reason receiving personnel must be concerned with the condition of the product when it is delivered and not just the grade of the product that was ordered.
        Receiving personnel should be prepared to receive items. This means that they should have the purchase orders available and a copy of the specifications on hand. The invoices received from the delivery person should be compared against the purchase orders for any discrepancies, and any discrepancies must be noted up front. Once all products are received, then the shipment should be signed for, and the forms should be forwarded to the purchasing office.

5.   The basic forms and documents that should be used during receiving.

Once a delivery arrives, all necessary forms should be reviewed for any discrepancies in price, quantity, or quality. If any changes have been made from the purchase request, they should be questioned at this time. This may prevent the waste of time and resources in unloading and having to reload the delivery because it was rejected even before further inspection. If there are no problems noted upon arrival, then the products can be unloaded and inspected. Once inspected, all forms can be completed. Forms and documents that receiving personnel should have on hand are as follows:

   a.   Standard purchase specifications
   b.   Purchase orders
   c.   Delivery Invoices
   d.   Credit memos
   e.   Receiving reports
   f.   Tags

6.   Procedures for handling credit memos.

The proper handling of credit memos is essential to preventing waste and theft within the operation. Too often, managers will be in a hurry or will become too familiar with the delivery personnel and they will accept the promise of delivery personnel without documentation. Storerooms throughout the hospitality industry are full of products that cannot be used. In many cases it was because someone ordered or accepted the incorrect size or ordered the wrong product altogether. If the wrong product is delivered, or a product that is on the invoice is not delivered, or the total amount of a requested product is not delivered, or if there is any reason for rejecting a product, a credit memo should be requested. Do not allow delivery personnel to say they will just bring the credit memo on the next delivery without some type of documentation.
If there is a rejection of a product for any reason a credit memos should be handled in the following fashion:

   a.   Request a credit memo from the delivery person.
   b.   Make sure the form is completed accurately reflecting the reason for the rejection.
   c.   Request the signature of the delivery person.
   d.   Annotate the rejection on the invoice so that the business office does not make payment for the product.
   e.   Give a copy of the credit memo to the delivery person and place a copy in a separate folder.
   f.   Store the remaining delivery.
   g.   Call the delivery company to make them aware of the discrepancy.
   h.   Attach credit memo to the invoice and forward to the business office for payment once the purveyor replaces the product or in some way satisfies the discrepancy.

7.   Activities to safe guard against during the receiving process.

During the receiving process products are very vulnerable. Products must be checked and stored as quickly as possible. Additionally, deliveries should only be made when receiving personnel have time to properly receive the products. Before deliveries are made, an inventory should be taken so that the correct number or amounts of products can be ordered. During this inventory process organize the refrigerators and freezers for storage of the new products upon arrival. Products should not be allowed to sit on the kitchen floor while storage facilities are reorganized to make space for storage. Only those individuals that are involved in the receiving process should be in the area where products are being received. Delivery personnel should not be allowed to enter storage areas to deliver products.

8.   Methods that can be used during the receiving process to examine the quality of different products.

Operations should examine products for basic quality and attempt to see if products have been mishandled. Some of the items to look for are as follows:

    a.   If the bottom of a case of berries or any other type of produce displays a lot of moisture then the products within the case should be checked for over ripeness or spoilage.

    b.   If the delivery person should drop a case of eggs, you will need to carefully examine the product or you may want to reject them as the products on the bottom could be broken. Bruising occurs easily in products such as bananas, pears, and apples. Crates containing these products should be set down gently.

    c.   Because of the danger of spoilage, any frozen fish that is going into the freezer should be checked to see if the temperature is still at least below 10 ° F.

    d.   Frozen products should be examined to see if there are any ice crystals.

    e.   Dated products or color-coded products should be checked to ensure freshness.

If products are accepted that are not usable, it will only increase the amount of food cost for the organization. If substandard products are used, the operation can develop a product of poor quality or unacceptable quality. This could cause the restaurant to lose return business. There are times when suppliers will be out of a product or may have to substitute a product. Any changes observed in cost, quality, or quantity should be discussed with the manager before the product is accepted.

9.   Delivery times are essential to the operation.

Deliveries must be scheduled for times that are convenient for the operation. This will prevent deliveries from arriving when delivery personnel are busy with other tasks. Having a set time for delivery will also ensure that the storage facilities are prepared and ready to receive the deliveries. In so doing, the possibilities of deterioration and theft of products can be reduced. Additionally, some purveyors may be willing to provide incentives for accepting products at off times. Since most facilities have the same time demands, if an operation has the capability to receive products at some other time, then incentives or discounts may be negotiated. Delivery times should be posted outside the facility so that delivery personnel will be aware of the available times.

10.   Procedures to be used when there is a suspicion of collusion

There needs to be some type of procedure in writing concerning collusion, as individuals are then more apt to understand the importance of these activities. Once an organization places policies in writing, it becomes very obvious to all that the operation wants certain procedures to be followed or in other cases will not tolerate certain activities or conduct. Those activities that should be in writing are as follows:

    a.   what procedures should be taken if collusion is suspected

    b.   how collusion affects the bottom line and affects all

    c.   what are considered acts of collusion

d.   what action will be taken against those individuals involved

e.   how silence can be misconstrued as acceptance

11.   The importance of the evaluation and receiving of nonfood supplies

There are several concerns associated with receiving nonfood supplies. One of the concerns is that some cartons have remained in storage sites for some time. Roaches are among the greatest hitchhikers in the world. Cartons should be opened outside if possible. Paper goods present a problem because roaches attempt to lay eggs among paper goods. Cartons containing napkins and paper towels should be inspected for these types of insects. If products received have to be thrown away or cause the operation additional cost or cause need for an exterminator, this takes away from the bottom line. Another major concern of receiving nonfood products is ownership. Be sure that there is a purchase order for any equipment received. There are so many scams to coax managers in to purchasing products that receiving personnel must ensure that the product was in fact ordered by the facility.

IV.   Definition of Key Terms

Credit memo - if there is a rejection of a product during receiving or if an order is incomplete the delivery personnel should issue a credit memo to account for this shortage.

Purchase order – informs receiving personnel of the quantity, quality, and price that was negotiated. Purchase orders (PO) should be on hand to indicate what deliveries are expected. This form is used to record the products ordered and to standardize the information about those products. The quantity and quality delivered should be compared against the purchase order and receiving report to see if there are any discrepancies.

Blind receiving – is a method of receiving in which the areas on the receiving report that would contain quantity and evaluation comments are blacked out. This requires receiving personnel to count, weigh, and give their own evaluation of products. The price can also be blacked out so that receiving personnel will have to ensure prices are correct for the products received. This would be a more effective way of ensuring that receiving personnel checked products and prices.

Inter-unit transfer – is used to transfer items within the same organization or that has the same owners.

Tagging – is accomplished during the receiving process to aid in first-in first-out (FIFO) procedures, which will help in preventing food from deteriorating. Tagging will also assist in maintaining sanitary procedures and will help to reduce theft. If prices are placed on products during tagging, prices will be readily available during the inventory process.

Receiving report – is completed once everything checks out during the receiving process. The receiving report provides the accounting department with a detailed breakdown of what has been received on a daily basis.

Receiving tools – is that equipment that should be available to open containers in order to verify the specifications or the order that is being received. At a minimum, receiving personnel should have the following equipment: thermometers, scales, rulers, knives, chippers, and chipboards.

V.   Teaching Outline

A.   The Receiving Process—A Quick Look
    1.   Layout of the Receiving Area
    2.   Receiving Personnel Must Be Trained
    3.   Receiving Equipment
B.   Procedures Involved in the Receiving Process
    1.   Blind Receiving
    2.   Forms and Documents Used During Receiving
    3.   Procedures for Handling Credit Memos
C.   Safeguards Against Certain Activities During the Receiving
    1.   Examine Products for Quality
    2.   Delivery Times
    3.   Procedures for Suspicion of Collusion
    4.   Nonfood Supplies

VI.   Questions and Answers

Review exercises

1. Credit memos should be used during receiving for all of the following except:

    a.   to identify price increases
    b.   to account for a shortage in products
    c.   to account for products that are rejected
    d.   to account for a missing case of tomatoes

2. Tagging can be used for all of the following except:

    a.   to record prices
    b.   to record a transfer
    c.   to record the date received
    d.   to record the time received

3. An inter-unit transfer would be used :

    a.   by purveyors to account for missing products
    b.   to transfer a product from one unit to another in the same company
    c.   to transfer products back to the purveyor
    d.   to act as a purchase request from purveyors

4. When a case of bananas is delivered and it is dropped by the truck driver, receiving personnel should:

    a.   check the products before signing for them
    b.   reject the bananas
    c.   make sure the bananas are cleaned before serving them
    d.   use them as quickly as possible

5. A case of frozen steaks being delivered has ice crystals in it. This could be an indication that :

    a.   they have been allowed to reach a temperature above freezing
    b.   a steak may have been removed and replaced with water
    c.   the steaks may have been in storage for a long time
    d.   all of the above

6. During the process of receiving there is a possibility of theft by:

    a.   the delivery personnel
    b.   kitchen personnel
    c.   someone passing by
    d.   all of the above

7. If equipment or products are in the storage room that are not being used, management should try all of the following except:

    a.   transfer it to another unit
    b.   return it for credit
    c.   sell it
    d.   give it to an employee

8. It is not a good receiving practice to :

    a.   sign for products before inspection
    b.   check all products against the purchase request
    c.   check all prices
    d.   none of the above

9. A French knife should not be used for the following:

    a.   to open cartons during receiving
    b.   to slice meat
    c.   to dice meat
    d.   to chop vegetables

10. Nonfood supplies such as paper goods and equipment:

    a.   do not need as much inspection as perishable items
    b.   can be signed for as soon as delivered
    c.   should be opened outside because of roaches
    d.   do not require a purchase order

Review Exercises Answers

1.   a
2.   d
3.   b
4.   a

5.   d
6.   d
7.   d
8.   d
9.   a
10.   a

11.   Make a list of five products for which you would want to inspect the bottom of the crates to

ensure the right quality is being delivered.

The products for which one may want to inspect the bottom of the crates to ensure the right quality is being delivered can be many. However, produce and meat products are probably the most important ones:
i.   Eggs - to examine the size of the products and check to see if any of the shells are broken
ii.   Tomatoes - again to check for size and quality
iii.   Apples - to check for the grade, size, and color among other characteristics
iv.   Oranges - to check for size/count and make sure that no rotten ones are on the bottom
v.   Pre-portioned steaks – to weigh the steaks and ensure that they are right weight and quality

12.   List at least five methods that can be used by receiving and delivery personnel in collusion.

The five methods can be:
i.   Receiving personnel signs for the product that the delivery personnel did not deliver. The two will resell those signed items to others and retain the profit.
ii.   Receiving personnel allow delivery personnel enter the storage area and remove items of the operation, claiming that they are wrong items. Again, the products will be sold at a later time.
iii.   Receiving personnel allow delivery personnel to enter the storage area and remove legitimate wrong items but the proper credit and debit memos are never filed. The delivery personnel will sell the products and share the profits with the receiving personnel
iv.   Receiving personnel allow substandard items to be delivered but pay the higher price to the delivery personnel. Delivery personnel will adjust accordingly and share the price difference.
v.   Receiving personnel allow deliveries at busy times to try to divert the attention of others and collude with the delivery personnel.

13.   Make a list of two produce products and two meat products and detail the specifications

that would be necessary when ordering these four products.

Produce:
Apples – for apples, specify the type, such as Golden Delicious or Granny Smith. The size (or count per case) is also important. The grade, being fancy or extra fancy, can affect the price and quality.

Potatoes – as in apples, the type (Idaho Russet, Russet Burbank, Norgold Russet), the count (70, 80 or 90), and the grade are most important. The potatoes are also expected to be uniform in size and shape, and free of dirt, cut and decay.

Meat:

Ground beef – the fat content of this product should be specified such as 80-20 (80 percent meat, 20% fat) or 75-25. For burgers to taste well and not to be too dry, a certain amount of fat is needed. Whether you will like a frozen or fresh product also needs to be specified. The USDA grade will also be helpful.

Chicken breast – the weight (4oz, 6oz, etc.), whether it should be frozen or fresh, bone-in or boneless, skin-on or skinless are all important.

14.   List the steps that would be necessary in handling a credit memo.

Rejection of a product may sometimes be unavoidable. In such instances, credit memos should be issued and handled in the following fashion:

i.   Request a credit memo from the delivery person.
ii.   Make sure the form is completed accurately reflecting the reason for the rejection.
iii.   Request the signature of the delivery person.
iv.   Annotate the rejection on the invoice so that the business office does not make payment for the product.
v.   Give a copy of the credit memo to the delivery person and place a copy in a separate folder.
vi.   Store the remaining delivery.
vii.   Call the delivery company to make them aware of the discrepancy.
viii.   Attach a credit memo to the invoice and forward it to the business office for payment once the purveyor replaces the product or in some way satisfies the discrepancy.

Examination Type Problems

1.   Explain the importance of tagging.

As the word tag suggests, tagging is simply putting a tag on a product. The tag is a card that records the price of the product, the date it was delivered, and other pertinent information such as count or weight. With the information on the tag, tagging aids in rotating inventory properly. It will also assist in maintaining sanitary procedures. If prices are placed on products during tagging, prices will also be readily available during the inventory process. Having prices on items may also reduce theft. Employees may be less apt to steal items when they know that management is able to quantify them. The perception of price can often reinforce the concept that food is money.

2.   List two food items that upon delivery would require a count.

Certain items need to be counted to ensure that theft does not occur. In a standing order where the delivery personnel will simply build the inventory up to the par level, managers need to count the number of products before and upon delivery so that the operation will not be overcharged. Milk and bread are two prime items that use the standing order purchasing method. It is also good practice to count items that are nicely packed. There are times that paper or other fillers might be added in the bottom of a box. Items that are bought by the count are good examples, such as apples, oranges etc. If the receiving personnel does not perform a count and the next person does not know that there should be 80 potatoes versus 70 in a box, the operation just lost 10 potatoes. Even worse, if 80 potatoes are needed, the operation will not only be short of the monetary value but will also need to buy more potatoes to meet the demand needed.

3.   List five items that would have to be measured during the receiving process.

Measurement can mean linear measurement, weights, and even temperature. Items that would have to be measured can include but are not limited to:
i.   Primal cuts (linear measure) – the difference between 1" lip (or fat) on a rib eye roll and that of a 2" lip is the fat that an operation paid for rather than meat. Thus, measuring the fat on these primal cuts is would be important.
ii.   Primal cuts (weight measure) – if an operation is buying whole tenderloins and then trimming and portion cutting into portions, the weight of the tenderloin is very important. A 7-up tenderloin is exactly what it should be, over 7 pounds and not under 7 pounds. Thus, besides measuring the fat, measuring the weight is as important.
iii.   Lobster/Portion cut meat (weight measure) – this is especially true for such high price items. If the weights were less than what they should be, the operation would have paid for something that they did not receive.
iv.   Lettuce – the temperature at which lettuce is transported is very important as extreme conditions can shorten its shelf life and quality. Thus, the receiving agent should spot check the temperature of these products.
v.   Cucumbers – certain produce of a certain grade means a certain weight should be achieved. Thus the weight of case of cucumbers is more important than the count of the cucumbers in the case.

4.   What could be an indication that a product had been allowed to thaw and was refrozen?

Ice crystals found on products can be an obvious indication that a product had been allowed to thaw and was refrozen. Other less obvious indications that cannot be easily seen but can be tasted would be the gritty texture in ice cream products.

Case Study

As a manager of Model, you do not directly order or receive the food items. The Purchasing Director and the Receiving Agent at Case-Study Hotel have both been in their positions for a good number of years and they both are very nice to their colleagues. One night, while you and your spouse were dining at an upscale restaurant, you observed that the Receiving Agent at the Case-Study Hotel was having dinner with the delivery driver who delivers meat products to the hotel. You recognize that particular driver because you were a bit suspicious when you saw him removing a case of food product from the freezer and placing it onto his delivery truck a week or so ago. When you saw that happen, you asked the Receiving Agent and he told you that the driver had previously delivered the wrong product. He also told you that you should pay more attention to your own duties and not concern yourself with other areas. As they finished their meal, you also observed that the delivery person paid for the meal and gave a white envelope to the Receiving Agent. All of the above incidents cause you to become suspicious and concerned. Below are three different choices for action:

1. Report the situation to higher authorities.

2. Do nothing unless you observe another similar situation.

3. Forget about it and pay more attention to your own tasks (as suggested by the receiving agent).

Discuss the pros and cons of each choice and recommend one.

As in any situation, it is always fair to accumulate all evidence before accusing somebody of an illegal or unethical act. Thus, this can be a very sensitive situation. For the first choice, to report the situation to higher authorities, the pros to this choice obviously is to clear up the situation. If this is true, then the higher authorities can take action and save the operation from these illegal dealings. They can conduct their own investigations and perhaps look at some other records to substantiate the stealing that might have occurred. In the end, if the receiving agent did not do anything wrong, he would be happy to have his name cleared also. On the other hand, if the situation is not true, then you will need to be able to apologize to the accused party and still be able to work together for the good of the operation.

If you choose to do nothing unless you observe another similar situation, this may also be wise to a certain extent since you only observe one situation. However, if you decide to put on Sherlock Holmes' hat and chase after the receiving agent and the delivery personnel, and not concentrate on your own job, this may not work out either. In addition, if you wait, the operation is going to lose more money in the interim.

The third choice is forgetting about the incident and paying more attention to your own tasks (as suggested by the receiving agent) may not be the best. One advantage perhaps is that you are out of the picture and need not to be concerned about this anymore. The guilty party, in this case the receiving agent, may also not hassle you. The cons obviously are that you are still allowing bad practices to remain unreported, that this person is still stealing from the operation, and this is hurting the bottom line. If other people also notice these practices and realize that these bad activities are tolerated, they may also get into the act and steal.

Thus, ethically, and also for the business, you should choose option one or two and not three.

References

Kotschevar, L.. H., & Levinson, C. (1988). <u>Quantity Food Purchasing</u>, third edition, New York: Macmillan, Inc.

Stefanelli, J. M. (1997). <u>Purchasing</u>. New York: John Wiley & Sons, Inc.

Warfel, M. C., & Waskey F. H. (1979). <u>The professional food buyer</u>. California: McCutchan Publishing Corporation.

CHAPTER 8

STORING AND ISSUING

I.   Purpose of the Chapter

The purpose of this chapter is to emphasize the importance of the protection of products from theft and deterioration.

II.   Overview of the Chapter

Proper storage is important to accountability and quality retention. In preparing items for storage, items must be tagged. This will make the procedures of first in, first out (FIFO) identifiable. But, most importantly tagging will force receiving personnel and storage room personnel to have to weigh and count products. Additionally prices are placed on items during tagging. This is beneficial to the control element in two ways. By having prices on items you can improve the perception and understanding that products are actually money. Also, it eases the inventory process because current prices are available when taking and extending inventory.

For control purposes all products in storage should have a specific location in the storage room. The shelves should be labeled and prices should be placed on the shelves. This aids in FIFO because items are not placed behind other items and forgotten. The procedures also speed up the inventory process and aid in sanitation of the storeroom. It can also help in identifying high cost times so that they will not be placed close to the door for easy pilferage. Expensive items should never be stored close to the door of the storeroom.

Delivery personnel should never be allowed in the storage room to store products. Only authorized employees should be allowed in the storage room. Delivery personnel may be tempted to remove items in empty cartoons on their way out. Therefore, do not allow delivery personnel to store products and keep storage areas locked at all times.

When issuing products a requisition should have been submitted. In all facilities products should be signed for when removed from storage. If products are not signed for you lose accountability. Products can come up missing and you will have no way of tracing them. The few minutes it takes to sign and date the removal of product from storage is a well worthwhile endeavor to the control process. A requisition form should be used if the organization is large enough, but even the smallest operations need to record any item that is removed.

It is important to point out that once products are issued, the management function of control is not finished. Products that are not used should be returned to storage personnel who should either hold the products for reissue or should see if the products cannot be returned to the vendor for credit. Management must understand that just because figures may balance it does not mean that the process is successful. It is only through constant observation and feedback from guests and employees that management can be assured that controls are functioning properly.

III.   Learning Objectives

1.   The six factors that must be considered when establishing a storage facility.

    a.   location and layout of facilities
    b.   temperature and humidity control
    c.   organization of placement of products
    d.   dating and pricing of stored products
    e.   record keeping, and
    f.   security

2.   The ideal factors associated with cold storage.

Cold storage is the preferred temperature for numerous perishable products. Eggs, butter, meats, fruits, and vegetables are held more safely at a temperature from 30°F to 45°F. This temperature is referred to as cold storage. It is important to remember that once food is removed from cold storage it should not be returned to cold storage. Produce should be located where air can circulate around the product. Products must also be stored to prevent the absorption of odors from each other.

3.   Some of the problems associated with the storage of beer.

Managers have to ensure the rotation of beer in storage, as beer does not mature with age. Beer begins to deteriorate as soon as it is processed and placed into containers for retail. Regular beer should be stored at a temperature of 40°F to 70°F while draft beer should be stored between 36°F and 38°F. As with all food products, it is imperative that first-in first-out procedures are used with the storage of beer and all other perishable products.

4.   How the copies of a requisition form should be distributed.

Maintaining and completing records is essential to proper control of products in storage. Whenever a product is required from storage, a requisition should be submitted to storage personnel. If the item is not in storage or has to be replaced to bring items back up to par, a standard purchase order form should be used. Orders placed in person, or over the telephone, should be confirmed on a purchase order form. One copy of the purchase order form should go to the vendor and a second copy should go to the accounting department. A third copy should go to the receiving clerk, and a copy should be kept on file in the storeroom or by the person that originated the request. The receiving clerk, who should be a representative of the accounting department, must receive all products. Once the receiving clerk is satisfied with the quantity, quality, and price of products, the clerk should record the quantity and description of the goods on the receiving sheet. The clerk would then place the products in storage if necessary or notify the department which ordered the products. The invoice would be sent to the auditor in the business office.

5.   How an operation would develop a reorder point.

Establishing the most effective reorder point is essential to controlling the amount of products in storage. The reorder point is the number of units to which the supply on hand should decrease before additional orders are placed. Before an operation can establish a reorder point for any item, it is necessary to know both normal usage and the time needed to obtain delivery. If products are essential to operational procedures, a safety level must also be developed to allow for delivery delays and for possible increased usage during that period. In the perpetual inventory method the reorder point is the equivalent of the desired ending inventory in the periodic method. Because purveyors are not willing to sell less than a case of certain products, management must be aware of these products before ordering and be prepared to stock products by the case. Once a par stock level and safety level has been determined, the amount that will be ordered each time the quantity of a particular item decreases to the reorder point can be determined. The calculation as to the quantity to reorder to bring inventory back to par stock is obtained as follows:

	Par stock	40
-	Reorder point	10
=	Subtotal	30
+	Normal usage until delivery	+ 5
=	Reorder quantity	35

As seen in the above example, 40 cases of French fries are needed as the par stock and the reorder point is set to be 10 cases. Therefore the subtotal of 30 cases is needed. However, knowing that you will normally use 5 cases once the order is placed but before it is delivered, this safety margin of 5 cases need to be added to the 30 cases to total the reorder quantity to 35 cases.

6.   The perpetual inventory method

The perpetual method is accomplished by recording the amount of products purchased, and as items are issued for use, the amounts issued are also recorded. The amounts recorded must reflect the movement of items into and out of storage. By following this procedure it is possible to examine the perpetual inventory records to determine how much of an item is in stock at the any given time. When a physical inventory is taken management can quickly determine if a product is over/under or missing. Information that is maintained in the perpetual inventory records is the name and address of the supplier, the most recent purchase price for an item, the par stock, reorder point, and reorder quantity.

7.   The importance of performing a physical inventory

For the purpose of control a physical inventory is a must. The physical inventory is the most commonly used control method of inventory in the hospitality field. This inventory is accomplished at the close of an accounting period. The process of taking a physical inventory requires that a physical count be made of each product on hand. It is best to have a list of products on hand before taking the inventory so that an item will not be omitted. Products should be listed in the inventory log in the same fashion as they are located on the shelves. This way, the individuals taking inventory can move in a logical manner through the storage facilities. It is advisable to list the items in stock in a book specifically for that purpose, in the same order in which they are maintained in stock. This facilitates a procedure that can be long and arduous, depending on the number of products in inventory. Two employees should be used to take a physical inventory. One person should count the products on hand, and the other person can record the amounts in the inventory log. Once quantities are determined for each item, total values can be calculated. Physical inventory can be calculated as follows:

	Opening inventory
+	Purchases during the accounting period
=	Total available for use
-	Closing inventory (number of units still available)
=	Amount consumed

8.   The importance of accounting for products after they are issued.

While storage, inventory, and issuing are very components of the control process it is essential for management to know what happens to products once they are issued. Just because all of the numbers balance and products are accounted for from the point of receiving to issuing, a manager has the additional responsibility of ensuring that the products are used for the purpose in which they were intended. If products are moved from storage they should be accounted for on some type of production sheet. If products are not used they should be returned to storage. All too often products that are not used are allowed to go unaccounted for and they eventually end up missing or written off. Managers must understand the importance of physically counting and comparing guest checks and the number of expensive items removed from storage to see if the items have been sold. Do not allow employees to take leftovers without asking. They may begin to generate leftovers through overpreparation. Eventually you will not be able to discern leftovers from other food products. Items that are issued that are not used should be returned to the storeroom.

9.   The correct method of storing products in a storage facility.

Products should be placed and located in storage in a manner where the most frequently used items are kept closest to the entrance. However, if all possible, do not place expensive items close to the entrance. Placing frequently used items close to the entrance will reduce the time required to move needed foods from storage, which will reduce labor costs over the long run. Additionally, the storeroom must be maintained in such a manner that each particular item has its on location and should be placed in the same location at all times. This will assist storeroom personnel in maintaining inventory by using first in and first out procedures and will make for easy access, as personnel will be come familiar with the location of products.

All food service employees must ensure first-in, first-out (FIFO) procedures. New deliveries should be stored behind the quantities already on hand. This will enable old items to be used before newer items which will help reduce the possibly of spoilage or infestation. All products should be stored 8 inches above the floor and shelving should be slatted to permit maximum circulation of air in refrigerated facilities for perishable foods. Solid steel shelving is usually preferred for non-perishables products. Food products should not be stored on the floor at anytime.

Beverages and food should be stored separately if possible as the humidity, temperature, and security concerns can be quite different. Alcoholic beverages can deteriorate or go bad very quickly. Because of the sensitivity of alcoholic beverages, thermometers should be used in both dry and refrigerated storage areas. The cork in wine bottles and the labels on alcoholic products can deteriorate because of humidity. Wines are also sensitive to vibrations and this must be a concern when storing expensive wine products. In addition, locking all liquor, beer, and wine storage areas may be a good practice in order to deter pilferage.

IV.   Definition of Key Terms

Bar codes - is a method for tracking products through an operation. It was invented with the idea that uniform symbols on items would facilitate control and tracking measures, reduce labor costs and increase inventory precision. Bar codes are printed on bundles of products, labels on products or the packaging itself. With the bar code method, a company assigns a number to every asset to be tracked and uses software to generate bar code asset tags encoded with the particular item's asset identification number. The number then links each item to its electronic file, which contains information such as the purchase date and cost, the person the equipment is assigned to, its location, the vendor, and any warranties, upgrades or license agreements. When the manufacturer provides bar codes, dealerships adapt them to their particular internal system. In this manner, all inventories that come in and out of their facilities are uniformly scanned, tracked and stored.

Cold storage - is the temperature from 30°F to 45°F and is the preferred temperature for numerous perishable products.

Directs - are usually inexpensive perishable products that are frequently purchased for immediate use, e.g., fresh produce, baked goods, and dairy products. For record keeping purposes, directs are treated as issued the moment they are received, and no further record is kept by receiving or storeroom personnel of these particular items.

Dry storage - is usually maintained at a temperature of 50°F to 70°F.

Freezer storage – is kept at a temperature of 0°F or lower.

Par stock - or "par" is the amount of product that should be on hand between one delivery and the next.

Perpetual inventory - is accomplished by recording the amount of products purchased, and as items are issued for use, the amounts issued are also recorded. The amounts recorded must reflect the movement of items into and out of storage. By following this procedure it is possible to examine the perpetual inventory records to determine how much of an item is in stock at the any given time.

Physical inventory – is a process that requires that a physical count be made of each product on hand.

Reorder point - is the number of units to which the supply on hand should decrease before additional orders are placed.

Requisition – is a form that is used to request supplies from storage.

Stores – are products that will be placed into storage as they have a long shelf life and will not be used for the delivery day's function.

V.   Teaching Outline

A.   The Storage Function
      1.   Location and Layout of Facilities
      2.   Temperature and Humidity Control
      3.   Organization of Placement of Products
      4.   Dating and Pricing of Stored Products
      5.   Record Keeping
      6.   Security
B.   The Issuing Function
      1.   Process
      2.   Requisition Forms
C.   Inventory
      1.   Par Stock
      2.   Order Quantity
      3.   Periodic Inventory
      4.   Perpetual Inventory

5.   Inventory Management
6.   Inventory Turnover
7.   Unused Products
D.   New Technology
1.   Bar Codes
2.   Retina Identification

VI.   Questions and Answers

Review Exercises

1.   It is important from a control point of view that when performing a physical inventory:

   a.   at least two people take the inventory
   b.   the inventory is done once a month
   c.   it occurs during the middle of an accounting period
   d.   includes items that are on order

2.   A method of assigning values to an inventory is:

   a.   last in first out
   b.   first in first out
   c.   actual purchase price
   d.   all of the above

3.   Excessive products on hand can cause the following disadvantage:

   a.   price of the item may increase
   b.   the item may become limited on the market
   c.   excessive capital tied up in the inventory account
   d.   all of the above

4.   The inventory turnover rate can be calculated by:

   a.   multiplying the amount of inventory by sales
   b.   dividing the cost of products sold by the average inventory
   c.   adding the ending and closing inventory amounts
   d.   dividing sales by the average inventory

5.   Which of the following is important when establishing a storage facility?

   a.   location
   b.   record keeping
   c.   type of inventory
   d.   only a and b

6.   A benefit of placing dates and prices on products is:

   a.   the vendor would be known
   b.   it will assist in rotating stocks

   c.   management would know when to reorder
   d.   all of the above

7. Products received by a food service operation normally fall into two categories:

   a.   directs and stores
   b.   directs and perishables
   c.   stores and perishables
   d.   frozen and dry

8. Stores are items such as:

   a.   canned goods
   b.   flour
   c.   sugar
   d.   all of the above

9. A par stock is:

   a.   the amount that is ordered for a new restaurant
   b.   the amount on hand between deliveries
   c.   is determined by the vendor
   d.   the amount on hand during a promotion

10. Which of the following is a major issue regarding storing?

   a.   security of products
   b.   linen products
   c.   bulk items such as flour and sugar
   d.   the time of delivery

Review Exercises Answers

1. a
2. d
3. c
4. b
5. d
6. b
7. a
8. d
9. b
10. a

11.   What are the procedures for distribution of a requisition?

       The key form for accountability in the issuing process is the requisition form. For control measures to work properly, the process always starts with a requisition form. Requisitions must always be used to obtain products from storage. A product should not be issued unless a requisition is received.

The procedure starts with a member of the operation listing the items and quantities needed from the storeroom on the requisition. The supervisor of the department in which the products are to be used then signs and thus authorizes the requisition. This supervisor should check to see if each item appearing is genuinely required and is in the amount listed. The requisition is then taken to the storeroom. It is also a good practice to submit requisitions in advance to enable storeroom personnel to prepare orders without having to rush. This will also train banquet and kitchen personnel to anticipate needs and plan for production. Storeroom personnel will then extend the cost of each requisition. The total dollar value of items issued would then be extended and totaled. One copy of the requisition should be maintained by the storeroom to be forwarded to the accounting department so that the cost of products used by each outlet can be easily identified and computed. The other copy should accompany the filled order to go back to the department that originated the requisition so that records can be kept and also to ensure that the products requested were filled correctly.

12. How would you establish the par level for flour if 10 pounds are used on a daily basis and

you receive deliveries every five days?

Before money should be invested in inventory, a par-stock level should be established. A par stock level or "par" is the amount of product that should be on hand between one delivery and the next. In this case, if 10 pounds are used per day and deliveries are made every five days, then the part level has to be at least 50 pounds (10 pounds per day X 5 days). Although on the fifth day, the delivery will come, you still want to count that day just in case the delivery was made toward the end of the day or there is an emergency and the delivery was not made on the fifth day. The par stock for items may have to change with the season and if there is a change in times between deliveries or a seasonal change in demand. This level of par stock must be evaluated from time to time to see if the amount being held in inventory is sufficient. When establishing par stock levels, management will have to consider the relative quantities of an item being used.

13. List six ways in which bar codes may be used to support the control function of a food

service operation.

i.   Bar coding provides a method for tracking products through an operation.
ii.   Bar coding, done electronically, can account for all inventory that comes in and out of an operation, and not only the high cost ones.
iii. It also aids in cost determination of prices since the cost of each product can also be linked to the bar code.
iv.   It can aid in product usage analysis.
v.   With such detailed reports, it may also deter theft.
vi.   Again with a more detailed reporting system, bar coding can definitely aid management in ordering the right amount needed.

14. What control procedure(s) would you use to ensure that physical inventory will be taken

accurately?

First, the process of taking inventory of the storeroom should not be completed by using only storeroom personnel. When taking inventory, two people will make a better control team. One will count and call out the amount while the other one will record the amount in the inventory book. This does not only cut the time of inventory taking but also reduces the temptation of stealing. Another point perhaps is that during the inventory process, the storeroom should be closed off. There should also not be any issuing of products during the inventory process as this will provide a chance of error or stealing.

Examination Type Problems

1.   What is the formula used to determine inventory turnover and what are some advantages

of performing this calculation?

Inventory turnover can be determined by dividing cost of the products sold for the period by the average inventory amount for the same period. In other words,

$$\frac{\text{Cost of products sold for the period}}{\text{Average inventory}}$$

Some advantages of calculating inventory turnover are:
i.   To account for spoilage, because food must be held too long before being used
ii.   To prevent excessive capital being tied up in inventory
iii.   To prevent incurring higher than necessary labor cost to handle the greater amount of food
iv.   To prevent greater than necessary space allocated to storage
v.   To provide unwarranted opportunities for theft

2.   What formula would you use to determine the amount of products consumed during the

accounting period?

The formula used for determining the amount of products consumed during the accounting period will be as follows:

	Opening inventory
+	Purchases during the accounting period
=	Total available for use
-	Closing inventory (number of units still available)
=	Amount consumed

3.   If you were operating an upscale steak house, in what order might you have products

stored in the refrigerator?

There are a few preferred methods to arrange the products in the storage area. First, products can be arranged alphabetically and thus the inventory book can be typed nicely, in alphabetical order. A better method is to organize the storeroom according to the way that the products will be used with those that are used most placed closer to the entrance for easy access. The inventory book will then be organized by the location of the products in the storeroom. This will make the taking of inventory a lot more efficient. Since this is an upscale steak house, steaks will obviously be used quite often. Yet, placing high priced items near the entrance of a storage area will not only provide easy access for employees but also provide easy access for those dishonest employees who may steal from the operation. Thus, the higher priced items may need to be placed further away from the storeroom entrance.

4.   Explain how a requisition would be extended and the importance of this activity.

Extending a requisition means that the unit cost of each item on the requisition will be multiplied by the quantity requisitioned of that item. The total dollar value of items issued would then be calculated by adding all the individual costs. This activity is important since the total cost of the products requisitioned can be maintained. This will aid in the calculation of the total product usage at the end of the accounting period.

Case Study

The Storeroom Manager of the Case-Study Hotel was talking to you over lunch at the employee cafeteria. He told you that one of your cooks went to him at 9 o'clock in the morning requesting a 2½ pound can of coffee. The cook said that they just ran out of coffee and they were still serving breakfast and the dining room was packed. The Storeroom Manager asked him for his requisition and he said he did not have time to fill one out and would try to look for the shift supervisor to sign it, as this was an emergency. He told you that this individual had the same problem a couple of weeks before with a different item. At that time the cook told him that he would get a requisition completed right after breakfast and it was two days later before he gave the Storeroom Manager the requisition. As the Restaurant Manager, write out the process of proper requisition and present it to your staff so that such incidents will not happen in the future. Please outline the process point by point starting with assessing the needs of the restaurant to receiving the products from the Storeroom Manager.

Case Study Answers

Requisition procedures for the food service outlets for the Case Study Hotel:
i.   Assess the product needs of the restaurant using sales information and other forecasts. This should be done during the shift for the products needed for the subsequent day.
ii.   Obtain the approval and signature of the shift supervisor.
iii.   Turn in requisition form to the storeroom personnel by the end of the shift. This will give the storeroom personnel ample time to pull the products.

iv.   Before the beginning of the shift of the subsequent day, obtain the products from the storeroom personnel.

v.   Check the products against the items listed on the requisition form. This will provide a chance for correction before the products leave the storage area.

CHAPTER 9

PREPARATION AND PRODUCTION

I.   Purpose of the Chapter

This purpose of the chapter is to make students aware that even though accountability for products has been maintained, unless control is given special attention during preparation and production waste and theft can occur on a consistent basis.

II.   Overview of the Chapter

Every effort must be made to prevent waste during the preparation and production phase. Standardized recipes, with specific procedures for measurements, weights, and amounts of yield must be in place. Tools must be available to ensure that ingredients can be measured during the production process. Equipment must be in place and maintained if the production process is to generate consistency and save labor costs. If personnel use equipment that is not appropriate for the task that needs to be accomplished, they may not maintain consistency and may also damage the equipment. Forecasting has to be as accurate as possible to prevent the development of leftover products. Production sheets must be completed with the required amount of yields, time of preparation, and the individuals responsible for preparing the products. If leftovers exist and they are still wholesome enough to be consumed, management should try and find a means of utilizing them as soon as possible to prevent further deterioration of the product.

Efforts must also be made to reduce waste through errors in production. If standardized recipes are not followed, mistakes in preparation and cooking will exist. Products may have to be discarded as inedible or because of a lack of appeal to guests. This can be the result of production errors or mistakes in recipe conversions. Recipe conversion must be taken very seriously because discarding a large amount of a product that has to be remade will double the food and labor costs of that product. Reducing the possibility of production errors is why, if possible, only one individual should be involved in the preparation of a food product. In special cases, to prevent an error in over or under production, management may want to devise a contingency menu for special occasions.

Accurate food costs of products have to be derived in order for products to be priced correctly. Additionally, portion control must be in place if standards are to be met. Employees should not be allowed to deviate from the standards. If management decides to substitute a product or ingredient to reduce cost, it must be realized that in most cases quality will be compromised.

Management must be aware that the public has a standard perception of consistency, taste, and appearance of certain products. If the taste, consistency, or appearance of a product is not as the perception of the norm, guest count may decrease. Therefore, management must be trained to recognize and evaluate standard products. This is true even if the products are specialties of the facility.

Because of trying to maintain consistency in products and portion control, the production process can be the most difficult step in the control process. Pilferage must be prevented though accountability and management attention to detail. During the production process, there are so many opportunities for pilferage through substitution and incorrect portion sizes. Management must constantly observe production personnel procedures and guests reactions. All of the control procedures in the previous processes can be lost if products are not consistent and at least adequate. The best quality of meat could have been purchased, received, and issued to the kitchen but if it is overcooked or cooked at a temperature that is too high, the product can be ruined. If spatulas are not used to get the remains out of cans and jars, servings can be thrown away. If someone accidentally puts too much salt in a product, it can be ruined. If potatoes are allowed to remain in an automatic potato peeler too, long portions can be lost. If too much of the ends of products such as carrots or onions are cut off, again you will lose portions. During the preparation and production process, management must constantly monitor standards to ensure that consistency is maintained and waste does not occur.

III.   Learning Objectives

1. Ways to prevent waste during production

Efforts must also be made to reduce waste through errors in production If standardized recipes are not followed, mistakes in preparation and cooking will exist. Products may have to be discarded as inedible or because of a lack of appeal to guests. This can be the result of production errors or mistakes in recipe conversions. Recipe conversion must be taken very seriously because discarding a large amount of a product that has to be remade will double the food and labor costs of that product. Reducing the possibility of production errors is why, if possible, only one individual should be involved in the preparation of a food product. In special cases to prevent an error in over- or under-production, management may want to devise a contingency menu for special occasions.

2. The importance of forecasting to the production process

A hospitality operation would like the last serving of a food product to be served to the last guest in the line. While everyone understands the difficulty of attaining this, every effort must be made to try and reach this point of efficiency when projecting for the volume of production. While forecasting for future sales is extremely difficult, hospitality operations must make these types of business decisions on a daily and weekly basis. Projecting sales in the hospitality industry is crucial to cost control as items cannot be placed back into inventory. Decisions must be made for production and personnel as well as for other components of the business. This type of planning requires forecasting future amounts of business that will probably occur. Forecasting is usually based on what is occurring at the present time and what has occurred in the past.

3. Recipe conversion procedures

Standardized recipes produce standard yields and they are usually developed to produce yields of 25, 50, 75, or 100 servings. Because an operation cannot afford waste and must forecast as accurately as possible for the exact number to be served, recipes must be converted to the number of sales projected. The standard yield of the recipe may be too large or too small and the recipe or formula has to be converted to yield the amount required. Before converting a standardized recipe, all of the items in the recipe must be reduced to a common denominator and a working factor must be developed. For example, all pounds should be changed to ounces. Once the amounts of all the ingredients have been changed to the same measurement, then the quantity of each ingredient is multiplied by the working factor. Once the multiplication process has been completed all ingredients can be changed back to useable measurements. Once the ingredients have been reduced to a common denominator, the working factor should then be developed. If the desired amount of the product is greater than the amount yielded by the standard recipe, divide the standard yield of the recipe into the amount desired to develop a working factor.An example as to how to develop a working factor is as follows:
The yield of the standard recipe is 50 and the amount required is 400

$$\frac{400 \text{ Amount required}}{50 \text{ Recipe yield}} = 8 \text{ Working factor}$$

This situation illustrates that the amount desired is 8 times the yield of the standard recipe. Therefore, multiplying the quantity of each ingredient in the recipe by 8 will establish the correct amount of ingredients to be used. The example shows that the working factor is a whole number, which makes multiplication simple; however, this is not always the case. Sometimes the working factor can result in a mixed decimal fraction.

Recipe Yield is 50 and the amount required is 440

$$\frac{440 \text{ Amount required}}{50 \text{ Recipe yield}} \quad = \quad 8.8 \text{ Working factor}$$

This example illustrates that the amount required is 8.8 times the amount yielded by the standard recipe. Therefore, multiply the quantity of each ingredient in the recipe or formula by 8.8 to obtain the required amount.

4. The importance of using measuring devices during production

Employees must be trained to use standardized recipes and measuring devices. Not only will the utilization of measuring devices aid in preventing waste through over usage; they can prevent ruining a product because of an incorrect measurement.

5. How to arrive at the food cost for a product

To arrive at the food cost for a particular product the cost of the ingredients to develop the recipe should be totaled. Then the cost for each ounce of a serving should be determined and the cost of each portion be determined.

6. Why only one person should be in charge of preparing a product

Only one person should be in charge of preparing a product because it reduces the possibility of production errors. One individual may place more or less of an ingredient in a product because he/she may not be aware that another individual has added the ingredient to the product.

7. How production errors can increase costs

Production errors can increase costs because products could become ruined and have to be discarded or they can lose consistency and become unacceptable to guest.

8. The significance of portion control to cost, time, and perception of value

Portion control has to be maintained if food cost is to remain within cost standards. If products are not cooked properly during production, servings and portions will be incorrect. If too much water is used when cooking vegetables, nutritional value as well as the dissipation of portions can occur. If meats such as spareribs, ham hocks, or baked chicken are over-cooked, portions can be lost due to the meat falling off the bone. If recipes and cooking times are not followed, expensive meat portions can be lost which will increase food cost. Not only must the cooking times of meats be adhered to, in many cases, additional portions will have to be prepared because of the overcooking and this wastes time as well as money. Management must be aware that the public has a standard perception of consistency, taste, and appearance of certain products.

9. Why it is important to have a production schedule

Providing a production schedule or cook's worksheet for controlling cost is essential in maintaining consistency and in preventing production errors. A production schedule will enable management to maximize the utilization of labor and other resources. A schedule will also help managers in estimating the utilization of personnel and equipment. If too many baked items are being prepared for the same meal the equipment may not be able to support the meal. The same can be said for the deep fat fryer and other equipment. A production schedule will assist managers in identifying these problems so alternatives can be made. When assigning personnel, management would be able to conserve labor hours by having personnel come in when needed, or if they are on a regular work schedule, other tasks can be assigned when production is not being done.

10. The cost relationship in substituting products

Food service operations are always looking for ways to reduce cost and increase profit. Maintaining and controlling costs is a continuous problem for food service operations. In order to increase profit an operation can select from four activities. These activities are as follows:
i.   reduce quality
ii.   reduce portion sizes
iii.   increase prices
iv.   substitute products

Any of these activities may have an effect on quality and the perception of value. If you reduce quality, guests are apt to identify this very quickly. There is a difference in substituting products that may have a cheaper cost than it is to substitute quality. If a cut of meat is tougher because of changing quality it will be noticed. If an operation attempts to reduce the size of their portions it will definitely be noticed. Once an operation begins to "play games" with prices, the laws of supply and demand will begin to take effect and you may decrease guest count. Therefore, the least threatening of the four factors in trying to control cost is to try and substitute an ingredient of the same quality that may have a lower price. An example of this would be to use walnuts instead of pecans in bakery products. Instead of using vine ripe tomatoes for cooking and by being very selective, other tomatoes can be used.

11. Effective ways to try to use leftovers

Even though management may attempt to forecast food sales as accurately as possible there are still so many uncertainties that cannot be anticipated. If there is a vast decrease in projected guest count, a full service facility can end up with a great deal of leftovers. When leftovers occur, management has the task of trying to prevent the waste of these products. When dealing with leftovers the following four factors must be considered:

i.   Leftovers must be used at the very next meal or as soon as possible.
ii.   They must be heated to an internal temperature of at least 165°F without interference of the heating process.
iii.   Management should change the face of leftovers.
iv.   Management should never attempt to offer leftovers a second time.

Because of the potential dangers of serving improperly handled leftovers, management must not allow the sole aim of reducing food cost to influence them in trying to serve questionable products. Because of the dangers of using leftovers, leftovers should be served at the very next meal. Food is always deteriorating. The longer food is held, the greater the possibilities for further deterioration, contamination, and bacterial growth. If leftovers are served as the same product, they may lack the consistency and quality that guests expect. Most importantly, leftovers could make someone ill. Because of the danger of serving leftovers, they should always be reheated to at least 165° F as quickly as possible. For safety reasons and prudent and ethical management, controlling cost should never be an overriding factor in using leftovers.

12. The importance of a contingency menu

It is important for production personnel to have contingency menus. Contingency menus are necessary in preventing the development of leftovers. There are times when a reduction in the amount to prepare may not suffice. Major events and other situations can cause a vast increase or decrease in guest count, and thus may entail using a different menu. If guest count increases significantly, the equipment in the facility may not be able to handle the regular menu. If guest count decreases significantly it may not be cost effective to prepare certain items. If there is an annual major event, management should anticipate this and develop contingencies for food production and labor volume in order to control cost. If the operation depends upon some type of seasonal product, contingency menus should be available as the length of seasons can vary from year to year.

13. The essential factors that should be listed on a kitchen production worksheet

As a minimum, a production schedule should have the following:

i.   What is to be prepared?
ii.   What method of preparation to use (Standardized recipe)?
iii.   What amount is to be prepared?
iv.   When it is to be prepared?
v.   Who will prepare the product?
vi.   Amount of leftovers?
vii.   Items returned to storage?

14. The importance of correct tools, equipment usage, and maintenance

Just as measuring devices are important to proper production procedures, so are other tools and equipment. Without the proper tools and equipment, it will be very difficult for production personnel to comply with control factors. Standards cannot be maintained if the correct equipment is not available. Additionally, if production personnel have to search for the correct tools, they are apt to take short cuts. Taking short cuts, again, can result in not performing the task completely or even to someone becoming injured because of not having the correct equipment ormalfunctioning equipment or tools. Personnel should be informed as to how to properly use tools and equipment. When equipment is filled over its capacity or if employees are allowed to abuse equipment, it will become very costly for the operation. Maintenance must be routinely done and not viewed as tasks to be completed because there is nothing else to do. Documentation as to how equipment should be cleaned and what type of cleaners should be used must be readily available or employees may use incorrect procedures or compounds. Schedules must be designed and posted as to how, when, and who should clean a piece of equipment.

15. Ways in which pilferage can occur during the production process

Food is stolen during production mainly through shorting the guest portion size, not returning products to storage, and unauthorized eating by employees. While there is a possibility of theft throughout the control process, it is during the production and serving process when the manager must really understand the techniques of control. Far too many managers believe that if numbers balance from purchasing through production, then the control process has been completed. Most students are indoctrinated with this process in mind. If input equals output, then all is okay. This is far from the truth when dealing with consumable products. Managers in the hospitality industry are constantly losing the profits and eventually their jobs, and food service facilities are constantly failing because of a reduction in sales and or increase in costs. In a large majority of cases, it is because the perception of value by guests has decreased. If guests do not perceive that they are receiving the amount and quality of food that is expected they will take their business to another facility. Guests may not always complain they will simply not come back.

IV.   Definition of Key Terms

Contingency menu – is a menu that is designed for major fluctuations in sales. Their could be a vast increase or decrease, but without being able to adjust the hospitality facility could incur a loss.

Leftovers – are products that are remaining because the total amount forecasted on the production sheet was not requested by the guest.

Pilferage – is to take or consume resources without permission.

Production errors – occur when mistakes are made in not following standard recipes.

Production schedule – is a worksheet designed to inform production personnel with thewho, what, and when, amount, and the standard recipe number of how to prepare products.

Recipe conversion – is the method used to increase or decrease the yield amount of a standard recipe.

Recipe yield – is the formula amount that is developed for a standard recipe. When the recipe is properly prepared, it will yield that amount.

Sales history – is the important data concerning previous sales. It may include any sales information that management may prepare it to retain.

Standardized recipe – is a formula for preparing a prescribed amount of a product and it provides all of the necessary information for preparing the product.

Substitution – is the replacing in a recipe of an item of similar texture and origin so as not to distort the recipe itself.

Time series – is a sequence of measurements for some variable or composite of variables arranged in chronological order of their occurrences. Therefore, the forecasting of sales will usually be far more successful when organized procedures of this type are used.

Working factor – is a fraction that can be used to convert the yield of a standard recipe. If the amount required is less than the amount yielded by the standard recipe, place the amount desired over the amount yielded by the standard recipe to form a fraction. Simplify the fractions to the lowest terms to find the working factor and multiply the quantity of each ingredient in the recipe by the fraction to get the desired amounts.

V.   Teaching Outline

A.   Employee Training
B.   Forecasting in Production
C.   Determining Purchases and Food Costs
D.   Recipe Conversion
E.   Production Schedule
F.   Measuring Devices
G.   Production Errors and Waste
H.   Portion Control
I.   Beverage Production Control

VI.   Questions and Answers

Review Exercises

1. The first step toward ensuring quality products and dining experiences that meet or exceed guest expectations is:

    a.   planning production
    b.   developing service procedures
    c.   ordering products
    d.   preparing products

2. A production schedule reflects a forecast and is used to:

    a.   set production goals for a chef and staff
    b.   establish production standards
    c.   list production techniques to be used in training
    d.   inform production personnel of new recipes

3. The chef needs to prepare carrots for 400 guests. The portion size is 4 oz. per guest. If carrots have a waste percentage of 10%, what is the total edible portion that needs to be prepared?

    a.   300 lb.
    b.   200 lb.
    c.   400 lb.
    d.   100 lb.

4. Referring to question #3, what is the total purchased amount needed?

    a.   90.0 lb.
    b.   110.00 lb.
    c.   111.11 lb.
    d.   120.00 lb.

5.   The working factor to convert a recipe if the standardized recipe is for 100 guests and the number of guests for a function is 500 is:

    a.   4.00
    b.   1.25
    c.   0.20
    d.   5.00

6.   Which of the following items is not necessarily pertinent information to be included in a production schedule?

    a.   method of preparation to use
    b.   amount to be prepared
    c.   when food is to be prepared
    d.   the name of the group the food is to be prepared for

7.   Standardized recipes should be used in:

    a.   restaurants in a hotel
    b.   restaurants in a club
    c.   food service outlets in institutions
    d.   all of the above

8.   What can sales history provide in forecasting for food production?

    a.   identify guest counts or trends for certain meal times
    b.   identify waitstaff performance level
    c.   identify the working factor for recipe conversion
    d.   identify how long the restaurant has been open

9.   Which of the following items is an activity that can cause errors in production?

    a.   day of the week
    b.   temperature
    c.   weather
    d.   number of guests served

10.   Which of the following is considered pilferage in the production process?

    a.   cooks using a different measuring device
    b.   cooks taking food home without permission
    c.   cooks giving waitstaff food as part of employees benefits
    d.   cooks not communicating well with the waitstaff

Review Exercises Answers

1.   a
2.   a
3.   d
4.   c
5.   d

6.   d
7.   d
8.   a
9.   b
10.   d

11.   List five activities that can cause production errors.

(The answers to this question may vary as there are many factors that can cause production errors. Seven factors are suggested here.) Five activities that can cause production errors are:
i.   not following standardized recipes
ii.   inadequate or incorrect employee training
iii.   inaccurate production forecast
iv.   confused AP and UP for production; may end up with more or less food products as required
v.   incorrect recipe conversion which again can lead to more or less food products
vi.   incorrect preparation of a production schedule/sheet
vii.   measuring devices were either not available or not used

12.   List five ways in which pilferage can occur during production.

(The answers to this question may vary as there are many reasons which pilferage can occur during production. Six factors are suggested here.) Five means in which pilferage can occur during production are:
i.   inconsistency in product quality either by incorrect preparation method or not following standardized recipes
ii.   incorrect portioning by waitstaff such as placing too much dressing on salads can be unacceptable as well as costly
iii.   incorrect portioning by kitchen staff, such as putting 4.5 oz of ham for a sandwich rather than 4 oz
iv.   cooking product at a higher temperature leading to more shrinkage and thus less yield
v.   simple cooking error to guests' requests causing orders to be sent back
vi.   pilferage can also occur when there is a breakdown in communication such as a drop in guest count and the kitchen is not notified of the change

13.   What is the working factor to convert a recipe of 50 to feed 220 guests?

The working factor is calculated by dividing the number of guests served by number of yield given in the recipe. In this case, it will be 220 divided by 50, or 4.40.

14.   In preparing the Mother's Day Lunch Buffet, you are estimating a total guest count of 450. Of the 450 guests, you forecasted that 200 would take the steamship round. The portion size for each guest for the steamship round is set at 4 ounces, and the waste factor

due to timing, cooking and the like is 25%. How much meat will need to be purchased for

the buffet?

The yield formula for deriving the correct amount is as follows:

$$AP = \frac{EP}{1 - W\%}$$ where AP = as purchased
EP = edible portion
W% = waste percentage

If management would like to serve 200 portions of 4 ounces cooked steamship round and 25 percent of the portion is lost during trimming, cooking, and portioning, then the amount that needs to be purchased would be as follows:

200 people x $\frac{4 \text{ oz}}{\text{person}}$ x $\frac{1 \text{ lb.}}{16 \text{ oz}}$ = $\frac{200 \times 4 oz}{16}$ = 50 lb. EP

Thus AP will be:

$\frac{50.0}{1 - 0.25}$ = $\frac{50.0}{0.75}$ = 66.66 lb. AP

15.   There is normally a 5% waste in cleaning iceberg lettuce. If 6 oz. per serving is needed for

each guest, how much lettuce will need to be purchased for a banquet of 60? If processed

iceberg is $1.10 per pound and regular iceberg is $1.00, should you buy the processed

iceberg (ignore the labor involved for calculation purpose)?

The yield formula for deriving at the correct amount is as follows:

$$AP = \frac{EP}{1 - W\%}$$ where AP = as purchased
EP = edible portion
W% = waste percentage

If management would like to serve 60 portions of 6 ounces of lettuce and 5 percent of the portion is lost due to preparation, then the amount that needs to be purchased would be as follows:

60 people x $\frac{6 \text{ oz}}{\text{person}}$ x $\frac{1 \text{ lb.}}{16 \text{ oz}}$ = $\frac{60 \times 6 oz}{16}$ = 22.5 lb. EP

Thus AP will be:

$\frac{22.5}{1 - 0.05}$ = $\frac{22.5}{0.95}$ = 23.68 lb. AP

Purchasing raw and processed at the operation:
    23.68 lb. X $1.00 per pound = $23.68
Purchasing as edible portion of 22.5 lb.:
    22.5 lb. X $1.10 per pound = $24.75
Thus, it will be more economical to buy them raw than processed (ignoring labor costs as indicated in the question.

Examination Type Problems

1.   Using the yield formula, determine how many pounds of beef rib would production

personnel have to request from storage to serve 200 people 6 ounces each when 40

percent is lost through cooking and trimming?

The yield formula for deriving at the correct amount is as follows:

$$AP = \frac{EP}{1 - W\%} \qquad \text{where } AP = \text{as purchased}$$
$$EP = \text{edible portion}$$
$$W\% = \text{waste percentage}$$

If management would like to serve 200 portions of 6 ounces cooked rib and 40 percent of the portion is lost during trimming, cooking, and portioning, then the amount that needs to be purchased would be as follows:

$$200 \text{ portions} \times \frac{6 \text{ oz}}{\text{portion}} \times \frac{1 \text{ lb.}}{16 \text{ oz}} = \frac{200 \times 6 \text{ oz}}{16} = 75 \text{ lb. EP}$$

Thus AP will be:

$$\frac{75.0}{1 - 0.40} = \frac{75.0}{0.60} = 125 \text{ lb. AP}$$

2.   Using the recipe conversion formula, convert the following recipe for dinner rolls from 12

dozen to 8 dozen.

1 pound 4 ounces granulated sugar
1 pound 4 ounces shortening
8 ounces dry milk
2 ounces salt
5 ounces whole eggs
6 ounces yeast
3 pounds cold water
7 pounds soft four

Working factor for this recipe conversion process is 8 divided by 12 or 0.67 (or 2/3). Thus the answer will be:
13.33 ounces granulated sugar
13.33 ounces shortening
5.33 ounces dry milk
1.33 ounces salt
5.33 ounces whole eggs
4 ounces yeast
2 pounds cold water
4.67 pounds soft four

3.   Describe four important procedures that should be adhered to when handling leftovers.

Four procedures that should be adhered to when handling leftovers are:
i.   Leftovers must be used at the very next meal or as soon as possible.

ii.   They must be heated to an internal temperature of at least 165°F without interference of the heating process.
iii.   Management should change the face of leftovers.
iv.   Management should never attempt to offer leftovers a second time.

4.   Describe two examples as to why only one person should be responsible for a product

during production.

There are a number of reasons to why only one person should be responsible for a product during production. This answer will outline two examples. First, specifying who should prepare the product will reduce any possibility of errors during the production process. If a specific person is not responsible for each product there can be a break down in one of these steps. An ingredient could be placed into a product twice or individuals may assume that the other person is going to take care of a specific procedure and it may never get accomplished. If one person completes the production task from beginning to end, there is less chance of a problem occurring.
Second, for sanitation purposes, if a product such as chicken salad is to be prepared and the ingredients are prepared at different shifts or by different people, any lag time will allow the product to stand at room temperature and a guest could become very ill from consuming the salad.

5.   A standardized recipe called for 10 pounds of julienne onions for making French Onion

soup. If the waste factor for onions is 10%, how much onion needs to be purchased?

The yield formula for deriving at the correct amount is as follows:
$$AP = \frac{EP}{1 - W\%}$$
where AP = as purchased
EP = edible portion
W% = waste percentage
If 10 pounds of julienne onions are needed and the waste factor is 10%, then the amount that needs to be purchased would be as follows:
$$\frac{10.0}{1 - 0.10} = \frac{10.0}{0.90} = 11.11 \text{ lb. AP}$$

6.   A conference group booked a banquet for 350 and has chosen zucchini as one of the

vegetables. If 2 ounces of zucchini batonettes are served to each guest and the waste

factor in preparing zucchini batonettes is 10%, how much is the "as purchased" amount?

The yield formula for deriving at the correct amount is as follows:
$$AP = \frac{EP}{1 - W\%}$$
where AP = as purchased
EP = edible portion
W% = waste percentage
If management would like to serve 350 portions of 2 ounces of zucchini and the waste/lost factor is 10%, then the amount that needs to be purchased would be as follows:

$$350 \text{ portions } \times \frac{2 \text{ oz}}{\text{portion}} \times \frac{1 \text{ lb.}}{16 \text{ oz}} = \frac{350 \times 2 \text{ oz}}{16} = 43.75 \text{ lb. EP}$$

Thus AP will be:

$$\frac{43.75}{1 - 0.10} = \frac{43.75}{0.90} = 48.61 \text{ lb. AP}$$

Case Study

As the manager of Model Restaurant, you are always concerned with controlling cost. You are walking through the kitchen and you see your baker making rolls for the day's business and he is not measuring his ingredients. This is the second time you have observed him not measuring ingredients and you had told him about it before. You question him about it and he tells you he has been making the rolls this way for over two years and there is no need for a standardized recipe for rolls. The baker is a very dependable and highly motivated employee. He is always willing to come in on call. However, he only works five days a week. You are concerned with the consistency of the products and the fact that when he is off for days, an inexperienced cook will have to prepare the rolls. You go back to your office and check the purchases of flour and you notice that there is a vast amount of waste in that product. You do not want to de-motivate the baker but you would like him to measure the ingredients so that you will be able to maintain the cost of all products and you will also be able to develop the same quality product when he is not working. What are some steps that you can initiate to have the preparation and production of dinner rolls followed? Give four suggestions and explain the importance of each suggestion.

Case Study Answers

The vast amount of waste in flour can be due to two main reasons. One is that the baker is actually using more flour than a normal recipe. If the product is better, and is what is preferred, then the recipe will need to be changed so that new cost structure can be used. The second reason can be that the inexperienced cook is also not following any recipe since there is no recipe to follow; thus flour is used. Following are five suggestions:

i. Have a meeting with the entire baking staff and show them the purchases of flour and the waste calculated. This can relate them to waste, costs, and the profit of the business. The more they understand the importance of their jobs, the more they are part of the operation.

ii. Ask them to do a trial batch of rolls and put different amounts of flour and taste the products. In doing so, they can taste the wrong product first hand and also can compared different quality.

iii.   Show them the importance of a standardized recipe and that how people of different skills can follow the same recipe and produce a product of consistency. When people actually do it, they will be more receptive to an idea than just being told to do something.

iv.   Show them how cost can be calculated very easily with a standardized recipe and how important that is in projecting profit. When they understand this, they can also understand that if profits are there, there will be a better chance for a raise than when the operation is losing money.

CHAPTER 10

SERVICE

I.   Purpose of the Chapter

The purpose of this chapter is to emphasize to students how control activities do not only consist of balancing numbers but must include controlling all operational activities and that guest services must be controlled.

II.   Overview of the Chapter

Controlling guest service can also be a difficult task for managers because as with the production process, it is also labor intensive. In order to control the service process, it is very important to have employees trained in your method of delivery and service. As stated earlier, controls rely to a great extent on perceptions. A manager must let it be known that poor guest service will not be tolerated. It is in this step of the cycle that a manager has an opportunity to lead by example. Employees must be made aware that it is far easier to get guests to come back than it is to attract new guests. If sales are lost as a result of poor guest service, other costs can suffer. Labor and product costs must still be paid for, while poor service can lose guests. Once sales drop you may not be able to meet your controllable and non-controllable costs.

Creative employees may count short shots by taking a penny from the penny slot and placing it in with the quarters until a certain amount is reached and then remove that amount at one time. Swivel sticks may be added or subtracted in a glass by the register until a certain amount is reached and then that amount is deducted from the cash drawer. A manager must monitor operations for these and other activities. An operation may have to use silent or mystery shoppers to keep employees honest. Honest employees are usually not disturbed by monitoring and evaluation. No matter how efficient the interviewing process and how references are checked, the hospitality field with its easily consumable products will have to deal with its share of dishonest employees. There are so many outstanding employees that have dedicated their careers to the hospitality industry, and yet, there are still those that will take advantage of it with a weak control system.

III.   Learning Objectives

1.   The importance of service as a competitive advantage

Numerous hospitality operations have found a competitive advantage through outstanding guest service. In the hospitality industry, differentiation and location are usually the major reasons why one operation is more successful than another is. If an operation has a great location, they may have a captive market. If not, it will usually take some form of differentiation to make guests select one facility of service over numerous others. Dominos Pizza made several other pizza organizations realize the importance of service when they opened with their speedy delivery service. Fast food operations and other types of service operations maintain their share of the market by providing a drive though service. Service, therefore, can provide a competitive advantage. In order to maintain this advantage, management must control the consistency of service. A competitive advantage through service can be one of the most cost-effective means of maintaining and gaining a better share of the market.

2.   Guest expectations

To be able to control the service process, whenever interacting with guests, management must set an outstanding example and then train employees to attain the level of set expectations. Management must also constantly impress upon employees the importance of their presence to the operation and how important their level of service to guests is to the success of the operation. Guests patronizing a food service establishment and guests patronizing a bar and beverage operation have basically the same expectations of the level of service and the type of service according to the type of facility. A guest in an up scale or medium scale restaurant would expect outstanding service. Guests in moderate priced facilities may only expect adequate service. The basic difference in the expectations of guests patronizing a bar and beverage operation from those patronizing a food service establishment is that guests patronizing a beverage facility may want to be able to talk and interact more with the bartender or other guests. Nonetheless, guests patronizing either one of these types of facilities would expect the following basic behavior from servers:

      a.   Courtesy
      b.   Timeliness
      c.   Knowledge
      d.   Accuracy
      e.   Honesty and ethical practices
      f.   Cleanliness

3.   The important elements of portioning

Portion control has been made a lot easier for the industry than it was in the past. However, the perception of value still belongs to the guest. Servers should communicate with cooks and management if it is perceived that portions do not appear to be in accordance with the standards or if a guest makes a comment concerning an insufficient portion. There will always be some guests who will complain; but if the complaints become frequent, management must investigate the problem. Remember that everything in the service industry is based on the perception of value to the guest. Trying to ensure consistency in portions can be very difficult when slicing cold cuts, portioning roast beef, or even serving salad and salad dressing. Management must ensure that employees are not shorting the portions in order to pilferage products. Management must also compare portions to see if the amount requested matches the amount served and constantly monitor servings to see if guests are receiving the correct amount. Serving sizes can be even more complicated in cafeteria lines where guest can see the inequities in their servings as compared to those of others. Also, remember that some guests frequent an establishment on a regular basis and they will be apt to notice if there is a decrease in the amount that they usually receive. Portions must be consistent and garnish must be consistent. Managers must be aware that it is through a reduction in portions that the greatest amount of theft actually occurs within a food service operation. It is important to constantly monitor and evaluate the size of portions and to let cooks and service personnel know that this is going to be monitored.

Managers have to ensure that cooks are not working in collusion with servers to try and gain larger tips through larger portions. If servers realize that they have some big tippers, they may get with the cooks to provide those guests with slightly larger portions and or have bartenders pour larger amounts only to split the tips later. Bartenders, cooks, and waitstaff may exchange drinks for food and tips. Adjustments for these factors can usually be found in decreased portions to the other guests. If standard portions are not followed, costs will eventually be out of line with budgetary expectations. Managers must periodically weigh portions and train employees to know what a standard portion of a product should look like.

4.   The need to control condiments

Employees will often place a small monetary value on items such as condiments in a restaurant, to bars of soap, and hair shampoo, etc., in guestrooms. Management may stand a better chance of controlling these items if they would explain to the employees how the pilferage of these items can substantially take away from the bottom line. Small signs may need to be posted in the back of the house to illustrate the cost of these items and how missing items can increase in cost over the long run.

Most employees do not understand that individual packaging or portioned items are very expensive. Employees may not take a large bottle of ketchup but will take the same amount in small packages in a short period of time. Employees must be made to understand the same amount in small packages that would equate to the amount in a bottle would be far more expensive because of the individual packaging. The airlines discontinued placing sugar in with their flatware several years ago. It was easy to see how much sugar could be saved in a day by just asking passengers if they wanted sugar. Food service employees should also be trained to ask guests about these types of items. Many guests do not want ketchup with their French fries. Yet several fast food operations will place a large number of packages into the takeout bag. Also, in a full service establishment, when guests request an order to go, they should be asked when picking up the order if they want the plastic flatware. In a majority of cases, guests are going home to eat and would prefer to use their own flatware to eat a complete meal. The amount saved in these areas, over the long run, can really help the bottom line. When delivering salads with dressing, the waitstaff should be instructed to ask the guests how much dressing would they like. Too much dressing on a salad can make some guest perturbed while more money is spent on food cost.

5.   The importance of quality control as it applies to service

All activities that occur in any business evolve around delivering a satisfactory quality product to the guest. If the guest is satisfied, then an operation is apt to be more successful. Because the hospitality industry is labor intensive, management must attempt to motivate all employees to deliver a product with the highest quality of service possible. The most important thing to remember about controlling the quality of service is that the guest is the one that makes the decision concerning quality and the expectations of service. Management may think that service is great and guests may feel totally different. Because employees have the responsibility of trying to deliver the highest quality of service possible, employees are the most important resource in a hospitality operation. If employees have a negative attitude, they can really turn guests away from an operation and dramatically reduce guest count. Outstanding service can make an average meal into an outstanding meal. By the same token, poor service can make a distasteful meal out of an outstanding meal. One of the most difficult tasks of management in the hospitality industry is to motivate employees to provide outstanding service.

The difficulty in motivating employees to provide outstanding service is even far greater in the hospitality industry than in other industries. In the hospitality industry, a majority of the employees are only earning minimum wage. Considering that the majority of employees are only making minimum wage, and in many facilities the annual turnover rate is usually over a 100 percent, management in the hospitality industry has to be concerned with controlling the quality of service. Regardless as to how much effort has been placed into other aspects of controlling an operation, without being able to control employees in providing quality service, all is lost.

6.   The pros and cons of empowerment

There are several pros and cons to the idea of empowerment in the hospitality field. Managers who are against empowerment feel that the majority of the employees in the industry are still not ready, or that they will abuse this power. Some managers think that employees are just not ready to make some decisions. These managers also would like to be in on any decision making process. The major reason for the rejection of empowerment by other managers is because of the control factor. Most managers feel that employees will take advantage of empowerment and abuse it in certain situations. Some managers feel that if employees are allowed to replace meals that are unacceptable without having to check with management, they may simply give meals to friends or relatives.

Those managers who are for giving employee's empowerment feel that it is cost effective in the long run. They feel that employees are better educated when empowered; and if cost control is explained to them, they will not abuse the privilege. Managers who are for empowerment feel that empowerment helps to motivate employees in making them a part of the organization and this in itself can aid in reducing turnover, which is very costly. Additionally, problems can be resolved far more quickly, or the perception of value of an operation can be heightened if a server can make a decision on the spot.

7.   Why different types of service require different methods of control

Different types of services require different controls. If a facility has very expensive china and silverware, the amount of concern over these products would have to be increased. The same can be said for paper goods in fast food operations. Paper goods in fast food operations must be used conservatively because a large volume of paper goods is used and employees have a tendency to waste paper goods. If an item represents a major cost to that particular hospitality operation then control of that item becomes a major concern.

Full menu table service restaurants usually have a major advantage over all other types of food service operations because these facilities normally sell alcohol and the sales and mark-up on alcohol can substantially cover up mistakes in other areas. The mark-up on alcohol is normally so large that it allows full menu, table service operations the ability to generate a profit. Wine sales in some of these facilities account for a large portion of sales. Because of the profit margin and cost of some of these wines, controls must be very tight. Also, the china, crystal, meat products, and silverware in some of these facilities make control procedures very important.

Limited menu table service restaurants would normally have other control issues. While these type of facilities may not have as much of the expensive wines and serving utensils, they would have to be even more concerned with controlling cost. These operations would probably not have the luxury of selling a lot of expensive wines to cover other costs. These types of facilities would have to focus even more on portion control and food cost. Limited service restaurants would usually have more difficulty controlling employees since they would have younger inexperienced employees and far great turnover.

Cafeteria style operations may truly be the most difficult to control when it comes to portion standards. Even though the facility may purchase convenient type of foods and thus may help in the production phase, this is usually not enough. The difficulty is that dishonest and/or experienced cooks and servers can manipulate products for pilferage. Servers who work on the cafeteria line may also waste products by portioning too much or upset the guests by not portioning enough. Servers should inform management if they think that products are inconsistent or if guests reject products because of their appearance.

8.   Difficulties in controlling the back and front of the house

The front of the house focuses to a great deal on quality control and guest services. Guest expectations and service are major concerns for front of the activities. The back of the house focuses on coordination of activities to ensure that the front of the house is able to accomplish the objectives of the organization. Accounting, engineering and maintenance, and housekeeping are but a few of the back of the house support systems that help to meet guest expectations and keep the operation functioning in a professional manner.

9.   The need for departmental relationships

Departments must coordinate with each other for an operation to be successful. Every effort must be made throughout the organization to control cost. Lines of communication must be allowed to remain open. Constant communication can prevent the possibility of breakdowns in services to guests. The entire organization must understand why guests frequent a facility. Guests are usually motivated by their biological, social, self-fulfillment, and psychological needs. Servers are the individuals that have contact with the guest in trying to satisfy these needs. If there is a breakdown in communication in attempting to satisfy a guest, the server or front desk employee will receive the brunt of the complaints. Therefore, all departments must interact to ensure that there is not a breakdown in expectations. Coordination and communication is the key to avoiding these types of problems.

10.   The importance of a POS system

Some point-of-sale systems can be linked to all areas of a facility. The more controls that are built into the system, the more security and information the system can provide. The system can easily maintain sales and inventory records. Some systems will link the bar operations to include types of drinks and brands used. Because prices can also be programmed into the systems, there is less chance of error. Numerous operations are finding that the new POS systems can provide greater control for managing operations and thus allow management the ability to spend more time with guests. The more items that can be extracted in a reporting system, the easier it is to detect mistakes or problems. Being able to extract this information and compare costs separately really makes purchasing these systems cost effective.

11.   Some of the problems that are associated with beverage operations and control

There are just many opportunities for a dishonest bartender to steal from the operation. Management has to be very selective when hiring bartenders. References should be checked any time employees are going to handle money, and a bartender should not be employed until his references have been checked to include his previous employer. Not only do bartenders have numerous opportunities to steal, but also because of third-party liability, management must try and make every effort to also protect the operation. Some of the ways in which dishonest bartenders can hurt the operation are as follows:

a.   Bring their own bottles to substitute for the operation's inventory
b.   Over-pouring to friends or to generate tips
c.   Short shots or under-pouring to other guests
d.   Substitutions of call brands with well brands
e.   Under ringing sales
f.   Adding water to alcohol products to fool the inventory process
g.   Leaving the cash drawer open
h.   Leaving the tip jar next to the cash register
i.   Padding the spill sheet
j.   Placing epoxy in jiggers
k.   Promotional abuse
l.   Voiding sales that were actually prepared

IV.   Definition of Key Terms

Beverage control – applies to the controls that are necessary to ensure efficient and effective operational procedures of service and security of beverage operations.

Competitive advantage – is to be able to accomplish some type of business activity more effectively and efficiently than the methods being used by competitors.

Empowerment – is to provide an employee with the decision making power over activities in their functional area.

Guest expectations – are the expectations of a guest based on his or her perception of value of the level of service and quality that would be anticipated as a guest in that facility.

Hand held server terminal – is a device that has been designed for efficiency in placing orders to prevent mistakes in reading orders and reduce the utilization of additional time and motion of having to walk to a POS system to place and order.

Point-of-sales (POS) – is an electronic computerized system that aids in accounting for cash and other resources and can be programmed for numerous functions. The system can easily maintain sales and inventory records and can be linked to any sales outlet in the facility.

Quality service – is the perception of service to the guest Management can establish a standard for service but it will always be the guest perception as to whether the service is regarded as quality. The standard of service should be designed to meet or exceed guests' expectations.

Suggestive selling - is a process of making suggestions or recommendations to help guests recognize true needs rather than to sell them unwanted products. In this process suggestive sell can be very beneficial to the guest and the hospitality facility.

V.   Teaching Outline

A.   Front of the House
1.   Quality Control
2.   Guest Expectations

a.   Courtesy
b.   Timeliness
c.   Knowledgeable
d.   Accuracy
e.   Honest and Ethical Practices
f.   Cleanliness
3.   Portion Control
4.   Controlling Condiments
5.   Empowerment
6.   Types of Services and Control
7.   Suggestive Selling
8.   Service of Alcoholic Beverages
B.   Back of the House
1.   Departmental Relationships
2.   Point-of-Sales Systems
3.   Closing of the Sale
4.   Theft is a Continuous Problem

VI.   Questions and Answers

Review Exercises

1.   Which of the following basic behaviors do the guests expect of the service personnel?

a.   courtesy
b.   accuracy
c.   timeliness
d.   all of the above

2.   Timeliness to a guest means:

a.   employees clock out at the assigned time
b.   servers and expeditors deliver the products to the guests as soon as the products are ready
c.   servers always get the drink order first even if a guest may want to order the food item
d.   know all questions regarding the menu when asked by the guests

3.   Accuracy to a guest entails:

a.   getting the information and requests of a reservation correctly
b.   getting the information and requests of a reservation quickest way possible
c.   know the name of all the guests
d.   smile at the guest at all times

4.   The service personnel has influence over portion control in the following instances:

a.   when filling drink orders
b.   when putting salad dressings on the salad
c.   when getting bread, crackers and butter for the guests
d.   when cooking the entree

5.   One of the best methods to increase sales by a server is:

a.   suggestive selling
b.   give the guest whatever he or she asks for
c.   sell the item that is the easiest to prepare
d.   pad the check for items that the guests did not order

6.   Good service in the beverage area includes:

a.   over-pouring to keep guests happy
b.   give complimentary drinks to guests
c.   getting the correct drink order to the guest in a timely manner
d.   diluting the drinks so that guests will consume less alcohol

7.   Good service is not important in which stage of the service cycle?

a.   when the guest first enters the operation
b.   when the guest is consuming the service or product
c.   when the guest is departing from the operation
d.   none of the above

8.   Cleanliness as a service point for a guest include cleanliness in:

a.   the equipment used to prepare and serve the food
b.   the personal grooming of the staff
c.   the loading dock and trash storage area
d.   all of the above

9.   The function of control is important in which type of operation:

a.   luxury
b.   mid-scale
c.   fast food
d.   all types of operations

10.   Which of the following actions should a manager take if he or she suspects that a bartender is pilfering from the operation?

a.   Terminate the bartender
b.   Do not schedule the bartender and give him/her a leave of absence
c.   Schedule a trustworthy mystery shopper to observe the bartender
c.   Check the bartender's personal belongings when he or she arrives at work

Review Exercises Answers

1. d
2. b
3. a
4. d
5. a
6. c
7. d
8. d
9. d
10. c

11.   Discuss the pros and cons concerning empowerment.

Empowerment, if carried out correctly, is a very beneficial concept. The cons about empowerment lie in both management and employees. There are managers who feel that the majority of the employees in the industry are not ready to make some decisions, or that employees will abuse this power. The major reason for the rejection of empowerment by other managers is because of the control factor. Others also feel that if employees are allowed to replace meals that are unacceptable without having to check with management, they may simply give meals to friends or relatives.

When empowerment works correctly, with the correct training of employees to make certain decisions, this is really a more cost effective in the long run. Management can now devote more time for guest relations and other issues and leave some of the other decisions to be made by the employees. Employees are better educated when empowered; and if cost control is explained to them, they will not abuse the privilege. Empowerment also helps to motivate employees in making them a part of the organization and this in itself can aid in reducing turnover, which is very costly. Additionally, problems can be resolved far more quickly, or the perception of value of an operation can be heightened if a server can make a decision on the spot.

Whether management is for or against empowerment, the truth of the matter is, hospitality managers are required to perform a large number of tasks during any given day. If employees are not utilized to their fullest, micro-management will cause numerous managers to leave the hospitality industry. The answer may be to try and be more selective when hiring employees. In order to control operations successfully, management may have to rely on a certain amount of empowerment.

12.   List five methods you would use to ensure that portion control would consistently

meet the set standards.

Five methods that could be used to ensure that portion control would consistently meet the set standards are:
i.   To spot check portioned products to ensure that the correct weight is being served

ii.   To provide the right utensils for serving. If a #8 scoop is used instead of the #12 scoop as designated, one will not have enough food to serve the guests or the cost of producing the product will increase

iii.   To spot check the amount of condiments given by the waitstaff

iv.   To watch for products being served and ensure that the waitstaff and the cooks are not colluding by providing guests with slightly larger portions so as to obtain a better tip

v.   To spot check how bartenders pour their drinks

vi.   To provide jiggers and other utensils for bartenders

13.   List five of the attributes you would look for when reviewing an individual for a

position as a server.

Six attributes are listed in the chapter. Thus any five of the six will be correct:
i.   Courtesy
ii.   Timeliness
iii.   Knowledgeable
iv.   Accuracy
v.   Honest and Ethical Practices
vi.   Cleanliness

14.   Explain how service can be used as a competitive advantage.

Numerous hospitality operations have found a competitive advantage through outstanding guest service. A competitive advantage is where one operation has something that distinguishes itself from others that do not posses the same characteristic. A competitive advantage through service can be one of the most cost-effective means of maintaining and gaining a better share of the market. This is where the service of one operation is of such a quality that guests will come back for the experience.

Examination Type Problems

1.   List five expectations that guests have of servers.

Six expectations are listed in the chapter. Thus any five of the six will be correct:
i.   Courtesy
ii.   Timeliness
iii.   Knowledgeable
iv.   Accuracy
v.   Honest and Ethical Practices
vi.   Cleanliness

2.   List eight ways in which bartenders have an opportunity to steal.

Dishonest bartenders can steal from an operation in many ways. Any eight items from the following will be correct. The instructor may also add in other ways:
i.   Bring their own bottles to substitute for the operation's inventory
ii.   Over-pouring to friends or to generate tips

    iii.   Short shots or under-pouring to other guests
    iv.   Substitutions of call brands with well brands
    v.   Under ringing sales
    vi.   Adding water to alcohol products to fool the inventory process
    vii.   Leaving the cash drawer open
    viii.   Leaving the tip jar next to the cash register
    ix.   Padding the spill sheet
    x.   Placing epoxy in jiggers
    xi.   Promotional abuse
    xii.   Voiding sales that were actually prepared

3.   Describe how servers can manipulate certain products in order to steal from the

operation.

        Server can manipulate products in different ways in order to pilfer from the operation. Pilferage is stealing but wasting products is also stealing from the operation, it is just done indirectly. Below are some suggestions. Instructors can make additional input.
    i.   Serve more food to the guest to obtain a better level of gratuity
    ii.   Serve less food to the guest so that they (the servers) can take the difference home
    iii.   Serve an inferior quality product and retain the difference
    iv.   Serve the product but do not charge the guests (their friends) the correct price
    v.   Serve the product but do not charge at all
    vi.   Serve the product but charge a higher price to those guests who may not be as detailed with the billing. Servers will then retain the difference
    vii.   Steal products directly and take them home
    viii. Serve products in the incorrect manner such as taking the wrong order, to preparing the wrong order, thus food has to be returned to the kitchen
    ix.   Waste the product when preparing it for serving, such as cutting the dessert in too big of a portion and wasting the other portion.

4.   Explain three instances in which servers can use a POS system to enhance control

activities.

        POS can provide various kinds of managerial information to aid in the control function. First, some point-of-sale systems can be linked to all areas of a facility. The more controls that are built into the system, the more security and information the system can provide. The system can easily maintain sales and inventory records.
        Second, some systems will link the bar operations to include types of drinks and brands used. Because prices can also be programmed into the systems, there is less chance of error. Numerous operations are finding that the new POS systems can provide greater control for managing operations and thus allow management the ability to spend more time with guests.
        Third, POS systems will also allow management to maintain records of sales history of different waiters and waitress. If the same individual has the lowest

guest check average every week, and there is not a valid reason, this particular individual may have to be retrained or terminated. Thus, POS systems can also be used in labor control.

Case Study

The Model Restaurant has been doing quite well and you are very satisfied with its operating results. In the last month, however, with an increase in business, you have hired a few new staff to take care of this increase in sales. One evening, while you are visiting with guests throughout the facility, you notice that a guest has just received a prime rib that appears smaller than the 10-ounce portion listed on the menu. You stop by another table and ask the guests if they are enjoying their meals and one guest complains that his meal is not really hot. You also notice that a party of four having just received their bread has to ask for butter. On your way back toward the kitchen, one of your regular guests tells you his meal tastes great. While continuing to make your way to the kitchen you observe two waiters leaning against the wall, smiling and talking with each other.

At the end of the business day you are going over these activities in your mind. Analyze and make a list of issues that you would like to discuss with both your service and / or kitchen.

Case Study Answers

(The answers to this case can vary. The instructor is welcome to make additional comments.) It is a good practice to do a short 3-5minute debriefing after every shift to give the employees some feedback. As a manager, you may not want to be always on the offensive and accuse your employees of not working. You also need to be mindful that they should be and have been trained properly before you tell them that they do something wrong. Thus, the following is a possible list of issues that you may want to discuss with the service and kitchen staff:

1.   that the portion size of the prime rib is not according to standard – you will need to explain to the kitchen staff why serving the 10 oz portion is important for the guest's perception of value and satisfaction level and for the food cost calculation of the operation

2.   that the food was not served at the appropriate temperature – you will need to emphasize to the kitchen staff that it is important since if the correct temperature is not maintained, this does not only change the quality of the food but also may lead to food safety issues. For the service staff, you will need to stress that food needs to be picked up from the kitchen and served to the guests as soon as possible to prevent the loss in temperature. The

point of guests' satisfaction will also need to be understood by all and how quality service can be a competitive advantage to the operation

3.   that butter was not served with the bread – this is strictly a service training issue. This might have happened because the new hires might not be trained well. It is important for you not to pinpoint the blame but rather make it a positive learning experience

4.   that the waitstaff needs to walk the floor to check on the guests' needs – again this will take care of a good number of issues mentioned above, such as spotting the table of four needing butter, etc.

5.   that one of the guest praises the taste of his food – always end the meeting on a positive note and leave your staff on a good feeling. Let them know all the good things so that these behavior can be reinforced

CHAPTER 11

SALES AND CASH CONTROL

I.   Purpose of the Chapter

This chapter is designed to provide information concerning the need and difficulty of controlling sales and cash.

II.   Overview of the Chapter

The theft of organizational funds and sales revenues can lead an operation into business failure. A good number of businesses fail because of theft and theft can cause a reduction in working capital. The guest check is the primary source of maintaining control throughout the hospitality operation. Employees must be informed, in writing, of the importance of guest checks and how the misappropriation of funds will not be tolerated. An organization should evaluate whether it is cost effective to use a POS system for controlling sales.

There are basically three forms of payment: cash, check, or credit cards. While all forms of card payment are referred to as credit cards, there is a major different between credit cards, charge cards, bank check cards, and debit cards. As society decreases the utilization of personal checks and currency, hospitality operations will have to consider the acceptance of some form of credit card. Once a decision is made to accept a particular card, management must then shop around to try and obtain the best proposal possible for the operation. Management has to be aware that the majority of guests who frequent a fine dining facility pay for their meals with some form of credit card.

III.   Learning Objectives

1.   The items that should be included on a guest check accountability log

If guest checks are issued by the operation there should always be a sign-out sheet or guest check accountability log for guest checks. This sheet or log must list the sequence numbers of the checks, the dates the checks were signed for, the time of day when the checks are issued and returned, and a place for the employee to sign checks in and out. Any unused checks should be returned at the end of the shift and the information should be noted on the sign-out sheet.

2.   How to handle missing guest checks

Every organization should have a procedure for dealing with missing guest checks. Some of the actions that can be taken are as follows:

a.   Every effort must be made to determine if the check is in the facility. It could have been misplaced in the kitchen, become folded in with a menu, or misplaced in some other area within the facility.

b.   The employee who is responsible for the missing check should write a statement as to the best of his or her knowledge of the whereabouts of the check.

    c.   Once it has been established that the guest check is not in the facility, all funds should be counted to estimate what is the amount of the check. This should be cross-checked against the cash register tape, kitchen production sheets, or back room printer to see if the amount of the order can be located. By determining the amount of the check, this can help in determining what was the amount of the mistake or pilferage that might have occurred.

    d.   The sales record for that day should be annotated with the approximate amount of the check and the name of the employee who is responsible for the check.

    e.   The employee must be given a written reprimand, as there may be no way of determining what is the exact amount that may have been lost. The employee should also be counseled on the outcome of a second occurrence.

    f.   If there is a second occurrence by the same employee then the employee should be given a last warning or terminated.

3.   Capabilities of a POS system

The majority of the systems can actually be programmed to handle any task that management requires. Functions such as programming in prices and being able to link to other departments are now basic functions of most systems. Some systems can be linked into the menu to include menu items and even brands of beverage sold at a bar and other beverage outlets. Systems can usually be programmed to provide your daily menu mix, amount of sales, amount of inventory, and amount and costs of items consumed. This information can be reviewed at any time and the systems can provide this information by the hour and also daily. Some systems also perform all time clock activities as well as the processing of authorizations for credit cards. There are also systems that are sophisticated enough to provide purchase requests to bring inventory back to par-stock level.

4.   The pros and cons of a POS system

A POS system is far more reliable than a manual system or a basic electronic cash register system. Manually, far too many mistakes can be made and it is very difficult to find errors or theft. Electronic cash register are often limited in the amount of functions that can be programmed into them. POS systems can have numerous controls programmed into them and thereby they are more effective to the control system.

5.   The three methods of payment or settlement of accounts and the convenience of each

The three methods of payments that are mostly used are as follows:

    a.   cash
    b.   check (personal, business, or travelers)
    c.   credit cards

6.   The criteria when selecting credit cards to be accepted by the operation

When making a decision as to which card to accept, management must be concerned with three factors. First, management needs to know the availability or frequency of the card being accepted. Second, the cost or rate of accepting the card is very important. With the income before tax of an average restaurant being around 4%, any cost that a credit card company charges the hospitality operation will further reduce this percentage. Third, the length of time it will take the credit cardcompany to reimburse the operation is also pertinent. There are several other cost factors that must also be considered but these activities are of major concern over the long run.

7.　　　Different types of credit card fraud

　　a.　　The majority of credit card fraud is from lost or stolen cards. Dishonest individuals often steal cards from the mail. Dishonest individuals may also fraudulently apply for credit cards through the mail. When most individuals receive advertisements from credit card companies, the advertisement will state that a card has been pre-approved.
　　b.　　When given a card by a guest, an employee can run two credit slips and use one for the next cash transaction.
　　c.　　Employees may also increase the amount of tips on credit cards.
　　d.　　When there is a party of four or more, quite often one person may pick up the bill, and pay for it by credit card, and the other members of the party may leave a cash tip. When guests leave, some employees will add an additional tip to the credit card slip.
　　e.　　Some employees may even run an invalid credit through the electronic equipment to credit their own accounts.

8.　　　Programs to prevent credit card fraud

　　　Therefore, management must make every effort to prevent credit card fraud. Management must insist that all purchases be processed through the electronic terminal. Signatures should be compared to observe if there are significant differences. The credit card agreement must be fully understood so limits will be well known. Employees should be trained to observe important information such as that of signature and expiration dates. In the age of technology, card companies do attempt to reduce fraud, but dishonest individuals will work just as diligently in trying to overcome security procedures.

9.　　　Why certain employees should be bonded

　　　To protect itself, a hospitality operation should have those employees bonded who may have access to large sums of money. If events are dependent upon subcontractors to supply equipment or services, bonding can eliminate some of the liability in these situations. If the situation warrants, added insurance must also be purchased to cover activity losses such as property, casualty, life, or workman's compensation.

10.　　The disadvantages of a manual system

　　　Some of the frequent disadvantages of manually performing sales activities are as follows:

　　a.　　Errors can occur in reading handwritings.
　　b.　　Guest checks from food and beverage outlets may not be posted to portfolios in sufficient time before guests' departure.
　　c.　　The possibility for theft and fraud is much greater.

d.   Mistakes in arithmetic can occur.
e.   It can be difficult to evaluate sales performance against time of occurrence.
f.   Management needs to be able to compare readings against cash received.
g.   Checks used for payments by guests cannot be validated as quickly as they can with the computerized system.
h.   A trail tape would not be available to compare sales and check for mistakes.
i.   Error can occur because prices of items are not coded into key functions.

11.   The differences between a credit card and a charge card

Charge cards are cards that require full payment at the end of a 20 to 30 days billing cycle, such as American Express. The benefit of these cards to the guest is the unlimited ceiling. Visa and MasterCard, along with several others, are credit cards. Guests receiving a credit card will receive a line of credit for utilization of the card. In return, interest is charged to the guests if the full balance is not paid off.

IV.   Definition of Key Terms

Bank check card - prevents the guest from having to write a check and allows those facilities that do not accept checks to have the backing of a credit card. The amount of payment owed to the hospitality operation is deducted immediately from the cardholder's checking account. In the case of hotel stays, a hold is placed on the account for the number of anticipated days plus an additional amount to cover other incidental expenses such as telephone, movies, etc.

Bonding employees – is accomplished to provide additional security to the hospitality operation because some employees may have access to large sums of money. If events are dependent upon subcontractors to supply equipment or services, bonding can eliminate some of the liability in these situations.

Cash bank – is the amount of change fund that employees would have access to start their business day.

Computerized systems – are electronic systems used to strengthen the control system as a larger volume of data and information can be maintained and accessed faster.

Credit cards – are given to customers to use and with the card is a line of credit that the customer can pay on a revolving basis.

Debit cards – are issued by a financial institution that maintains cash holdings of the card user. When the card is used the amount is automatically deducted from the card user account.

Effective discount rate – is the rate associated with using a credit card. The effective discount rate must be known before making a decision as to whether to use or accept a particular card.

Guest checks – are the documentation that is used to record orders from guests to have the orders prepared by the hospitality facility.

Missing checks – are guest checks that have been misplaced or stolen This creates a very complicated situation because management may not have any real means of determining the amount, honesty, or method for having a misplaced check.

Overages/shortages – the amount of different between the cash bank that was given an employee and the amount of cash that should have been tendered. The difference in the amount could be more or less.

Statement analysis formula – allows a business to evaluate the true cost of accepting a credit card.

Voids or over rings - occur when employees entering sales into a system enter the incorrect amount. Because an over ring or void is a cash transaction, management should ensure the correctness of the occurrence and the amount.

V.   Teaching Outline

A.   Sales and Cash Control Analysis
B.   Guest Checks
    1.   Types of Guest Check
    2.   Missing Guest Checks
C.   Cash Register/POS System
    1.   Types of POS Systems
    2.   Manual Versus Computerized
    3.   Cash Banks
    4.   Accounting for Overages and Shortages
    5.   Procedures for Change
    6.   Processing Transactions and Deposits
    7.   Fraud and Theft During Cash Transactions
    8.   Reports and Reconciliation
D.   Methods of Payment
    1.   Cash and Checks
    2.   Types of Cards
    3.   Which Card to Accept?
    4.   Processing Credit Cards
    5.   Signage
    6.   Fraud
    7.   Electronic Equipment
    8.   Bonding Employees
    9.   Theft by Guests

VI.   Questions and Answers

Review Exercises

1.   Which of the following is not a normal method of settlement used in the hospitality industry?

a.   cash
b.   credit cards
c.   charge to a house account
d.   checks

2.   The guest check accountability log should include the following:

a.   name of waitstaff
b.   sequence number of missing check
c.   waitstaff's signature
d.   all of the above

3.   What might be a reason why a computerized POS system is better than a manual system to process guest checks?

a.   it is more economical
b.   errors in reading handwriting causes confusion whereby an order can be reduced or eliminated
c.   sales performance reports are easier to compile using a manual system
d.   a trail tape is not necessary when using a manual system

4.   What certain information can a POS system include on a guest check automatically?

a.   waitstaff or server identification number
b.   tax calculation
c.   menu items ordered and their prices
d.   all of the above

5.   The amount of sales recorded in a POS system should equal to:

a.   the total amount of cash, credits, and checks in the cash drawer
b.   the total amount of cash, credit and checks in the cash drawer minus the beginning amount issued in the drawer
c.   all voids
d.   the number of guest checks used in that particular day

6.   Which of the following will be a good procedure for making change?

a.   bills over $5 should be put under the currency tray
b.   cashiers should try to complete multiple transactions in order to service the guests faster
c.   cashiers can use personal funds so that time will not be wasted to track down management for change
d.   drop box for cash should remain locked during the shift

7.   If the cash, credit card vouchers, checks, and coupons do not balance with the register reading, management must check for:

a.   the quality of food
b.   the total amount of cash collected

c.   mistakes or voids not reported
d.   the deposit slip

8.   The real rate that a manager needs to be aware of when deciding which credit card to accept is the:

a.   effective discount rate
b.   statement fee
c.   per transaction cost
d.   volume of business of the operation

9.   The three steps in processing a credit card, in the correct sequence, are:

a.   settlement, authorization, handling
b.   authorization, settlement, handling
c.   handling, authorization, settlement
d.   authorization, handling, settlement

10.   It is good business practice to bond the following employees:

a.   cash handling employees
b.   all waitstaff
c.   employees who have worked more than 5 years with the operation
d.   all employees

Review Exercises Answers
1. c
2. d
3. b
4. d
5. b
6. d
7. c
8. a
9. c
10. a

11.   Explain in detail the factors that must be considered when making a decision as to which credit card or cards to accept.

When making a decision as to which card to accept, management must be concerned with three major factors. First, management needs to know the availability or frequency of the card being accepted. There are now so many cards available in the market that management has a large number of cards to choose from. Management also has to consider the operation's clientele. If an operation such as a hotel is in a major metropolis that has in international airport, it may be heavily involved in the international market; this can make it an even more difficult choice. Also, credit cards are viewed as providing utility and convenience, and charge cards usually illustrates prestige. Guests patronizing a full service, medium scale restaurant or cafeteria would expect the restaurant to accept credit cards.

Guests patronizing an upscale restaurant would expect the facility to accept credit cards and charge cards.

Second, the cost or rate of accepting the card. This is important because any cost that the credit card company charges the hospitality operation will further reduce this percentage. To determine if using the card is cost effective, management must evaluate the effective discount rate. Once the effective discount rate is known, the hospitality operation should negotiate for the best offer possible. The volume of sales, the amount of an average check, and the methods of processing the credit card vouchers all play a part in determining the effective cost. Using the electronic process would be the most effective way to control these transactions, reduce fraud, mistakes, and maintain cash flow.

Third, the length of time it will take the credit card company to reimburse the operation. The more electronics there are in the processes of handling, authorization, and settlement, the quicker the money can be directly deposit into the bank accounts of the business.

12.   Explain in detail two reasons why a guest check may be missing.

(A guest check could be missing because of various reasons. Two reasons are

provided below. However, instructors are encouraged to add in other reasons.)

One reason why a guest check can be missing perhaps is the sheer carelessness on the part of the waitstaff. They may not view the guest check as an important document and might have used it for scratch paper or just plain do not keep track of the use. On the other hand, there may be many problems in theft and controls associated with a missing guest check. The waitstaff might have used a check to obtain food from the kitchen, destroyed the check, and given the food away to their friends. They might also have given the food to the guests and after settling the bill (especially if settled by cash payment), pocketed the cash and destroyed the check afterwards. Therefore, whenever there is a missing check, management needs to find out the reason, correct any misunderstanding or mistakes, and train and reprimand employees if necessary.

13.   Make a list of ten methods that can be used to during cash transactions to commit

fraud.

As mentioned in the text, the following are ten methods of fraud during the cash transaction process:

i.   Managers become busy and give their keys to the POS system to an employee to take care of a managerial transaction. Managers must never allow employees to have access to their keys. Even if it is a large facility, the access of such keys should be limited and documented.

ii.   Managers will sometimes allow the detail tape to run out and the continuity of transactions is lost; and with some systems, records of transactions are also lost. Managers should check the detail tape to ensure that there is enough supply before re-setting the register. The detail tape should also be monitored from time to time to see if there are rings for no sale, voids, and guest checks closeouts that are widely out of sequence.

iii. Managers may use a key or a code to by-pass buzzers or bells on cash register systems that are in place to alert management and employees that the cash drawer is being opened. Not only should buzzers and bells not be by-passed, but also managers should monitor cash register operations as a part of their managerial duties. Surprise cash register audits are a must to ascertain if an employee is trying to steal from a cash bank.

iv. Employees should not be allowed to cash personal checks at the facility where they work.

v. The cash register should not be used as an imprest fund. One of the problems of small businesses is using the cash register as a petty cash fund and eventually there is no accountability for the funds.

vi. The amount of sales that are rung into a register should be visible and convenience for guests to see.

vii. The readings from a POS system should agree with the amount of cash received.

viii. Management must be concerned when employees do not want to take a vacation or a day off. This is a signal that employees do not wish to have their crime found out.

ix. Cash registers should be emptied and left opened when the operation is closed to prevent thieves from breaking into them and damaging a piece of equipment that does not contain any funds.

x. Employees may collect cash and say that a guest walked out.

14. List five reasons why a hospitality facility may want to use a POS system rather than a manual cash register.

Nine reasons are listed in the text. Any five of the following will be acceptable. Instructors are also encouraged to add in additional reasons:

i. Errors can occur in reading handwritings.
ii. Guest checks from food and beverage outlets may not be posted to portfolios in sufficient time before guests' departure.
iii. The possibility for theft and fraud is much greater.
iv. Mistakes in arithmetic can occur.
v. It can be difficult to evaluate sales performance against time of occurrence.
vi. Management needs to be able to compare readings against cash received.
vii. Checks used for payments by guests cannot be validated as quickly as they can with the computerized system.
viii. A trail tape would not be available to compare sales and check for mistakes.
ix. Error can occur because prices of items are not coded into key functions.

15. Given average monthly credit card sales of $60,000 and an average number of monthly credit card transactions of 2,800, you are asked to calculate the effective discount rate of accepted a credit card. Company A quotes you a discount rate of

3%, a statement fee of $30 and a transaction fee of $0.50 per transaction.

Company B proposes only a 2.5% discount rate but a $10 statement fee and a

$0.75 per transaction fee. Which credit card company would you go with?

The calculation of Company A is as follows:

Required information Calculation	**Formula**
A. Annual Volume of Credit Card Sales	not needed
B. Average Monthly Volume of Credit Card Sales	$60,000 given
C. Average Number of Credit Card Transactions per Month	C = given e.g., 2,800
D. Average Check $60,000 \div 2,800$ $= \$ 21.43$	$D = B \div C$
E. Discount Rate $3.0 \div 100 = 0.03$	E = given by credit card company 3.0%
F. Statement Fee $20 \div 60,000$ card company $\div$ B = 0.0003	F = fee given by credit e.g., $20
G. Transaction Fee $0.50 \div 21.43$ $=0.0233$	G = fee given by credit card company $\div$ D e.g., $0.50
TOTAL EFFECTIVE DISCOUNT RATE 0.0536 or 5.36%	E + F + G

The calculation of Company B is as follows:

Required information Calculation	**Formula**
A. Annual Volume of Credit Card Sales	not needed
B. Average Monthly Volume of Credit Card Sales	$60,000 given

C. Average Number of Credit Card
    Transactions per Month

C = given
e.g., 2,800

D. Average Check
    60,000 ÷ 2,800

     = $ 21.43

$D = B \div C$

E. Discount Rate
    2.5 ÷ 100 = 0.025

E = given by credit card

company 2.5%

F. Statement Fee
    10 ÷ 60,000
    card company ÷ B = 0.0002

F = fee given by credit

e.g., $10

G. Transaction Fee
    0.75 ÷ 21.43

    =0.0350

G = fee given by credit

card company ÷ D

e.g., $0.75

TOTAL EFFECTIVE DISCOUNT RATE
    0.0602 or 6.02%
You should choose Company A.

$E + F + G$

Examination Type Problems

1.   What three factors are used to determine credit card rates?

    The three factors that are used to determine credit card rates are the volume of sales, the amount of an average check, and the methods of processing the credit card vouchers. They all play a part in determining the effective cost. The higher the volume and the higher the amount of an average check, the lower the discount rate should be as the operation will now have more negotiating power. The per transaction fee is charged no matter how much the average check would be. Thus the higher the average check, with the transaction fee remaining the same, the lower the effective rate percentage. Using the electronic process would be the most effective way to control these transactions, reduce fraud, mistakes, and maintain cash flow. Is also reduces the cost since less labor is involved in the processing of the credit card vouchers.

2.   What are the three methods of payment and how does each benefit the guest?

    The three methods of payments that are mostly used are cash, check (personal, business, or travelers), and credit cards. The advantage of cash is that it is widely accepted and it helps hospitality operations to maintain a good amount of working cash flow. From the guests' point of view, cash may not be the best method because it will reduce their cash balance as soon as the cash is paid out.

The only advantage perhaps is that no follow up in paying bills or balancing checkbooks would be necessary.

Checks are similar to cash but they provide guests with a record of payment. Checks have traditionally been used more than any other form of payment; however, the amount used is now on the decline. Traveler's checks are usually used by international or out of town guests. The near 100 percent replacement value on lost or stolen traveler checks makes them as convenient to both the guests and the hospitality operations, especially hotels, when dealing with travelers.

The third method of payment, the utilization of credit cards, provides the same amount of convenience and records to the guest as check and more. If used properly, it can give the guests a line of credit and preserves the cash outflow from the guest's bank account. In addition, most cards provide incentives for guests to use their cards by giving away trips and other bonuses. If a card is lost, a guest will just need to call in to cancel the card and there are also other means of extra protection available at a certain cost if so desired. Credit cards are also accepted internationally; thus they are really convenience for travelers.

3.   Why is it important that some employees be bonded?

Management must be aware that a dishonest employee can be detrimental to an operation and can cause an operation to fail. There is little that can be done in trying to prevent theft by individuals who are prone to steal. Dishonest employees will exist regardless of how effectively and diligently management may go about hiring practices. Even though management may make every effort to check references and try and verify the conduct of past employment, a thief can still be difficult to detect.

Bonding of employees, therefore, protects the hospitality operation in case of employee theft of funds or when a subcontractor fails to complete a job within an agreed upon time. In hotel and motel operations, an employee may have opportunities to steal the belonging of the guests. The same holds true with credit cards, sales revenue, and other types of funds within hospitality facilities. To protect itself, a hospitality operation should have those employees bonded who may have access to large sums of money. If events are dependent upon subcontractors to supply equipment or services, bonding can eliminate some of the liability in these situations. If the situation warrants, added insurance must also be purchased to cover activity losses such as property, casualty, life, or workman's compensation. Thus, all employees who handle cash or have access to expensive properties of the business or the guests should be bonded, when feasible.

4.   Your restaurant has just completed its first anniversary and has been doing quite

well. The annual credit card sales of your restaurant are $500,000, while the

average number of credit card transactions per month is $3,000. Company X offers

you a great discount rate of 2% with a transaction fee of $0.50 and a statement fee

of $40. Company Y, however, charges a much higher discount rate of 3%. Its transaction fee is considerably lower at only $0.25 and the statement fee is also lower at $20. Which company is offering you a better business plan?

The calculation of Company X is as follows:

Required information Calculation	Formula
A. Annual Volume of Credit Card Sales	Given: $500,000
B. Average Monthly Volume of Credit = 500,000 ÷ 12 Card Sales =41,667	B = A ÷ 12
C. Average Number of Credit Card Transactions per Month	C = given e.g., $3,000

D. Average Check
      41,667 ÷ 3,000
 	
      = $ 13.89
	D = B ÷ C

E. Discount Rate 2.0 ÷ 100 = 0.02	E = given by credit card company 2.0%

F. Statement Fee
      40 ÷ 41,667
      card company ÷ B
	F = fee given by credit
	
	= 0.0010
	e.g., $40

G. Transaction Fee
      0.50 ÷ 13.89
 	
      =0.0360
	G = fee given by credit
	
	card company ÷ D
	
	e.g., $0.50

TOTAL EFFECTIVE DISCOUNT RATE 0.0570 or 5.706%	E + F + G

The calculation of Company Y is as follows:

Required information Calculation	Formula
Steps A through D will be the same	
E. Discount Rate 3.0 ÷ 100 = 0.03	E = given by credit card company 3.0%

F. Statement Fee
    $20 \div 42{,}667$
    card company $\div$ B

F = fee given by credit
= 0.0005
e.g., $20

G. Transaction Fee
    $0.25 \div 13.89$

    =0.0180

G = fee given by credit

card company $\div$ D

e.g., $0.25

TOTAL EFFECTIVE DISCOUNT RATE
    0.0485 or 4.85%
You should choose Company Y.

E + F + G

Case Study

One of the waitresses at the Model Restaurant is missing a guest check and this is the second time this week that this has occurred. This waitress has been working there for about three years and she has lost two or three tickets in the past. She is very efficient in her work and friendly toward the guests and you feel that a lot of local guests frequent the facility because of her presence and service. However, you also realize that you cannot afford to keep losing guest checks. Each time you talk with her about a missing check she always states that a guest must have taken it. As the manager of Model, establish a policy of guest check control by putting in writing the following.

1.   The procedure for the issuance and return of guest checks, and

2.   The responsibility of employees regarding missing guest checks

If guest checks are issued by the operation there should always be a sign-out sheet or guest check accountability log for guest checks. This sheet or log must list the sequence numbers of the checks, the dates the checks were signed for, the time of day when the checks are issued and returned, and a place for the employee to sign checks in and out. Any unused checks should be the responsibility of the waitstaff to fill in the time issued and returned, the sequence numbers of the unused and missing checks if any, and their signatures. By instituting a program such as this, the importance of control and accountability will be highlighted to your crew.

Missing guest checks should be viewed in the same manner as missing funds. Some of the actions that can be taken are as follows:

i.   Every effort must be made to determine if the check is in the facility. It could have been misplaced in the kitchen, became folded in with a menu, or misplaced in some other area within the facility.

ii.   The employee who is responsible for the missing check should write a statement to the best of his or her knowledge of the whereabouts of the check.

iii. Once it has been established that the guest check is not in the facility, all funds should be counted to estimate what is the amount of the check. This should be crosschecked against the cash register tape, kitchen production sheets, or back room printer to see if the amount of the order can be located. By determining the amount of funds of the check, this can help in determining what was the amount of the mistake or pilferage that might have occurred.

iv.   The sales record for that day should be annotated with the approximate amount of the check and the name of the employee who is responsible for the check.

v.   The employee must be given a written reprimand, as there may be no way of determining what is the exact amount of funds that may have been lost. The employee should also be counseled on the outcome of a second occurrence.

vi.   If there is a second occurrence by the same employee then the employee should be given a last warning or terminated.

Management must inform employees of the need to maintain security of their guest checks and the consequences of losing a guest check. These procedures should be placed in writing so that employees will be aware of such policies and procedures. Employees should also be asked to add their signatures, acknowledging that they are aware of the consequences. Employees perceive issues to be more important when management takes the time to place the outcomes of those issues in writing. Guest checks are the same as blank checks. It is very difficult to discern the amount of actual losses when a guest check is missing.

CHAPTER 12

SALES ANALYSIS

I.   Purpose of the Chapter

The purpose of this chapter is to prepare managers with an understanding of how essential it is to track sales, as a missing guest check is the same as a missing check without having any idea of the amount of the check.

II.   Overview of the Chapter

Sales analysis can be more accurate if information is provided in a useable fashion. Managers should not be placed in operations or situations wherein they will be confronted with information overload. If the structures of organizations are very flat, management will end up with having to make a vast number of decisions and information overload can occur. Employees and guests should be provided with correct information while management should attempt to disseminate accurate and quality information that will be beneficial to all constituencies of the organization.

If an organization understands its target market, it can more effectively develop a menu mix that will have a sufficient contribution margin and sales to generate a significant profit for the organization. When developing a menu mix, managers must understand that contribution margin is a component of pricing that deals specifically with the profitability of each item.

The performance of the waitstaff must be evaluated in order to maintain control and to know which waitstaff are doing an outstanding job of selling and which ones may need additional training. Management must constantly identify and reward those individuals that are contributing to the success of the operation if that behavior is to be continued. Conversely, management must understand the importance of either retraining or terminating those employees who are not helping the advancement of the operation. The success of the service industry is usually generated more around service than the tangible products that are being sold. Employees are important to the success of an operation and their performance must be monitored.

Guest counts provide information and knowledge for the operation to forecast future sales, production, and labor. Management must occasionally count guests and compare this count with the reading from the computerized system to see if a dishonest employee is circumventing the system. Guest count is also helpful in booking future business and in determining the seat turnover and in informing guests of the average wait involved before seating.

The number of items sold per meal period provides management with information for forecasting the popularity of such items. In doing so, the amount of production of certain items may need to be increased or decreased on certain days of the week. Management may also find that some items may need to be relocated on the menu or completely removed from the menu.

When completing a sales analysis, an organization must take into consideration the menu mix, operating expenses and required profit for that particular facility. It is important to understand that the menu mix must be based on the operational expenses and the amount of sales that are required for the continued success of the operation. There is a continuing myth regarding what should be the average food cost or labor cost of certain types of operations. While industry standards for prime cost percentages may not be that far off, they cannot account for all of the nuances of every operation. Through sales analysis, management can determine how sales, production, and the workforce are performing as compared to the established standards of its own operation. Management can then evaluate the menu mix and implement control factors to ensure that the standards and quality of that menu is maintained.

III.   Learning Objectives

1.   The need for accessing information to be disseminated

Those managers who are willing to search for information concerning market conditions may be able to remain competitive by adjusting very quickly to anticipate changes in the market place. With this information at hand, strategic plans can be developed to maintain or enhance market share.

2.   Why it is important to control information

Controlling certain information from employees and the public is often necessary. Information is power and the company may need to control access to different pieces of information. Timing is also very important in the business arena and timing can influence the impact of a message. Additionally, because of information overload, information should be limited to that which is necessary. When it comes to information, more is not always necessarily better. The thought that managers need all of the information they can obtain is far from the truth. Increasingly, the quantity of information might not improve the decision making process. Managers can become overwhelmed with too much information and some of it may be of little value. The theory that it is always best to obtain as much information as possible before making a decision does not always fit. Too much information may actually hinder the decision-making process.

When dealing with the public there may be information about the company that management may want the public to be aware of and there may be additional information that may not be of interest or could be detrimental for the organization. You may not want the public to know that the company is having financial problems or problems with products if this is not a threat to the public. The public does not have a need to know this information and it could cause a decrease in sales if they were to find out.

In this same manner information can be used to gain a competitive advantage. Any time computerized systems can be used to take advantage of historical data as opposed to individuals who must evaluate information manually, a competitive advantage is possible. In most cases a competitive advantage gained by an information system will not be a permanent advantage because, as with other products and services, organizations will either duplicate or improve on the methods used.

3.   Why training must be an ongoing process

Training improves productivity as well as enhances the motivational level of employees. This is why training must be an ongoing process even if according to a sales analysis all activities appear to be within standards.

4.   The importance of knowing the guest check average

Tracking the guest check average can point out trouble areas in the operation. Guest check averages may be down when a certain special is on the menu or when certain production personnel are on duty. Managers must talk with the waitstaff when they are not generating sufficient guest check averages. Managers may find that it is due to poor service from the waitstaff.

According to the menu mix and the clientele mix, management should have an idea of the average guest check and establish a standard based on the average. This is how management will often project sales for a given period. If waitstaff are not reaching that average, then there may be a reason for evaluation of products, procedures, and personnel. If check averages are down from standards then management must attempt to pinpoint the problem.

5.   Why guests should be counted

It is extremely important that management consistently monitor guest counts. From a control standpoint, this is important for several reasons. Mangers can try and evaluate whether guest checks are missing, being reused because of time lapses, or if some servers have far less guest checks than others do. While guests must always be counted, the count should usually coincide with the number of entrees sold. Employees should also be made aware that managers are going to do a guest count as this may deter the possibility of theft.

6.   Why it is important to understand the length of time between seat turnover

The number of seats and the capacity of equipment must be known for managers to plan for busy periods, and to book and handle large functions. By using guest counts, management can project how long guests may have to wait for a table. Seat turnover is derived by using the number of guests served during a given meal or period divided by the number of seats available.

7.   The importance of perception in the pricing of a specialty item

In many cases in the food service industry, management feels that specialty products have to be inexpensive products to attract guests. This is often not the case and food service managers need to change their perception of this. If a restaurant decides to have a specialty or signature product such as a 32-ounce steak, this does not mean that the steak should be inexpensive. Guests who may order these products would do it for the prestige of the experience; hence price may not be as much of a factor. When beverage operations sell drinks in a particular glass and allow the guest to take the glass, the guest has usually paid an expensive price for an inexpensive glass. Therefore, developing specialty items can be extremely cost effective. Management simply needs to market the product. A house specialty becomes a house specialty because the house says so. Most specialty items are well marketed; and because of the marketing, a certain clientele will be motivated to purchase these products.

8.   Why employees should be awarded for outstanding performance

Employees must be made aware of their own performance results and the overall performance of the organization. Without providing feedback, employees may perceive that either everything is all right, standards are not important, or their input into the organization is not important. Therefore, if standards are being met or even if they are not being met, employees should be informed and their opinions of how to improve operational procedures should be solicited. Just because standards are being met is not an indication that they cannot be improved. If a business is generating a profit, managers should always investigate as to whether they can generate even more. This is another reason why average check size and average number of guests served must be tracked and evaluated. Through evaluation, managers would be able to determine which members of the waitstaff have the highest average so that they can be commended. The only way to encourage the same behavior is to show that the behavior is appreciated.

IV.   Definition of Key Terms

Contribution margin - is the dollar amount remaining after variable costs have been subtracted from the sales dollar.

Formal communication – within an organization is usually information that comes from the top down through the chain of command and may or may not be in writing.

Guest comments – should be solicited as guest will often inform management if service or quality is meeting, exceeding, below expectations. These comments can also assist in identifying possible flaws in the control system.

Guest count – is the number of guests that enter or order from an establishment. If the hospitality operation does a large amount of takeout and a large amount of in-house business management may want to maintain separate counts.

Informal communication – is communication that is basically horizontal in nature with the best know source being the grapevine.

Menu mix – alludes to the different products that are on the menu and their amount of contribution margin.

Popularity of items – defines the number of times that an item is chosen as compared to other items on the menu.

Publicity – is information that is disseminated to attract public notice that differs from advertisement in that it is free.

Seat turnover – is the number of times a seat or table is turned over in a hospitality facility during a specific business time or period.

V.   Teaching Outline

A.   Pertinent Information
    1.   What Information Do I Want?
    2.   How Do I Obtain That Information?
    3.   What Information Do I Want Other People to Know?
    4.   How Do I Distribute Such Information?
B.   Sales Analysis and Pricing
    1.   Who Are the Target Guests?
    2.   What is the Type and Location of the Facility?
    3.   What Are the Prices of Competitors?
    4.   What Are the Costs of Preparing and Providing the Products or Services?
    5.   What Amount of Profit Does Management Want to Generate?
C.   Sales or Menu Mix Analysis
    1.   Identify the Contribution Margins of Items
    2.   Identify the Popularity of Items
    3.   Special Sale Item
D.   Waitstaff Performance Tracking
    1.   Analyze Items Sold per Waitstaff
    2.   Point Out Trouble Areas

       3.   Additional Training if Needed
       4.   Praises and Awards When Appropriate

E.   Guest Counts
       1.   By Meal Period
       2.   By Waitstaff
       3.   By Dining Areas
       4.   Aid in Calculating Seat Turnover
       5.   Aid in Forecasting

F.   Items Sold
       1.   Menu Mix Analysis Per Meal Period
       2.   Item Placements on Menus
       3.   Signature Items

G.   Other Useful Measurements
       1.   Guests' Comments
       2.   Per Person Average
       3.   Food Cost Percentage
       4.   Beverage Cost Percentage

VI.   Questions and Answers

Review Exercises

1. When gathering information management usually has all of the following concerns except:

      a.   how much information is available?
      b   what information do I want?
      c.   how do I obtain that information?
      d.   what information do I want other people to know?

2. When assessing the utilization of information the following is true:

      a.   An information system provides management with information in a usable fashion and not just data
      b.   the majority of information that is used in most organizations comes from computer-supported applications
      c.   Managers need information that will assist them in the performance of their duties and will aid them in remaining within their budgetary constraints
      d.   all of the above

3. Questions that management may find pertinent in generating pricing information are as follows:

      a.   what is the type and location of the facility?
      b.   what are the prices of competitors?
      c.   what are the costs of preparing and providing the products or service?
      d.   all of the above

4. Management would like to control all of the following types of information from the public and competitors except

      a.   three cases of food borne illness that have occurred since yesterday's lunch

    b.   a new product is being tested in the test kitchen
    c.   sales figures that have been down for the last month
    d.   developing a faster process to produce certain items

5. The dollar amount remaining after variable costs have been subtracted from the sales dollar is

    a.   profit
    b.   contribution margin
    c.   break-even
    d.   controllable cost

6. If a menu item is not popular management may try doing one of the following:

    a.   change the face of the item to make it more acceptable
    b.   advertise the item more if the item has a low contribution margin
    c.   remove the item from the menu if the item has a large labor cost
    d.   management may try a and c

7. Management has the following considerations when advertising:

    a.   use radio for special events
    b.   make sure advertising is addressed to the target market
    c.   make sure advertising is cost effective
    d.   use a shotgun approach

8. Placing too many food products on a menu can cause an operation to:

    a.   lose focus as to the type of business they are in
    b.   lose sales
    c.   increase spoilage, waste, and quality
    d.   can reduce the requirement for storage space

9. Food cost percent can be obtained by

    a.   dividing sales by food cost
    b.   dividing food cost by food sales
    c.   dividing food cost by total sales
    d.   multiplying food cost by cost of food sold

10. By analyzing the number and type of items sold managers will obtain the following:

    a.   which items should be removed from the menu
    b.   which items are the most attractive to customers
    c.   how much suggestive selling is being used
    d.   all of the above

Review Exercises Answers

1. a
2. d

3. d
4. a
5. b
6. d
7. d
8. a
9. b
10. d

11.   Name, explain, and give an example of three reasons why it is important to monitor the

per person average of guest checks.

There are many reasons why it is important to monitor the per person average of guest checks. Three reasons will be discussed while the instructor can accept other answers as appropriate. First, from the check averages, management may find out whether servers are aware and selling the items that have the highest contribution margin. Through suggestive selling servers can persuade a number of guests to select items with higher contribution margins.

Second, guest check averages can also be increased through up selling products. The numbers of desserts or appetizers sold will often be an indication of the amount of suggestive selling. If suggestive selling is applied, the number of these products consumed should increase. Therefore, by analyzing the check average, the effectiveness of the waitstaff can also be determined.

Third, check averages can also point out trouble areas in the operation. Guest check averages may be down when a certain special is on the menu or when certain production personnel are on duty. Managers must talk with the waitstaff when they are not generating sufficient guest check averages. Managers may find that it is due to poor service of the waitstaff. According to the menu mix and the clientele mix, management should have an idea of the average guest check and establish a standard based on the average. This is how management will often project sales for a given period. If waitstaff are not reaching that average, then there may be reason for evaluation of products, procedures, and personnel.

12.   Explain four different ways how guest counts can aid an operation to become more

effective.

It is extremely important that management consistently monitor guest counts. From a control standpoint, there are a number of ways how guest counts can aid an operation to become more effective.

First, when guest counts are performed by meal periods, managers can project labor usage, food cost, and forecast production sheet items accordingly. This way, managers can complete production sheets and employee work schedules differently for the volume of business on special days of the week.

Second, if guests are counted by each waitstaff and if one always serves 30 more guests than another waitstaff during the same meal period, management should check into the situation. The assignment of the stations may always favor the waitstaff that serves more guests. However, if this is not the case and guests' satisfaction is still higher and service quality is not compromised, this is good news. If not, some adjustments may need to be made. Therefore, guest counts by waitstaff will provide some very useful data for management.

Third, by maintaining guest counts by dining, problems may be easier to identify. This is especially helpful if there is a POS outlet in that area that is being used to place orders. Then, the performance from each outlet can be monitored and evaluated rather than aggregating all food and beverage data in one single sales figure or costs figures. By monitoring the guest count of each dining area, improvements in those that are less frequented by the guests can be made.

(Other possible answers can be aid in calculating seat turnover or aid in forecasting for future periods)

13.   Calculate the food and beverage cost percentages given the following data:

Beverage sales for the month are at $50,000 while total sales post a record of $275,000. Food costs are totaled at $100,000 and beverage costs are calculated to be $15,000.

Note in this question that the $275,000 is the figure for total sales. Thus if beverage sales were $50,000, then the food sales would be $225,000. The food cost percentage is calculated by dividing food cost into food sales. Therefore,

$$\text{Food cost \%} = \frac{100,000}{275,000-50,000}$$
$$= 44.44\%$$

The beverage cost percentage is calculated by dividing beverage cost into beverage sales. Therefore,

$$\text{Beverage cost \%} = \frac{15,000}{50,000}$$
$$= 30.00\%$$

14.   Calculate the contribution margin of the daily special served given the following cost and

sales figures:

Special of the day: Grilled Tuna Steak

Food Cost = 30%
Total Food Sales = $50,000
Food Cost for each Tuna Steak = $7.00
Menu Price for Tuna Steak special = $15.00

In calculating the contribution margin of an item, only the food sales and food cost figures are need of that particular item. Thus, the calculation is as follows:

Sales – Cost = Contribution Margin
15 – 7 = 8

Therefore, $8 is the contribution margin. If the contribution margin ratio were asked in the question, the answer would be to divide $8 into $15, or 53.33%.

Examination Type Problems

1.   Evaluate the importance of ongoing training for the waitstaff.

2.   List and evaluate three reasons as to why it is important to analyze sales.

3.   What are the food and beverage percentages of the Bayshore Restaurant given the

      following income statement

Food sales	$200,000
Beverage sales	$100,000
Total sales	$300,000
Food cost	$ 75,000
Beverage cost	$ 20,000
Total cost	$ 95,000

The food cost percentage is calculated by dividing food cost into food sales. Therefore,

Food cost % = $\dfrac{75,000}{200,000}$

= 37.50%

The beverage cost percentage is calculated by dividing beverage cost into beverage
sales. Therefore,

Beverage cost %   = $\dfrac{20,000}{100,000}$

= 20.00%

4.   What is the contribution margin that is reflected for Bayshore Restaurant in

      Question 3?

      In calculating the contribution margin, only the sales and cost figures are need.
Thus, the calculation for the contribution margin for food is as follows:

      Sales – Cost = Contribution Margin
      $200,000 - $75,000 = $125,000

      Therefore, $125,000 is the contribution margin. If the contribution margin ratio
were asked in the question, the answer would be to divide $125,000 into $200,000, or
62.50%.

      And, the calculation for the contribution margin for beverage is as follows:

      Sales – Cost = Contribution Margin
      $100,000 - $20,000 = $80,000

      Therefore, $80,000 is the contribution margin. If the contribution margin ratio
were asked in the question, the answer would be to divide $80,000 into $100,000, or
80.00%.

Since this question simply asks for the contribution margin, it will be the total sales and the total cost. Thus, the calculation for the contribution margin is as follows:

Sales − Cost = Contribution Margin
$300,000 - $95,000 = $205,000

Therefore, $205,000 is the contribution margin. If the contribution margin ratio were asked in the question, the answer would be to divide $205,000 into $300,000, or 68.33%.

Case Study

After being the Restaurant Manager at Model for six months, you have noticed in your Profit and Loss statements for the past few accounting periods that even though sales have remained the same your profit level is declining. You have checked prices of food and supplies and you have also checked inventory and everything appears to be in order. According to your evaluations the problem is not occurring within the purchasing, receiving, issuing and production areas. You know something is wrong and you cannot find the problem. Finally, you determine that perhaps some sales analysis tools or reports may give you some information on this declining profit level. Name 5 reports or measurements that you would collect data for and explain what information each report and measurement will contain and why they are selected.

Case Study Answers

The five reports or measurements that you would collect data for are all related to the sales analysis area, since it has been eliminated that the challenges are not from purchasing, receiving, issuing and production. First, a menu mix should be performed. This can tell what the operation is selling. Perhaps sales are there but the right items, those that have higher contribution margins, are not sold. Thus, sales can still be good but the profits are not there.

Second, a report that analyzes the items sold per waitstaff will also be helpful. This will not only point out whether the preferred items are sold but who sold it. Perhaps there is a new employee who is not aware of suggestively selling the higher contribution margin items. Or that the waitstaff know but they just are not selling. Therefore, a report like this can be helpful.

Third, a guest count report may also be helpful. This tells the number of guests served. If the number of guests served has decreased, sales may still be there because of up-selling or other activities. However, without the volume, profits cannot be generated as easily. Thus, a guest count report can provide such information.

Fourth, in addition to an aggregate guest count report, a guest count report by meal period can also help to determine where the problem area lies. If breakfast is where the guest count has suffered, management may need to take action to increase guest count and thus sales in this meal period.

Fifth, using the same logic, a guest count report by waitstaff and by dining areas again can provide more detailed information for management to discover the true problem instead of a general symptom.

Other possible answers can also include, but are not limited to, average check per meal period, per waitstaff, and by dining areas. The same can also be said for sales mix analysis.

CHAPTER 13

LABOR PLANNING AND FACTORS AFFECTING LABOR COST

I.   Purpose of the Chapter

Since labor cost is one of the prime costs for the hospitality industry this chapter is designed to inform students of how essential it is to monitor and control labor at all times.

II.   Overview of the Chapter

Food and labor costs are the prime costs of hospitality businesses. While food cost affects all foodservice areas, the impact of labor costs affects all areas. Thus, a good control of labor is vital. It all begins with the selection and hiring process, then orientation and training. Moreover, management also needs to equip employees with a workplace that is conducive to efficiency. Employees' input should be sought to improve work processes. Management should use incentives to motivate rather than de-motivate. Once everything is in place, standards should be set, communicated, and maintained so that each person knows his or her performance expectations and can work toward a better goal.

III.   Learning Objectives

1.   The importance of the five (5) functions of human resources as they relate to cost control

The five categories under human resources management that can greatly impact labor quality and costs are selection, hiring, orientation, training, and termination. From a cost control point of view, when management looks at labor cost, management concentrates on the total payroll figure, that is, the number of hours worked multiplied by the different hourly rates. However, the actions of management in the selection, hiring, orientation, and training processes actually heavily influence the amount of money that is needed to spend every accounting period on payroll and benefits.

2.   The various sources of labor

Management can find quality and dedicated employees in many different sources. Most of the time, management thinks of labor as full-time personnel. However, there are other categories such as part-time, on-call lists, agency staffing, and co-operating units.

3.   The various factors influencing labor costs

While it is a fact that we multiply the hourly wage and the number of hours worked to obtain our payroll, there is still a fairly long list of factors that can directly and indirectly affect payroll as well. These factors are all controllable. It is up to us, the management, to manage all these factors and make adjustments as needed.

To begin with, we can directly control physical facilities, equipment, hours of operation, menu type, service type, and product. Though they all seem quite broad, we do have control over them and can increase the efficiency and productivity of the staff so that a lesser amount of payroll can be achieved.

4.   Time and labor saving devices for various job positions

There are many measures that management can take to better the productivity of employees so that labor costs can be well spent and not wasted. Front desk personnel can be empowered to handle more managerial activities to prevent guest from waiting while employees search for management.

Uniforms can also play a part in employee work effectiveness. Nicely designed pockets to hold guest checks and pens will help waitstaff to be more organized and professional looking. If they can get a check and pen ready to take the order, the entire process can be sped up.

Supplies and equipment need to be strategically placed to save time for the waitstaff. Computers and point of sale systems can add up guest checks and compute guests' totals accurately and efficiently. Having the appropriate equipment in this area can save time for the waitstaff and thus labor costs. Technology today can also print menu items in different languages, which can be most useful in ethnic restaurants.

As for the back of the house, equipment and utensil placement is important in helping employees to accomplish their tasks. Access to food items needs to be regulated but once the items are requisitioned and to be used, they should be stored and placed in a fashion that is convenient to the employees.

One way to seek out these labor and time saving devices is to listen to the employees themselves. Solicit their input. They are the people who are doing these tasks on a daily basis. If there is a better way, they will use it. In considering the opinions of the employees, management is also establishing trust and respect for and from the employees. This fosters teamwork and motivates all. At the end, the operation comes up with better processes and the employees are all working more effectively.

IV.   Definition of Key Terms

Absenteeism – is referred to as being habitually absent from work.

Fringe benefits – are employee benefits that are given to employees in addition to their wages or salary.

Hiring – is to engage someone for their services and to pay them for such.

Incentives – is some type of reward or punishment that induces a certain type of action and incentives are usually used to motivate employees to take some type of positive action.

Labor legislation – is any type of law that is enacted that can affect labor laws.

Labor sources – the labor sources normally consist of the labor market within the demographic area surrounding the hospitality operation.

Orientation – is an important part of having employees adjust to the new working environment and all new employees should have an orientation.
Selection – is the process of trying to choose the right person for the job.

Termination – is to bring to an end the employment of an employee.
Time and labor saving devices – any procedure that management or employees can develop to reduce labor time and these procedures be found through the utilization of equipment, or other forms of time an motion.

Training – is the process of making employees proficient with specialized instruction and training is essential in successfully accomplishing organizational goals and objectives.

Unionism – is the principle of forming a union and once a union is formed employee cost may increase and therefore the best way of preventing unionization is to treat employees fairly.

V.   Teaching Outline

A.   Human Resources Management
1.   Selection, Hiring, and Orientation
2.   Training
3.   Termination
B.   Sources of Labor
1.   Part-time Staffing
2.   On-call and Agency Staffing
3.   Co-op Services
4.   Cross-training of Labor Pool
C.   Factors Influencing Labor Costs
1.   Physical Facilities
2.   Equipment
3.   Hours of Operation
4.   Menu
5.   External Factors
6.   Training, Benefits, and Accidents
7.   Skullduggery
D.   Time and Labor Saving Devices
E.   Setting Labor Standards

VI.   Questions and Answers

Review Exercises

1.   Which of the following is not one of the categories included in human resources management as discussed in this chapter?

a.   selection
b.   orientation
c.   labor cost calculation
d.   training

2.   Sources of labor for the hospitality industry include:

a.   part-time employees
b.   on-call lists
c.   agency staffing
d.   all of the above

3.   A disadvantage of using part-time staff in your hotel include:

a.   working at the establishment is their top priority
b.   staff is trained with the procedures and policies of your hotel

      c.   staff may not be available at the time needed by your hotel

      d.   staff is committed to your hotel

4.   What might be a potential problem when using various co-op services or staffing agencies?

      a.   such services may conflict with union regulations where applied

      b.   such services are always less expensive

      c.   staff is always better trained

      d.   there is an obligation to employ the same people from the staffing agencies

5.   Which of the following is not a factor that will affect labor cost?

      a.   hours of operation

      b.   equipment available

      c.   menu

      d.   cost of food

6.   The category of external factors that would affect labor cost consists of:

      a.   labor legislation

      b.   union contract

      c.   labor supply

      d.   all of the above

7.   Accidents can increase labor cost through:

      a.   increase in workman's compensation claims

      b.   decrease in paper work needed

      c.   paid time-off for the injured party

      d.   a and c only

8.   Some examples of labor saving devices are:

      a.   where property management system is placed in the front office area

      b.   the way that a kitchen is designed

      c.   the proper equipment to be used by the waitstaff

      d.   all of the above

9.   Setting labor standards can be useful in:

      a.   determining food cost

      b.   determining labor schedule

      c.   determining the type of services

      d.   determining the guest mix

10.   An example of employee theft in direct labor cost is:

      a.   stealing food products

      b.   punching in before the scheduled time without authorization

      c.   giving food to friends
      d.   short-changing the guests

Review Exercises Answers

1. c
2. d
3. c
4. a
5. d
6. d
7. d
8. d
9. b
10. d

11.   Describe the importance of the five functions of human resources as they relate to cost control.

      The five functions of human resources are selection, hiring, orientation, training, and termination. From a cost control viewpoint, the actions of management in the selection, hiring, orientation, training and termination processes actually heavily influenced the amount of money that needed to spend every accounting period on payroll and benefits.

      Since the industry is very labor intensive, the need of personnel is of utmost importance. When a restaurant or hotel hires new employees, there needs to be a systematic selection process of interviewing. This is the start of the control of labor by selecting new hires with the right qualifications, attitudes and other characteristics.

      Once selected, employees need to be hired into the organization. The hiring process is important as the necessary paper work needs to be documented. If something is missing, and new employees are not processed into the system properly, the correction of such work will not only waste time but human and monetary resources.

      After the hiring process, to ensure that new employees will assimilate and be part of the organization, an orientation is needed. An orientation can convey to the new hires the philosophy of the workplace, the importance of customer services, the general attitude of making the guests feel welcome and the like. This will eliminate certain mistakes that could be made and any process that can be improved will simply improve the efficiency of labor and thus labor cost in the long run.

      Training can also help in cost control. Training should not be done only when the crew is hired, it should be an on-going process to emphasize and remind the employees of the correct way to perform their jobs and to update them with new improvement techniques and information. When employees are trained correctly, they will be better and more effective and thus help in the labor cost.

      Last but not least, termination is traumatic to both the organization and the people involved. However, this can easily be avoided if the other functions of human resources are carried out properly. Termination also puts a strain on the rest of the crew because there is one less person to get the work done. This means that a new person needs to be hired as a replacement and thus the whole human resources cycle has to start all over. Even worse, the guests can feel the effects of short staffing. Scheduling can probably alleviate some of these issues in the short run; yet, in the long run, it may also hurt the profits of operation.

In labor cost control, if one will start well from the beginning so that the problem of constant turnover will not pose a problem to the operation, the more effective an organization will be.

12.   Identify and explain five sources of labor.

The five sources of labor are full-time, part-time, on-call, agency staffing, and co-operating units. Full-time normally means that a employee works 40 hours per week, although some organizations will recognize over 30 hours per week as full-time. For full-time employees, these jobs are probably contributing to a major part of their income and, thus should be important to them. They would put their job as one of the priority items in their daily lives and would be more skillful and knowledgeable in their work procedures and practices. They are often more dependable.

Part-time staff normally works 20 hours or less per week. They provide flexibility in scheduling. During peak check-in times at a hotel or special functions for a food service operation, management can have enough staff on hand to handle the demand. Benefits and other fringe items available to full-time staff may not be available to part-timers. Thus, hospitality operations can save some monetary resources here.

Using an on-call list of people for emergency purposes is another source. This list of on-call people can be ex-employees who might have sought a career change, but would still enjoy working with their previous co-workers once in a while. They can also be college students who might have worked with the establishment and know the ins and outs of the workplace. Today, with staffing companies, one can ask for a certain number of staff to be present at the establishment with little notice.

Co-op services are the fourth source. For hotels or restaurants that are chain affiliated or clubs that are managed under the same management company, they can set-up co-operative services whereby Hotel A can call Hotel B for two room attendants to help out for a day and will return the favor to Hotel B when Hotel B needs extra help. The advantage obviously is the trained personnel.

Last, but not least, in larger operations such as a hotel, mega-resort, or even in smaller operations such as independent restaurants or clubs, labor sources can cross-trained. Since the philosophy of the company is the same, once an employee at the front office has also learned the skills needed for a host/hostess in the fine dining restaurant, he or she now is more valuable for the establishment. At the same time, he or she can also understand the difficulties that his or her counterparts have in the other departments so everybody now can be more compassionate and appreciative and able to work together better as a team.

13.   Identify and explain five factors influencing labor costs.

Nine factors are discussed in the chapter as factors that can influence labor costs. They are physical facilities, equipment, hours of operation, menu, external factors, training, benefits, accidents, and the unfortunate event of stealing. Any five of these factors will be correct. Again, the instructor is welcome to provide additional factors.

Physical facilities include the design of the building itself and the placement of all furniture and equipment. For instance, a well built hotel and conference center would have storage rooms for banquet tables of various sizes and banquet chairs right next to the conference rooms and banquet ballrooms. This saves employees the time needed to roll the tables and chairs from one place to another when setting the rooms for different events. A well-designed clubhouse will not have the locker rooms next to the main entrance. Rather, there should be an exit from the locker room to the golf course, and another exit to the clubhouse.

Second, in equipment, if one purchases a wrong piece of equipment an establishment does not need, this equipment may also hinder the productivity of labor and thus, increase the labor cost. Even a pair of tongs, a very minute piece of equipment for kitchen, can hinder the effectiveness of labor and increases labor costs.

Third, the hours of operation can definitely influence labor costs. The longer an establishment is open, the more labor costs will be incurred. Thus, by controlling the hours of operations sensibly, the number of employees scheduled can be done at an optimal level to ensure that costs are contained.

Fourth, menu also dictates the product and specifies the service style in an establishment. The more the menu items are made from scratch, the more labor will be needed in the preparation process.

Fifth, products can also affect labor cost. The differences in the product, whether it is a limited service hotel or a luxury establishment can affect staffing in all areas, and thus labor costs. In a luxury hotel, due to the amenities and services provided in a guest room, the time needed to clean such a room is often more than that needed to service a limited service hotel. Thus, labor cost may, therefore, be more in a luxury hotel.

14.   Describe how one would go about determining time and labor saving work procedures

for room attendants.

The methods that one can use to design time and labor saving devices are various. One way would be observing a random selection of room attendants at work. Videotaping can be very useful in documenting the event and for timing a process. All the steps of a task, such as making a bed, would be listed. Then, the manager will observe the employees and analyze their work task according to the listed steps. The time that is used to complete each step within the task would be marked. The manager will then determine if the given steps are most efficient and ascertain if some employees have used some other steps which result in a quicker completion time or a better quality product.

All of the tasks that a room attendant would perform, including the way that the linen cart is loaded, should be studied. The placement of certain items on the linen cart within easy reach may cut the work time and thus make the process more efficient.

The goal here is to provide employees with the tools and processes that they can use to perform at a higher level. Another way to seek out these labor and time saving devices is to listen to the employees themselves. They are the people who are doing these tasks on a daily basis. If there is a better way, they will use it. In considering the opinions of the employees, management is also establishing trust and respect for and from the employees. This fosters teamwork and motivates all. At the end, the operation will benefit.

Examination Type Problems

1.   Describe the advantages and disadvantages of part-time and full-time staff from the cost

control point of view.

There are obvious advantages with a full-time staff. Full-time staff makes scheduling a lot easier task for management. Since they work more hours than the part-time staff, they would be more skillful and knowledgeable in their work procedures and practices. They are often more dependable. However, when one or a few of them do not show up to work during the same shift, it may not be easy for management to call in another person to replace them temporarily.

Part-time staff, on the other hand, offers flexibility in scheduling. They do not expect 30 to 40 hours of work per week and thus their hours can be cut back during slower periods. During peak periods, management can have enough staff on hand to handle the demand. Benefits and other fringe items available to full-time staff may not be available to part-timers. Thus, monetary resources can be saved. Some work force also prefers a more flexible schedule and part-time positions work well for this group and also for the company. However, the fact that these part-time jobs are not at the top of the employees' priorities may lead to less desired level of performance in rendering services to the guests. Again, because of their major commitments, part-time staff may, sometimes, not be available at the specific times that the establishments need extra help.

2.   Describe the advantages of having on-call personnel.

There are some advantages of having on-call personnel. On-call people can be ex-employees who might have sought a career change, but would still enjoy working with their previous co-workers once in a while. These people know the ins and outs of the operation and will not require extensive orientation and training. If the on-call staff is obtained from a staffing company, one can ask for a certain number of staff to be present at the establishment with little notice. Staffing companies will also perform all of the human resources functions for the hospitality operations and this can help in reducing the amount of paper work in selection and hiring personnel. These agencies and companies are quite handy and dependable and the hospitality establishments have no obligation to re-employ these on-call personnel.

3.   List and explain three fringe benefits or incentives that you would use to motivate your

employees and explain why you chose these particular types of fringe benefits.

The first fringe benefit will probably be health insurance. In today's economy where an average health insurance policy will cost an individual $300 to $500 per month, this benefit will add a tremendous value to the position. Additional health benefits that are available to family members at a reduced cost are also welcomed. This will relieve the employee from the constant worry that if his or her family member is ill, he will need to take off from work to take care of them or that he does do not have the money to take the sick individual to the doctor.

Another benefit will be vacation time. Paid vacation is a reward that employees would treasure. They can have the income while they are able to spend time to do the things that they enjoy with the people that they like.

One incentive that employees would like will be a cash bonus. This can be performance based to reward good performance. This can also be a reward for a sales contest or recognition for perfect attendance. This extra cash can always be a little lift to the spirit and give employees something to look forward to.

(Other answers can also be acceptable.)

4.   Describe how labor standards can be set for a bus person in a 100-seat restaurant.

To begin with, one may search for some good sources of industry averages and standards. Good sources for such standards can often be obtained from trade or professional associations. Once the industry standards or guidelines have been obtained, management needs to assess its own operation. Depending on the type of service and the menu type, the expectation from guests will be different. In a limited service or fast food restaurant of 100 seats, perhaps one busperson will be enough. This is especially true for fast food restaurants when most guests will clean up their own area.

In a mid-priced restaurant, however, the labor standards will be different as more china, glassware, and silverware might be used. The bus person may also help in refilling drinks. In a 100-seat up-scale restaurant, a bus person will be assigned to a team of waitstaff and a captain. Their job may not just be bussing the table when the guests leave but also cleaning out ashtrays, scraping off the breadcrumbs, and others.

Therefore, depending on the characteristics of the 100- seat restaurant, the end result standards will be different. However the process remains the same in that all characteristics of the operation need to be considered and testing need to be carried out to see if the quality of level of service can be maintained.

Case Study

Your best friend has just received a job offer at Lawrencetown University (LU). LU is a new private college. It has a dining facility that can serve the 3,000 plus student population and the 500 plus full-time and part-time faculty and staff. The food service will be open for breakfast five days a week from 6am-10am; lunch for five days a week from 11am-3pm; and dinner from Monday through Thursday from 5pm-8pm. The style of service is cafeteria style. Average estimated count is 500 for breakfast, 1,000 for lunch and 500 for dinner. The majority of the guests will be students with board plans. The food service also has a boardroom that can hold up to 25 people. Catering events are normally held there but the food service can be expected to cater fairly large parties on and off-campus, mainly utilized by the administration of the university. Annual food and beverage sales are estimated to be about $3 million.

Your friend has been hired as the new Assistant Food and Beverage Director and has also helped estimate the $3 million sales level. In three weeks, the university will start its fall semester. Your friend needs to hire and train a large group of employees to handle the business. In addition, since Lawrencetown is situated in a college town, he is also wondering what he needs to do in order to hire the best people possible. One other challenge about this food service is the layout and design of the dining facilities. The university has a boardroom that is located down the hallway on the other side of the kitchen. There is a back hallway that links the back door of the boardroom and the kitchen but servicing out of the kitchen directly would be quite challenging. The hallway is a good 300 feet long. Thus, if the waitstaff forget something from the kitchen, it will take a while to rectify the issue.

After assessing the situation and given the number of guests served per meal, your friend calls you up for some advice. He knows that you have been working with the Case Study Hotel and has extensive experience. He would like your help in the following:

a.   Identify the various sources of labor available and determine how to reach them.

The five sources of labor available are full-time, part-time, on-call, agency staffing, and co-operating units. To reach full-time labor and part-time labor, the best way is perhaps through a local newspaper advertisement. Spots on local radio stations will also be helpful. Since this is a college environment, students can be a great source for part-time labor. Thus, an advertisement in the student newspaper, flyers at the college's bulletin board and notices in the dormitory areas will be useful. Obviously, word of mouth and references from other employees will be a good start. At this point in time when your friend is "opening" the place, there is not a pool of people readily available who have worked in the operation. Thus, the on-call list may not be too feasible. Even if there are on-call students or part-timers, they will not be familiar with the layout of the operation. Training will therefore be required. However, if there is a staff leasing agency available, the agency can be the source of on-call staff. It is true that people from staffing agencies may not know the layout of LU but they do know the job skills. This will help in decreasing the amount of training that your friend will need.

Co-op service will be the next source. For this one to work, your friend will need to network with other food service operations in the area and negotiate some mutually beneficial agreement. This will turn out to be a very helpful source in the long run. Once your friend has gotten the operation off the ground and has done all the basic training, he can then select certain people for cross training. Again, this source will benefit the operation in the long run rather than in the shortrun.

b.   Develop a checklist of table settings for a regular three-course banquet service for 25 people. This will include all tableware, stemware, glassware, condiments, and the like so that a banquet set-up crew can use this checklist to pull the necessary equipment to set up the room correctly.

The following will be a suggested list of items for servicing 25 people. Given the fact that the board room is quite a distance from the kitchen, the utensils for 26 people will be pulled so that if something is missing or there is another guest, the waitstaff will not have to run back to the kitchen. A 5% safety factor is normally recommended:

- 26 salad forks
- 26 dinner forks
- 52 knives
- 26 butter knives
- 26 dessert forks
- 26 teaspoons
- 26 butter plates
- 26 saucers
- 26 coffee cups
- 26 water glasses
- 4 – 6 tea pots (for those who may ask for tea)
- 4 – 6 sets of salt and pepper shakers
- 4 – 6 sets of sugar/condiments
- 4 – 6 sets of coffee creamers
- 26 napkins
- 4 – 6 table cloths (depending on size of table cloths)
- 4 – 6 bread baskets
- 4 – 6 napkins for the bread baskets
- 2 towels for wiping off spills if necessary

c.   Develop a checklist of service items needed for a regular three-course banquet service

for 25 people. This will include beverages, condiments, all food items, rolls, butter,

serving utensils, refills and the like so that a banquet service crew can use to prepare

itself for servicing the room appropriately.

This will be similar to the previous answer with the following additional items:
- 52-60 dinner rolls (2 per person with some extra)
- 55-60 butter pads (2 butter pads per person)
- 4 – 6 butter plates for center of table (if desired to put butter as condiments in the center of the table rather than on the butter plates of the guests)
- 4 – 6 pots of coffee as a start and with an urn of coffee as back-up
- 4 – 6 jugs of iced tea
- 4 – 6 jugs of water
- 4 – 6 tea bags (if assorted tea will be served, the assortment box will also be needed)
- 2 pots of hot water
- 26 iced-tea spoons (for those who desire iced tea)
- 2 pair of tongs for the bread (if the waitstaff will serve the bread rather than the guests passing the bread)

d.   Develop a list of at least 10 questions that you would ask when interviewing for your new

employees in order to find the best crew for your dining facility.

A list of questions that can be useful are as follows (instructor can modify as needed):

i.   Explain to them the job descriptions of the various jobs available and ask if they believe they will be able to perform at the required levels as stated
ii.   Amount of work experience in the food service industry
iii.   What types of service has the person been exposed to (cafeteria, a la Carte, fast food, etc.)?
iv.   Preference of positions of the interviewees: waitstaff or kitchen staff
v.   If interviewees are students, what are their class schedules?
vi.   Whether they have handled money before in another job
vii.   Whether they have any cooking experience
viii.   References that they can give you
ix.   Pose a scenario of guest complaints and note the reaction of the interviewees
x.   What is their expectation of the wage level?
xi.   How many hours will they be willing to work?
xii.   Would they like to be consider on the on-call list?

CHAPTER 14

STAFFING AND SCHEDULING

I. Purpose of the Chapter

The purpose of this chapter is to show students how important the staffing and scheduling processes are to labor cost and the morale of employees.

II. Overview of the Chapter

Try to be as creative and fair as possible in staffing and scheduling. Last but not least, be consistently inconsistent. Come up with the unexpected from time to time. Be creative and think out-of-the-box. To increase productivity and attendance, one hotel company has a $1 million stock option awarded to the one property that has the highest guest comment card score for the year. The $1 million stocks will be divided up among all full-time employees, hourly and management alike. One may ask, is this much money worth it? To this company it is. Guest satisfaction is important to the company's mission and they reward their employees for a job well done.

III. Learning Objectives

1.   The four steps in analyzing your labor needs

To accomplish an analysis of the labor needs of an operation, management has to perform the following four steps:

   a.   perform a business demand analysis
   b.   complete a productivity scheduling
   c.   complete the actual payroll budgeting, and
   d.   provide the assignment of task.

All four steps go hand-in-hand and they are essential in accomplishing an analysis of labor needs.

2.   A business demand analysis

Business demand analysis provides the answer to the question—what does a business need? Well, what an operation needs depends on what the operation has. Questions that need to be answered are as follows:
   a.   What will be the estimated sales level in each meal period, day, place, or outlets?
   b.   Are there any special promotions that may change the normal demand?
   c.   What local events are happening?
   d.   What about our competition?
   e.   Will they take away some of the sales?
   f.   Is a particular day a weekday, a weekend day, or a holiday?

These are all important questions to consider before an operation can determine what is needed in terms of labor. A checklist or a chart can also be created so that notations can be made. The more information a hospitality operation has, the more accurate the forecast will be.

3.   A productivity schedule

Productivity scheduling is like putting a puzzle together. It is taking the estimated sales from the business demand analysis and using the standards that have been set to schedule and estimate the labor needs.

4.   A payroll budget

Once positions are scheduled, an estimated payroll amount can be generated. Payroll budgeting is a blue print that lets management know the monetary resources that will be needed in order to achieve the estimated sales level with the proper and appropriate service standards.

5.   Tasks and develop a schedule

Once management knows how many people are needed for each meal period, function or event, and day, the next step is to assign the tasks. The productivity schedule and the payroll budget will now serve as guides to a manager. The manager will then need to schedule specific employees and assign the tasks to them.

6.   Measure and evaluate the efficiency of your staff

It is pertinent to measure efficiency, both for the good of the employees and for the operation. The best way is to have this written out as performance-based objectives. Then, managers will award an employee a rating as to how these objectives are being accomplished. This process may take some time but it is worth it.
One method to measure employee efficiency is through a good amount of observation. Managers will observe employees during their work periods, and assign each a rating on an hourly basis. These ratings can be on a scale of 1 to 5 with 1 being the lowest to 5 being the highest. They can also be as simple as 0 to 3 where:
0 is when the employee is idle, such as during the lunch hour
1 is under-expectation; not performing up to par
2 is average, right at par, and
3 is over-expectation, performing over par.
Thus, for an 8-hour shift of 7:00 a.m. to 3:00 p.m., the employee will have a total rating of 0 to 24. Since there is an hour off for lunch and breaks, the scale can be modified to rate only 7 hours, thus a scale of 0 to 21.

7.   Evaluate the different means of increasing morale

Because of the vast amount of turnover in the hospitality industry it is very important to try and increase employee morale as higher morale translates into increased productivity. The following factors can help in increasing morale:

a. select and train accordingly
b. treat everybody with respect
c. give credit where credit is due
d. award some monetary bonuses or increases when appropriate

IV.   Definition of Key Terms

Measuring efficiency – in the area of labor, is a means of determining how efficiency the hospitality operation is in spending its labor dollars. Methods of measuring efficiency of labor dollar spent is sales per labor dollar, sales per man-hour worked or sales per employees and use those standards for comparison.

Payroll analysis – is the evaluation of the sum of wages as to how successful the operation is utilizing these wages.

Payroll budgeting – is a blueprint that lets management know the monetary resources that will be needed in order to achieve the estimated sales level with the proper and appropriate service standards.

Productivity scheduling – is a method wherein management looks into each job category to see how the estimated sales will affect each job category and during what hours. Then, managers will plan the payroll by scheduling the full, part-time, and other personnel accordingly. In certain restaurants, specific operating hours are busier while others are slower.

Tolerable variance – is the amount of overage or shortage that management is willing to accept. Thus, variances on either side may occur. Management will need to decide what percentage of variance is acceptable. Normally, any amount with plus or minus 1% is deemed acceptable.

Work production standards – are measurements of work performance that may be expressed in different ways. They can be expressed in terms of rooms sold, sales dollars generated, guests served, net profit level and the infamous labor cost percentage. Different departments in a hospitality operation will have their own standards.

V.   Teaching Outline

A.   Work Production Standards
    1.   What Do We Produce?
    2.   Measurement Standards
B.   Analysis of Labor Needs
    1.   Business Demand Analysis – What Do We Need?
        a.   Forecasting Using Daily Statistics
        b.   Competition
        c.   Local Events and Holidays
        d.   Advertising and Promotion
    2.   Productivity Scheduling
    3.   Payroll Budgeting
        a.   Budget versus Actual
        b.   Tolerable Variance
    4.   Assignment of Task
        a.   An Example
        b.   Measuring Efficiency
C.   Morale and Turnover
    1.   Cost of Turnover
    2.   Increasing Morale and Productivity
    3.   Fringe Benefits

VI.   Questions and Answers

Review Exercises

1.   Which of the following will not be normally regarded as a productivity measurement?

    a.   number of management
    b.   guests served
    c.   sales per meal period
    d.   rounds of golf played

2.   To take full advantage of measuring productivity and planning labor, productivity measurement and standards need to be set for:

    a.   each shift
    b.   each meal period
    c.   each work category
    d.   a and c

3.   The following are all factors affecting the sales level except:

    a.   competition
    b.   weather
    c.   local events
    d.   labor needs

4.   What is an effective method to track the success of a particular advertising and promotion program for a hotel?

    a.   ask the advertising agency
    b.   use of a 1-800 number for reservations to track the origination of the call
    c.   look at past history
    d.   analyze the weather element

5.   Which of the following is not one of the steps in the analysis of labor needs?

    a.   business demand analysis
    b.   morale assessment
    c.   productivity scheduling
    d.   payroll budgeting

6.   An increase in food cost dollars may not signal a problem in a restaurant if

    a.   it is accompanied by an increase in sales
    b.   food has consistently been thrown away due to spoilage
    c.   the food cost percentage also increases dramatically
    d.   employees are allowed to take leftovers home

7.   When measuring employee efficiency a scale of 1 through 5 was used. If an employee works for 7 hours and the average score is 3 per hour, an employee receiving a score of 28 is said to be at a _____% level.

a.   100
b.   125
c.   133
d.   148

8.   Which of the following may not be regarded as a motivator to hospitality employees?

a.   increase in pay
b.   better work schedule
c.   fringe benefits
d.   none of the above

9.   If the normal scheduling standard is to have one server for every 25 seats in a restaurant, the manager will need to schedule _____ waitstaff to ensure thatan 180-seat restaurant will have sufficient personnel for a very busy night.

a.   5
b.   7
c.   8
d.   9

10.   One rule that a manager may want to avoid in the assignment of tasks is:

a.   to schedule employees of different competency levels on the same shift to complement each other
b.   to schedule two weak employees in the same function room for them to assist each other
c.   to schedule a captain to assist the new employee to "learn the ropes"
d.   to schedule according to the level of business

Review Exercises Answers

1. a
2. d
3. d
4. b
5. b
6. a
7. c
8. d
9. c
10. b

11.   Explain the four steps in analyzing labor needs.

To accomplish an analysis of the labor needs of an operation, management has to first perform a business demand analysis, then a productivity schedule, the actual payroll budgeting, and finally, the assignment of task. Business demand analysis provides the answer to the question—what does a business need? It includes forecasting using daily statistics, analyzing the competition, and noting of all local and special event and holidays and the operation's advertising and promotion efforts. In some establishments, there is a column for remarks on a daily recap sheet for the manager to input data such as weather, special event, holidays, major advertising and promotion dollars spent and also to determine if correlation exists between those factors and sales. The more information an operation can have and understand, the better it will be able to prepare for the guests by staffing accordingly.

The second step is productivity - taking the estimated sales from the business demand analysis and using the standards that have been set to schedule and estimate the labor needs. In productivity scheduling, management needs to look into each job category and see how the estimated sales will affect each job category and during what hours. Then, managers will plan the payroll by scheduling the full, part-time, and other personnel accordingly.

Once the positions are scheduled, an estimated payroll amount can be generated. This is the third step of a labor needs analysis. Payroll budgeting is a blueprint that lets management know the monetary resources that will be needed in order to achieve the estimated sales level with the proper and appropriate service standards.

Finally, once management knows how many people are needed for each meal period, function or event, and day, the next step is to assign the tasks. The productivity schedule and the payroll budget will now serve as guides to a manager. The manager will then need to schedule specific employees and assign the tasks to them.

12.   How can local events affect the volume of business in a hotel? How would that be different in a restaurant situation?

Local events can affect the volume of business in hotels and restaurants. If a local event is scheduled in a hotel, the occupancy of that hotel may increase, especially if there are out-of-town participants. With the increase in in-house guest count, the food and beverage facilities within the hotel should also be benefited. If the local event is held nearby a hotel, the occupancy may not increase as much. Depending on the time of the event, the hotel may advertise for some special meals for some room packages to attract guests to dine and stay with them.

In the case of a restaurant, the timing of the event will either greatly increases, the guest count or it may have no effect at all. If an event that is held nearby the restaurant is scheduled to end right before the lunch period, the restaurant may have many hungry guests who may not want to fight the crowd in traffic and would patronize the restaurant. Therefore, businesses should always plan accordingly for such functions. The local Chamber of Commerce and the Convention and Visitors Bureau can provide a listing of local events and holiday promotions.

13.   Calculate the total score and efficiency percentage rating for the following housekeeping staff: Scale: 0 = idle, 1 = lowest, 5 = highest. Use 21 (3 x 7) as the average score, with 3 being the average and 7 as the number of hours worked.

Name	Time of Day								Total	%
	7-8am	8-9am	9-10am	10-11am	11-12pm	12-1pm	1-2pm	2-3pm		
Anne	2	1	2	3	3	4	0	2		
Betty	3	3	4	4	0	2	4	4		
Carol	3	3	3	3	3	3	0	2		
Diane	4	4	4	0	4	4	4	4		

The answers can be calculated as follows. First, total the scores earned by each employee and put this total under the total column. For example:
Anne = 2+1+2+3+3+4+0+2 =17
Once the total is calculated, divide the total by the average score of 21
Thus, $\frac{17}{21}$ = 80.95% and Anne will be rated below average (100%)

Name	Time of Day								Total	%
	7-8am	8-9am	9-10am	10-11am	11-12pm	12-1pm	1-2pm	2-3pm		
Anne	2	1	2	3	3	4	0	2	17	80.95
Betty	3	3	4	4	0	2	4	4	24	114.29
Carol	3	3	3	3	3	3	0	2	20	95.24
Diane	4	4	4	0	4	4	4	4	28	133.33

14.   Referring to question #13, who are the employees that are above and who are those that are below the average?

In this scenario, Anne and Carol are below average while Betty and Diane are above average. It is important to note that these are simply the average levels. An operation may choose to set a higher standard for all employees, for instance, 28. Then 28 (4 X 7) rather than 21 will become the denominator for the efficiency percentage calculation.

Examination Type Problems

1.   Calculate the total score and efficiency percentage rating for the following kitchen line cooks: Scale: 0 = idle, 1 = lowest, 2 = average, 3 = highest. Use 14 (2 x 7) as the average score, with 2 as the average and 7 as the number of hours worked.

Name	Time of Day								Total	%
	3-4pm	4-5pm	5-6pm	6-7pm	7-8pm	8-9pm	9-10pm	10-11pm		
Joy	2	1	2	3	0	1	3	2		
Kim	3	3	2	2	0	2	3	2		
Lucy	3	3	3	0	3	3	3	2		
Mary	2	2	2	0	3	3	1	1		

The answers can be calculated as follows. First, total the scores earned by each employee and put this total under the total column. For example:
Joy = 2+1+2+3+0+1+3+2 =14
Once the total is calculated, divide the total by the average score of 14
Thus, $\frac{14}{14}$ = 100% and Joy will be rated right at the average (100%)

Name	Time of Day								Total	%
	3-4pm	4-5pm	5-6pm	6-7pm	7-8pm	8-9pm	9-10pm	10-11pm		
Joy	2	1	2	3	0	1	3	2	14	100
Kim	3	3	2	2	0	2	3	2	17	121.43
Lucy	3	3	3	0	3	3	3	2	20	142.86
Mary	2	2	2	0	3	3	1	1	14	100

2.   Referring to question # 1, who are the employees that are above or below the average?

According to the data, all are either at or above the average. In this case, the operation may want to use incentives to reward some or to challenge the employees by setting a higher goal with some added bonuses and the like.

3.   What are five strategies that you can use to improve the efficiency of those who are below average?

Strategies to improve efficiency can be various. First, before any retraining or counseling, the manager may want to observe the work habits of the individual. It may just be that the individual was performing the tasks but went about it the longest way possible. In this case, perhaps a quick retraining session will be all that is needed. If the individual is doing things the wrong way and thus is inefficient, then the strategy of an organized retraining plan may be warranted. In the third case, if the individual simply has an attitude issue and does not like to work at hard, some counseling may be needed. In the fourth case if this attitude is not only found in just one person but is a general attitude that exists in the entire operation, management will then need to address the morale issue. In this case, meetings for employees and managers to sit together and discuss the goals of the business or other issues may provide an avenue for discussion to solve some of these problems, and thus increase efficiency in the long run. Finally, if itis a miscommunication issue between management and the staff, again, a meeting to serve as a forum for the various parties to discuss the issues would be helpful. Therefore, before instituting a strategy, do investigate the reason of inefficiency and then address the issues accordingly.

Case Study

Your friend has recently inherited a restaurant from a distant relative. Knowing that you are successfully managing the Model Restaurant, she is seeking some advice from you in the area of labor staffing and scheduling. The restaurant she has is a 100-seat mid-scale casual dining establishment. It is situated in the downtown business district. Therefore, most of the clients are business folks in the office and bank buildings. The operating hours for lunch are from 11 a.m. to 2 p.m. with the majority of the business arriving between 12 noon and 1 p.m. Since most people only have one hour for lunch, quick and efficient service is of utmost importance. Using the four steps of labor needs analysis:

1.   List ten factors that can affect her business demand.

The following is a list of 10 factors that can affect the demand of her business:

i.   Holidays (since this is a downtown location and her clientele are mainly business people)
ii.   Economic boom and bust
iii.   Weather (most downtown buildings are not connected by walkways or underground tunnels; thus if it is a rainy day, people may order delivery items to the office rather than going out to eat)
iv.   Parking availability
v.   The viability of the downtown area (many major cities are having downtown rebuilding projects. If this is the case, then your friend will start seeing some dinner business also)
vi.   Quality of service employees that she can hire and retain (with good service employees who are efficient, guests will be served within their short lunch hour in an effective and yet quality manner)
vii.   Quality kitchen personnel to ensure that the food is cooked properly and in a timely fashion
viii.   Menu design (the menu needs to be changed every so often as she seems to have the same guest base. The items also need to be easy to make so that time can be saved)
ix.   Effective advertising and promotion that she has will increase business and generate good will
x.   Competition (she needs to stay in touch with the competition to ensure that her business is ahead of her competitors)

2.   If the business serves 200 during lunch, how many front of the house personnel would you recommend to your friend? Please specify the number in each category such as host/hostess, waitstaff, buspersons, etc. Explain the rationale of your recommendation.

Since the majority of the business is between the 12-1 time period and people all come in pretty much in a rush, your friend will need to ensure that the guests are all served. The following could be one suggestion:
Hostesses: 3 – one can come in before the 11am opening hour to set up. The second person can come in at about 11:15 to 11:30 and the third may come in at 11:30 to handle the crowd. In this case, one can be taking the names of the guests while the others will be seating the guests.

Waitstaff: Again, due to the arrival time of the guests, the waitstaff has to be very efficient. It takes about 5 minutes on the average to take the drink orders, deliver the drinks, and then take the food order for a table of 4. This is if the guests know what they would like instead of asking all sorts of questions about the menu, the special, the types of dressing etc. Therefore, with 100 seats, 5 good waitstaff would be sufficient. Each will be in charge of 20 guests in a one seating. If they are not very efficient or if they are new and do not know of all the details of the place, perhaps a 6th person may be helpful. Again, the hours that they work could be staggered as those of the hostesses.

Busperson: The buspersons may not need to be on the floor until 11:30 or so. They can, however, help prepare water, drinks, cracker baskets or other items and help out in the servicing of the guest. Three may be all that is needed while a forth one can help out at the back as an expeditor when the food starts coming out from the kitchen.

3.   Using a spreadsheet program, formulate a spreadsheet file for a payroll budget for the

front of the house for the lunch period. Use Figure 14-3 as an example for the format.

The answer to this will vary according to the type of spreadsheet used. The following is an example of an EXCEL spreadsheet.

A payroll budget for the front of the house for lunch on

Shift : 11-2	Time	Hours	Name	Rate	Extension (#of Hrs X Rate)
Hostess 1	10 to 3	5		7.50	37.5
Hostess 2	11:15 to 2:15	3		6.25	18.75
Hostess 3	11:15 to 2:00	2.75		6.25	17.1875
Waitstaff 1	9 to 4	7		3.00	21
Waitstaff 2	9 to 4	7		3.00	21
Waitstaff 3	9 to 4	7		3.00	21
Waitstaff 4	10 to 3	5		2.35	11.75
Waitstaff 5	10 to 3	5		2.35	11.75
Waitstaff 6	11 to 3	4		2.35	9.4
Busperson 1	11 to 3	4		5.50	22
Busperson 2	11:30 to 3	3.5		5.50	19.25
busperson 3	11:30 to 3	3.5		5.50	19.25

If the formulas are reviewed, it will be as follows where column C stands for the hours worked and column E stands for the rate.

A payroll budget for the front of the house for

Shift : 11-2	Time	Hours	Name	Rate	Extension
hostess 1	10 to 3	5		7.5	=E3*C3
hostess 2	11:15 to 2:15	3		6.25	=E4*C4
hostess 3	11:15 to 2:00	2.75		6.25	=E5*C5
waitstaff 1	9 to 4	7		3	=E6*C6
waitstaff 2	9 to 4	7		3	=E7*C7
waitstaff 3	9 to 4	7		3	=E8*C8
waitstaff 4	10 to 3	5		2.35	=E9*C9
waitstaff 5	10 to 3	5		2.35	=E10*C10
waitstaff 6	11 to 3	4		2.35	=E11*C11
busperson 1	11 to 3	4		5.5	=E12*C12
busperson 2	11:30 to 3	3.5		5.5	=E13*C13
busperson 3	11:30 to 3	3.5		5.5	=E14*C14

4.   Explain how you would suggest your friend measure labor efficiency. Following the

format of Figure 14-4, work out a numerical example to help explain your suggestion.

One method to measure employee efficiency is through a good amount of observation. Managers will observe employees during their work periods, and assign each a rating on an hourly basis. These ratings can be on a scale of 1 to 5 with 1 being the lowest to 5 being the highest. They can also be as simple as 0 to 3 where:

0 is when the employee is idle, such as during the lunch hour
1 is under-expectation; not performing up to par
2 is average, right at par, and
3 is over-expectation, performing over par.

Thus, for an 8-hour shift of 7:00 a.m. to 3:00 p.m., the employee will have a total rating of 0 to 24. Since there is an hour off for lunch and breaks, the scale can be modified to rate only 7 hours, thus a scale of 0 to 21.

	Time of Day									
Name	7-8am	8-9am	9-10am	10-11am	11-12pm	12-1pm	1-2pm	2-3pm	Total	%
Waitstaff A	2	2	2	2	0	3	3	3	17	121
Waitstaff B	1	1	2	2	0	3	2	2	13	93
Waitstaff C	3	3	3	0	3	3	3	3	21	150
Waitstaff D	2	2	1	0	1	1	1	2	10	71

As seen from the chart above, using a 0 to 21 scale, with 14 being average, waitstaff A has a total rating of 17 and an above average percentage, as expected, of 121% (17 ÷ 14 = 121%). With this score card, your friend can identify her best performers so that she can recognize the good work and give pats on the back. She can also have discussions with the poor performers and decide what the next steps would be. Most importantly, she now has the master plan for assigning the tasks.

5.   Perform a literature search and recommend to your friend five strategies in combating poor morale.

        The answers to this question will vary.

CHAPTER 15

MANAGING OTHER CONTROLLABLE AND NON-CONTROLLABLE EXPENSES

I.   Purpose of the Chapter

This chapter is designed to reinforce to students the importance of control and how many activities are actually under the control of management. Additionally, it is pointed out that management ability to control is extremely important to the success of the hospitality operation.

II.   Overview of the Chapter

This chapter discusses the controllable and non-controllable expenses that are common in our industry. Too often, management and owners are concerned about the prime cost, meaning food and beverage and also labor costs. While they unequivocally represent a large percentage of the costs to operate a business, there are still many other costs that need to be addressed and controlled. If management and owners only control food, labor and beverage costs and let the other categories go unattended, the profit of a business will slowly, and at times, even quickly, be wiped out. Some expenses are non-controllable at the manager's level but are controllable at the owner's level. Therefore, care needs to be taken in managing all costs.

We have also seen form examples of how savings in these costs can either lower our taxes paid and/or increase our net income. Therefore, it is up to both management and ownership to make that profit.

III.   Learning Objectives

1.   The differences between controllable and non-controllable expenses

Controllable expenses are controllable by management within the department or the operation, such as utilities, marketing, and administrative and general expenses. Non-controllable expenses are still expenses but they are normally controlled at the owners' level. Some examples are rent and interest. An understanding of these two categories can help managers and owners to classify and thus manage those costs more effectively.

2.   The various sub-items in each major expense category

There are a number of major expense categories besides food, beverage and labor. These major categories are direct operating expense, music and entertainment, marketing, utilities, administrative and general, repairs and maintenance, occupation costs, depreciation, and interest. A good understanding of where and why various sub-items belong to which of these major categories can help management track expenses accordingly. The figures in this chapter help outline the sub-items under each expense category.

3.   The effectiveness of a department or expense category by examining its expense
      schedule

At times, it is difficult to decide where money was spent in a category such as utilities. Is the utility account high this month due to an increased use in air-conditioning or gas? If management can examine an expense schedule, this question can be answered. In addition, if management is trying to track the usage of any item, an expense schedule can delineate these items very easily.

4.   The different types of depreciation and their effects on taxes and profits

There are many methods of depreciation. In this chapter, the two main types, straight line and accelerated depreciation, are discussed in detailed. The higher the depreciation expense, the lower the taxable income since depreciation expense is treated as any other expenses. However, since it is a non-cash expense in the sense that the operation is not writing a check to pay this depreciation amount to any person or entity, the money stays in the bank account of the business. With a lesser amount of taxable income, the amount of taxes that is needed to be paid to the government also decreases. Depreciation is one way where the government gives businesses a tax break with the intention that these non-cash expenses will be saved up so that when it is time for an equipment to be replaced, the businesses will have the funds to do so.

5.   Actions to improve the effectiveness of a department or expense category

Once management understands what it can control, it will then need to find methods to control the items. Certain items such as rent and interest are controlled at the owners' levels. Unless the owners have solicited the help of management and have given them some authority to negotiate such expenses, management can try to control such costs but their efforts will be wasted. Thus, once management understands the various categories of controllable expenses and knows the sub-items, they need to assess the effectiveness of the operation and seek improvement to the controllable expense categories.

IV.   Definition of Key Terms

Administration and general expense – this category of expense encompasses items that are related to the administrative functions of the business. Examples include credit card collection expenses, information systems and general office supplies, from photocopies to pencil sharpeners, are all included.

Contracts and services – these are contracts and services that the operation uses. They may include maintenance contracts, contracts for cleaning vents and hoods or even a contract with a credit card company.

Controllable expense – this is an expense that a manager should have influence over and the authority to make decisions regarding. Examples of this category are utilities and marketing.

Direct operating expense - Direct operating expenses include items such as uniform and laundry, china, glasses, silver, linen, kitchen fuel, cleaning supplies, paper supplies, bar supplies, menus, dry cleaning, and the like.

Expense category – expenses can be monitored more easily and effectively if like items are grouped together. In so doing, if one category is very high, management can take action and see if there are some issues that need to be resolved.

Insurance expense – as the name suggests, any types of insurance for the business excluding employee health insurance will be part of the employees' benefits package) will be included. Examples can be general business insurance or flood insurance.

Marketing expense – this is an expense that will help market or promote the operation to its guests. Examples include direct mailings, radio spots, and newspaper advertisements.

Music and entertainment expense – this will include royalties paid to music associations for playing certain music in the establishment or hiring an entertainer to perform in the operation.

Non-controllable expense – this is an expense in which management has no control over. The owner normally is the party that negotiates all these expenses. For instance, rent is negotiated by the owner and although it is an expense under the income statement, management can also do its best to best utilize the space rented but will not decrease the amount of rent that owners need to pay.

Utilities expense – this includes all kinds of utilities from electricity to gas, and from water usage to sewage charges.

V.   Teaching Outline

A.   Direct Operating Expenses
B.   Music and Entertainment
C.   Marketing
D.   Utilities
E.   Administrative and General
F.   Repairs and Maintenance
G.   Occupation Costs
    1.   Rent
    2.   Property tax
H.   Depreciation
I.   Interest

VI.   Questions and Answers

Review Exercises

1.   For departments where food and beverage costs do not apply, which cost is the largest portion of a department's budget?

    a.   advertising
    b.   utilities
    c.   labor
    d.   property tax

2.   Which of the following will not be considered as controllable?

    a.   labor
    b.   food
    c.   beverage
    d.   interest

3.   Marketing expenses will normally include:

    a.   postage for mailing

b.   signage
c.   direct mail
d.   all of the above

4.   One important point about marketing expense is:

a.   tracking the success of each marketing program and idea
b.   do not waste time in calculations and analysis
c.   the more money spent, the more sales will be generated
d.   record keeping is not needed

5.   Which of the following is not an example of saving on utilities?

a.   maintenance of water heater temperature at a constant level all year round
b.   linen re-use program
c.   towel re-use program
d.   compact fluorescent bulbs

6.   One fact that management should not lose sight of while saving energy is:

a.   guest satisfaction
b.   employee satisfaction
c.   dollars spent
d.   dollars saved

7.   Credit card commission fees are dependent upon one of the following factors:

a.   number of employees
b.   total revenues
c.   total costs
d.   tax paid

8.   Occupation costs may include:

a.   rent
b.   utility
c.   property tax
d.   all of the above

9.   Property taxes:

a.   are fixed
b.   can be appealed
c.   are in opposite relation to the property's value
d.   are always paid by the tenant

10.   Depreciation methods that are used include:

a.   straight-line
b.   quadruple declining balance

c.   modified accelerated cost recovery system
d.   a and c

Review Exercises Answers

1. c
2. d
3. d
4. a
5. a
6. a
7. b
8. d
9. b
10. d

11.   Name two controllable and two non-controllable expenses. Explain why they should be

        categorized as such.

        Two examples of controllable expenses are marketing and utilities (direct
        operating expense, music and entertainment, administrative and general, repairs and
        maintenance, and obviously food, beverage and labor costs can also be included). They
        are deemed controllable because managers, with their regular responsibility and
        authority, can control these costs. A manager can decide whether a direct mailing should
        be used rather than a flyer for a neighborhood party advertisement. A manager can
        decide whether a gas or electric oven will be better for the operation, thus affecting the
        utility expense.
        On the other hand, interest and rent are two examples that are deemed non-
        controllable. Non-controllable means that it cannot be controlled normally at the
        manager's level, but they can be controlled at the owner's level. The owner is the one
        who will go to bank to negotiate a loan for the business; the owner is also the one who
        will negotiate with the landlord on the rent.

12.   List three pieces of equipment in a fast food restaurant and explain why a maintenance

        schedule will be needed for them.

        This answer will vary. The aim is to let students know that there needs to be a
        regular maintenance schedule so that equipment can be correctly maintained. First, a
        maintenance schedule can be set up for the POS equipment of the fast food operation. It
        is the manager's expertise to operate a restaurant but not his or her expertise to fix a
        POS system, especially if the system is a more fancy one. Thus, a contract in this case
        can give the business regular maintenance and protection. The maintenance staff of the
        Contract Company will come in every so often to check if all the parts of the POS system
        are working correctly. The second piece of equipment is the vent and hood system that
        is over the cooking area. These hoods need to be cleaned at regular intervals. A
        maintenance schedule can be set so that the cleaning company can clean the hood and
        ensure that the hood is working properly. The third piece of equipment can be the oven.
        This could be done easily in house. Besides cleaning the oven at regular intervals, it also

needs to be calibrated. Otherwise, food will be cooked at the wrong temperature and will not meet the standards of the operation.

13.   Discuss how you can evaluate the effectiveness of an advertising or promotion

campaign.

One can evaluate the effectiveness of an advertising or promotion campaign by tracking of the success rate of each marketing program and idea. Calculations should be done so that the results can be analyzed.

For instance, if a hotel is advertising a Valentine's Day weekend special on three different cable channels, the hotel may want to have separate 1-800 number lines for each of these radio spots. In doing so, the reservations agent can track the source of the calls. Using special promotion coupons in direct mail can also achieve the same purpose. When the results are tabulated, management can easily ascertain which of the ideas, programs, or direct mailing agencies yields the best return on the investment. It will also be a good idea to train employees to ask the guests whether it is their first time visiting the operation, and if so, how they learned about the property. Employees can then make a notation on the voucher, coupon, or reservation to track the amount of new business each advertising program is generating.

14.   Discuss the differences between the straight-line depreciation method and one modified

accelerated cost recovery system.

The straight-line method is achieved where owners and management or owners deduct the salvage value from the cost and divide the depreciable base by the estimated number of years of its useful life to obtain the annual depreciated amount, hence the depreciation expense. Thus, the annual depreciation expense is the same for the entire useful life of the equipment.

Accelerated depreciation is where the owner and management can write off a larger sum of money as depreciation expense and thus pay lesser taxes in the early years. Many start-up businesses or even established ones would opt for this method because in the first few years of a start-up business, cash flow normally is the tightest. Thus any extra penny that does not need to be paid out could be retained in the business for other purposes. The more commonly used accelerated methods are double declining balance and the modified accelerated cost recovery systems.

15.   You have found a perfect spot for your fast food operation in a new mall. You also have

a choice of 3 leases: variable, fixed and mixed. For the variable contract, the lease or

rental charge will be 5% of sales. The fixed contract offers a rate of $55,000 per year

while the mixed contract charges a base minimum rent of $25,000 plus 3% of sales over

$350,000. What will you choose if your sales level is:

a. $500,000

Sales = $500,000

Rental payment:
Under Fixed lease $55,000
Under Variable lease $25,000 $500,000 x 0.05
Under Mixed lease $29,500 $25,000 + ($500,000 - $350,000) x 0.03
            Best option: Variable lease

b. $200,000

Sales = $200,000
Rental payment:
Under Fixed lease $55,000
Under Variable lease $10,000 $500,000 x 0.05
Under Mixed lease $25,000
            Best option: Variable lease

c. $1,000,000

Sales = $1,000,000
Rental payment:
Under Fixed lease $55,000
Under Variable lease $50,000 $1,000,000 x 0.05
Under Mixed lease $44,500 $25,000 + ($1,000,000 - $350,000) x 0.03
            Best option: Mixed lease

Examination Type Problems

1.   You have recently purchased some new equipment for the office area and they fall

      under the 3-year class life of the modified accelerated cost recovery system. Given that

      the equipment cost $100,000, has 4 years of useful economic life and a salvage value of

      $25,000, calculate the:

   a. depreciation expenses of the four years using the straight-line depreciation method.

            Cost $100,000
            Salvage $ 25,000
            Life   4 years

            Depreciation expense = 100,000 - 25,000
                                   ────────────────
                                          4

                        = $18,750 per year

   c. depreciation expenses of the four years using the double declining balance method.

            In the double declining balance method, one will first need to calculate the
         double declining rate. This is essentially doubling the straight-line rate. Thus:

$$\text{Double Declining Rate} = \frac{100\%}{\text{useful life}} \times 2$$

Using the same date from the example of the straight line depreciation:

$$\text{Double Declining Rate} = \frac{100\%}{4} \times 2$$
$$= 50\%$$

The depreciation expense of the double declining rate is calculated by multiplying the rate to the cost of the asset. Salvage is not used until the depreciated value approaches the salvage in later year. To fully depreciate the $100,000 amount using the DDB method with a $25,000 salvage:

Year	Calculation	Expense	Accumulated Depreciation	Salvage	Book Value
	Acquisition	0	0	25,000	100,000
1	100,000 x 50%	50,000	50,000	25,000	50,000
2	50,000 x 50%	25,000	75,000	25,000	25,000
3				25,000	25,000
4				25,000	25,000

In this case, since the total value was fully depreciated after year two, there will no be any depreciation expense for years three and four.

c. depreciation expenses of the four years using the modified accelerated cost recovery

system.

This equipment is under the 3-year class life of the MACRS system, thus the appropriate percentages are 33%, 45%, 15% and 7%. In this method, the cost is 100% depreciable. Therefore, the depreciation expenses for the four years will be as follows:

Year	%	Depreciable base		Depreciation Expense
1	33%	x $100,000	=	$33,000
2	45%	x $100,000	=	$45,000
3	15%	x $100,000	=	$15,000
4	7 %	x $100,000	=	$7,000

2.   Name three items under the direct operating expense category and discuss how costs

can be controlled and evaluated on these items.

Three items under direct operating expenses can be cable/satellite television in a hotel room, china in the food and beverage area and refuse or trash removal in the others area. For cable and satellite television, the main point to look for is the initial installation costs and then all the monthly charges, charge backs, paper work, field support charges, and any other miscellaneous fees. Most companies will provide hotels with similar services and types of movies or even video games if desired. However, the price structure is very different.

For china items, it is not just the cost but also the usage by employee and pilferage by employees and guests. China items are very expensive and care needs to be used when handling such items. The amount spent on replacing china items should be well documented and monitored. If an uncharacteristically high amount is used, management needs to investigate. It is also good practice to take a china inventory on a regular basis. This will also deter employees from taking them home if they know that management keep track of these items.

It may not appear that one can do much about trash removal since all hospitality operations will have to incur the cost. Therefore, managers need to control cost here by controlling the services that these companies will give. For example, if the prices quoted by two companies is the same, the one that can come at the times you want rather than during the time that you are receiving your food products would be more beneficial to your operation. In addition, if they also provide recycling bins and other services, it will be a better option for the business.

3.   Internet and homepages are some new ways to market your hotel, restaurants and food

service operations. Discuss three methods to examine if you should have your own

homepage for marketing purposes.

First, you may want to determine if your existing guests will have access to the Internet and may use the homepage and know of your new marketing program. Second, you also need to ask the Internet provider the number of hits that they have on record and where they are generated. For a hotel, this will be better if the hits are not from the same city because people do travel from state to state and also internationally. For restaurants however, the guests are usually local. People very infrequently will fly to another state to have dinner. So, this information will be important. Third, you may want to evaluate the pricing of creating the homepage and updating information. For marketing purposes, the homepages need to be updated to attract the attention of the guest. It will not be good if such homepages have old information. Therefore the services that the Internet company will provide and the costs associated with it are also important.

4.   You have a choice of three leases (variable, fixed and mixed) for your fast food

operation space. For the variable contract, the lease or rental charge will be 7% of sales.

The fixed contract offers at rate of $60,000 per year while the mixed contract charge a

base minimum rent of $30,000 plus 4% of sales over $400,000. What will you choose if

your sales level is:

a. $250,000

Sales = $250,000
Rental payment:
Under Fixed lease $60,000
Under Variable lease $17,500 $250,000 x 0.07
Under Mixed lease $30,000 $30,000 + no extra over $400,000
        Best option: Variable lease

b. $600,000

Sales = $600,000
Rental payment:
Under Fixed lease $60,000
Under Variable lease $42,000 $600,000 x 0.07
Under Mixed lease $38,000 $30,000 + (600,000-400,000) x 0.04
        Best option: Variable lease

c. $900,000

Sales = $900,000
Rental payment:
Under Fixed lease $60,000
Under Variable lease $63,000 $900,000 x 0.07
Under Mixed lease $50,000 $30,000 + (900,000-400,000) x 0.04
Best option: Mixed lease

Case Study

You have managed the Model Restaurant so well that your hotel corporation has asked

you to consult on a restaurant of another sister hotel. The General Manager of the sister hotel

explains to you that even though sales have remained the same for the last few months, there

has been a constant decline in profit. Several efforts were also used in advertising and

promotion to increase sales. Since you are not the owner and you have no control over the non-

controllable costs, your only alternative is to try and reduce the amount of controllable costs. List

five specific controllable expenses and evaluate how each can be improved.

Case Study Answers

These five items suggested are not in any particular order and additional
items can always be added as long as they are listed as one of the controllable expenses in this
chapter. Food, beverage and labor costs however, will not be included here since they have
been discussed in the previous chapters. The restaurant should probably look into the budgeted
figures and compare them with the actual figures to see it some accounts will need more
scrutiny than other.

The first item that you may want to evaluate will be the efforts in the advertising and promotion expenses to see if sales have increased. You know that the campaign has been carried out but the sales figures were not given, therefore, this will be one of the items. It is the hope that there is a tracking device somehow attached to these advertisements so that the net increase in sales through the advertisements and promotions can be documented. If not, this may be fairly difficult to ascertain if the net increase in sales in due to that particular advertising and promotional effort.

The restaurant may also want to look into the amount spent on uniforms and laundry. If the cooks are using their aprons and towels to clean equipment improperly and ruin them, the linen company may charge the operation more. This is also true when the buspersons use napkins to clean the tables rather than a kitchen towel. In addition, when receiving linen, do count not only the bundles but the individual napkins in a bundle. A bundle of 25 may only have 24. However, you are now charged for 25 and when the linen company picks up the dirty one, you are now one short and they will then charge you the replacement cost of the napkin that they never delivered.

China, glasses, silverware is another bug category under direct operating expenses and they are very costly to the operation. This is especially true when high grade stainless steel, silver-plated, or real silver utensils are used. Care needs to be used when handling such items. The amount spent on replacing these items should be well documented and monitored. If an uncharacteristically high amount is used, management needs to investigate. It is also good practice to take a china, glassware and silverware inventory on a regular basis. This will also deter employees from taking them home if they know that management keep track of these items.

A fourth item can be found in the utilities area. Energy used improperly can create an enormous amount of waste and decrease profit margins. Therefore, energy conservation is not only the right thing to do to help preserve the earth, but is also the right thing to do for a more profitable business. Check all the lighting and replace incandescent bulbs with compact fluorescent bulbs. Window shades can help block sunlight and reduce the amount of energy used. An energy audit can be useful to this restaurant. Most energy providers have a free energy audit for business and also residential accounts. A phone call to set up a free energy audit is most beneficial to this restaurant.

The last area might be credit collection policies and credit card commissions. If the credit policy is not reasonable and strict enough, guests may take advantage of the system and more bad debts will have to be written off. This is a cost. In today's society where credit cards are so widely used, a high credit card fee can erode a big part of an operation's profits. These fees need to be re-negotiated down as the average check and/or per transaction revenue and total revenue increases. It is advisable to update credit card commission quotes at least every two years since the revenue levels can change.

CHAPTER 16

FORECASTING AND BUDGETING

I.   Purpose of the Chapter

This chapter emphasizes the need for forecasting and budgeting in a hospitality operation. Though it may be perceived as a quite time consuming project, forecasts and budgets provide a plan for a business to work towards. The chapter also stresses the importance of ratios and variance analyses once the actual performance data are collected.

II.   Overview of the Chapter

If management would like to have a successful business, they need to have three key points in mind when they are preparing their forecasts and budgets. First, forecasting and budgeting are important. Once that is completed, continuously monitoring the actual figures becomes paramount. Ratios and variances will need to be calculated to assess the health of the operation. Third, if necessary, the budgeted amounts may need to be modified to reflect the realistic picture of the business.

To begin, forecasts and budgets need to be accurate. Use all data and personnel available inside and outside of the operation in establishing forecasts and budgets. Historical data are important yet future events that have impact on your hospitality concern are also vital. Even if the first go-around has deficiencies, management and responsible parties should not simply abandon the forecasts or budgets and "go by experience."

When the actual data are collected and the forecasts or budgets are not on target, management needs to provide updated reforecasts and new budgets to reflect the current situation. Timely reports are crucial. It will not help a hotel if a forecast is wrong and the revised version is not calculated for the staffing to take actions that are needed until it is too late. Contingency plans should have been established during the original forecasting or budgeting period so that when actions needed to be taken, the plans will all be in place. Besides timeliness, relevancy is also pertinent. How many times has one heard management complaining about the stack of reports on their desks? Reports need to be concise, to the point, describe the situation, and stop. They should not be given pages after pages of peripherals that do not concern the main situation. Information overload has an adverse effect on the efficiency of the operation.

III.   Learning Objectives

1.   The importance of forecasting and budgeting

As a sound and solid strategy is imperative to winning a war, a budget is essential to the profitability of a hotel. Effective preparation of forecasts and budgets can lead to better knowledge of probable income on a departmental or unit level and thus efficient control of operating expenses. Forecast is the planning of what sales level one may achieve given a set of circumstances. Forecasting is useful in many ways including staffing properly, controlling cost, making decisions, planning strategically, maximizing profits, and having a standard of comparison, setting prices accordingly and others.

Budgeting is different from forecasting in that it gives information not only regarding the level of sales but all the costs needed to generate that one level of forecasted sales and the possible profits that can be generated.

2.   Methods of forecasting

A number of methods are used in preparing forecast and this chapter discusses these following methods: sales force estimates, moving averages, decomposition, juries of executive opinion, smoothing, simple time series, market research, the Delphi method, and regression. Which is the best method will depends on the type of operation, the type of customers, the level of demand, the efforts spent on sales and marketing, seasonality, specific events, and availability and accuracy of past data.

3.   Forecasting using simple time series and moving averages

These two methods are more important than the others mentioned in the chapter because they also are the most used. A simple time series is where simple rules such as forecast equals last period's actual activity, or adding/subtracting a certain percentage from last period's data is used to complete a forecast. This is especially useful for smaller scale hospitality operations where time, technology or expertise is lacking. Moving averages are compiled based upon average past values of a time series. This method is also very popular due to its simple and quick calculation.

4.   Static and flexible budgets

Static and flexible budgets are each a different form of an operation's budget. An operations budget reflects the projected revenues and expenses. It mirrors the income statement by providing the operator an estimate of the income or loss potential before the actual accounting period. It is good to have a static budget, as it will be simple and clear with only one level of sales. However, to be more effective, management will need a flexible budget where more than one level of sales is given, along with their respective expenses. It is therefore one of the objectives of this chapter for students to understand the worth of both types of budgets and also know when to use them. The mechanics of such budgets is normally covered in more detail in an accounting versus a controls class.

5.   The five major categories of ratios

When students finish this chapter, they need to have an understanding of the five major categories of ratios. These are like the major subjects in a report card of an operation. If all five categories exhibit good ratios, the health of this organization should be solid and should be a good company for one to work for or to invest in. The five categories are liquidity, solvency, activity, profitability, and operating. Liquidity ratios measure the ability of the operation in meeting its short-term debts. Solvency or debt measure the degree of debt financing and indicate the operation's ability to meet its long-term debts. Activity or turnover ratios reflect the company's use of assets that are available, prompt payment of trade payables and expenses. Profitability ratios is the most often discussed category since these ratios show the amount of money earned, such as return on assets and return on sales. Last but not least, operating ratios such as sales mix, average daily rate (ADR), revenue per available room (REVPAR), all help determine the efficiency of how the hotels are managed.

6.   Perform variance analysis

Variance analysis tells how well an operation is performing when compared to the planned figures. The aim of forecasting and budgeting, obviously, is to be on target. However, when variances occur, management will be looking for favorable variances.

Students need to understand and also be able to perform a variance analysis, as variance is a fact of life because the probability of a budget that is 100 percent of the actual figures is minimal. Variance should never be ignored, even when it is favorable. If such is the case, better planning may enable the operation to capture a bigger margin to the bottom line.

7.   Take action and follow up on significant variances

It is also important to know that having all the analyses and figures all neatly computed will not do the operation any good if actions are not taken to correct the significant variance. This business is very hands on. Information is important and is much needed but they also need to be acted upon. Thus, students must understand the need to following-up on the significant variance.

8.   Avoid the problem of stock out

Stock out occurs when an operation does not have enough inventories to fill the orders. It is a situation that neither management nor guests will enjoy. Guests may look at this negatively and may never return to this one establishment because his or her demand is not met. This should never even be allowed to happen. Again, this is why good and accurate forecasts and budgets are essential to the success of a business.

9.   Contingency plans for unforeseen circumstances

Just as there is a hurricane escape route and that cities have emergency plans for natural disasters, hospitality operations also need contingency plans for unforeseen circumstances. The more a crew is prepared to deal with certain situations, the easier it will be on everybody, including the guests, if such situation does ever occur. Therefore, it is good to have contingency plans for stock outs and other circumstances.

IV.   Definition of Key Terms

Budgeting – is a "formal" plan, normally expressed in terms of the dollar revenues and expenses of an operation over a period of time.

Contingency plan – is simply a plan in place when a particular event that was expected to have a possibility of happening did in fact happen.

Decomposition – this is a time series that is broken down into trends, cyclical, seasonal, and randomness to offer the user more in-depth information.

Delphi method – When performing a forecast for the entire industry, the Delphi method, a formal process conducted with a group of experts to achieve consensus, is often used.

Flexible budget – is an operations budget with more than one level of sales, thus the adjective flexible. This is a more preferred method for an operations budget as management can ascertain the effect on costs and income if the projected sales level change.

Forecasting – is similar to budgeting in that it is also used to predict some future outcomes. However, it normally is used to predict the outcomes of future events such as sales level or the number of room nights and not the expenses.

Juries of executive opinion – this is where the opinions of top executives jointly served as the basis to prepare forecasts.

Market research – this is where information about the perception of the product is gathered from potential customers to estimate the rate of demand.

Moving averages – are compiled based upon average past values of a time series. This method is also very popular due to its simple and quick calculation.

Operations budget – is also known as the revenues and expense budget. It mirrors the income statement by providing the operator with an estimate of the income or loss potential before the actual accounting period. It serves as a benchmark for the company for comparison with past efforts and also as a realistic and yet attainable goal.

Ratio analysis – is essentially a mathematical calculation of one value divided by another, expressed in the form of times or percentages. It is from the presentation of such relationships that ratios generate new information, making the numbers and values more meaningful, informative, and useful. Primarily, financial ratios are used to assess the performance of businesses. Through financial ratios, absolute numbers are transformed into meaningful relative terms where owners and managers can then extract more invaluable information.

Regression – regression is a statistical method to determine the effect independent variables has on dependent variables using the least squares method. The R^2 statistic, derived from regression, will have a value of 0 to 1 and it indicates the percentage of how much the independent variable can explain the changes that occurred in the dependent variable. Thus a higher R^2 value indicates that the independent variable is a better predictor of the dependent variable. For example, rooms sold can be a predictor of labor costs in the rooms department.

Sales force estimates – this is a bottom-up approach to forecasting by aggregating unit managers' forecasts to compile one for the entire organization. At a unit or departmental level, this will be done by gathering data from the first-line employees.

Simple time series – simple rules such as forecast equals last period's actual activity, or adding/subtracting a certain percentage from last period's data are called simple time series. They are especially useful for smaller scale hospitality operations where time, technology or expertise is lacking.

Smoothing – smoothing is similar to moving average except that it gives more weight to the more recent past values of a time series, thereby discounting the older data that may not have as much impact on the forecast.

Static budget – when an operations budget reflects only one level of sales, it is known as a static budget.

Stock out – this is when an operation does not have enough inventory to fill the orders.

Variance analysis – the difference between the budgeted figures and the actual performance of the hospitality operation is the variance. Depending on whether it is a revenue variance or cost variance, a positive or negative difference may be favorable or unfavorable.

V.   Teaching Outline

A.   Forecasting the Volume of Business
B.   The Whens, Whos and Whats of Forecasting
C.   Preparing a Budget
D.   The When, Whos and Whats of Budgeting
E.   Measuring Success and Budgetary Control
          1.   Ratio Analysis
          2.   Variance Analysis
F.   Stock Outs and Contingency Plans
G.   Computerization - Technology Today

VI.   Questions and Answers

Review Exercises

1.   Which of the following is not an important factor to consider when estimating sales incomes?

          a.   food costs
          b.   sales histories
          c.   inflation
          d.   nearby street improvement

2.   Over a 60-day period, 600 guests are served and 120 prime rib dinners sold. What is the percentage of guests ordering prime rib dinners?

          a.   12%
          b.   20%
          c.   40%
          d.   45%

3.   Past records show that 40% of the dinner guests order some sort of a chicken entrée. If 160 guests are forecasted for next Tuesday's dinner, how many chicken entrees will be sold?

          a.   40%
          b.   46%
          c.   60%
          d.   64%

4.   When budgeted sales are at $17,000 and the actual sales are at $15,000, the variance will be:

          a.   +$2,000 favorable
          b.   +$2,000 unfavorable
          c.   -$2,000 favorable
          d.   -$2,000 unfavorable

5.   Which is not a method used in forecasting as discussed in the chapter?

    a.   guests' comments
    b.   simple time series
    c.   market research
    d.   decomposition

6.   Which is a good method to use if forecasting for the sales of new products or services?

    a.   guests' comments
    b.   Delphi method
    c.   moving average
    d.   market research

7.   If Great Food Restaurant uses a 4-week moving average to predict customer counts, what would be the count predicted for week 8?

Week	Count
3	1000
4	1020
5	1040
6	980
7	1008

    a.   1000
    b.   1012
    c.   1020
    d.   1028

8.   A simple series of add 5% will make the last guest count of 200 for lunch become:

    a.   201
    b.   205
    c.   210
    d.   220

9.   What is the occupancy percentage of Sky Lodge if it has 300 rooms and housed 200 guests last night? (Assuming all single occupancy)

    a.   40%
    b.   60%
    c.   67%
    d.   70%

10.   Referring to question 9, if 50 rooms were each occupied by two people, what will be the double occupancy percentage?

    a.   20%
    b.   25%
    c.   30%
    d.   33%

Review Exercises Answers

1. a
2. b
3. d
4. d
5. a
6. d
7. b
8. c
9. c
10. d

11.   The Red Fish Cafe uses the 3-week moving average method in forecasting. Given the following data, what will be its expected guest count for week 20?

Week	Actual Guest Count
15	1,840
16	1,760
17	1,882
18	1,823
19	1,799

To calculate the forecasted guest count for week 20, we will need to add the counts for the last 3 weeks and divide that total by three. Therefore, the expected guest count for week 20 will be:

$$= \frac{1,882 + 1,823 + 1,799}{3}$$

$$= 1,834.67 \text{ or } 1,835 \text{ guests}$$

12.   The Golden Eagle, a 300-room hotel, uses simple time series to forecast its guests and thus occupancy percentages. The current month, April, records a guest count of 5,400. As the summer months approach, the hotel expects an increase of 1% in guest count per month for the next five months. What will the guest counts and occupancy percentages be for the months of May through September? (Assuming all single occupancy)

Month	Guest Count	Occupancy	
April	5,400	$\frac{5,400 \text{ guests}}{300 \text{ rooms} \times 30 \text{ days}}$	= 60%

May	5,400 x 1.01 =5,454	$\dfrac{5,454 \text{ guests}}{300 \text{ rooms X 31 days}}$ = 58.65%
June	5,454 x 1.01 =5,509	$\dfrac{5,509 \text{ guests}}{300 \text{ rooms X 30 days}}$ = 61.21%
July	5,509 x 1.01 =5,564	$\dfrac{5,564 \text{ guests}}{300 \text{ rooms X 31 days}}$ = 59.83%
August	5,564 x 1.01 =5,619	$\dfrac{5,619 \text{ guests}}{300 \text{ rooms X 31 days}}$ = 60.42%
September	5,619 x 1.01 =5,675	$\dfrac{5,675 \text{ guests}}{300 \text{ rooms X 30 days}}$ = 63.06%

13. Given the following information, prepare a budget for Restaurant Max Profit for the month of April.

Average check $15.40
Customer count per day 302
There are 30 days in April
Food Cost 33.4%
Salaries and Wages 28.6%
Employee Benefits 4.0%
Direct Operating Expense 6.9%
Music and Entertainment 0.5%
Marketing 2.5%
Utilities 2.9%
Repairs and Maintenance 1.1%
General Administrative 3.0%
Interest 5.5%
Occupation Cost $3,110
Depreciation $1,337

A Budget for Max Profit for the month of April

Revenues:

Food Sales ($15.40 x 302 x 30days)	$139,524.00

Controllable Expense:

Food Cost 33.4%	46,601.02
Salaries and Wages 28.6%	39,903.86
Employee Benefits 4.0%	5,580.96
Direct Operating Expense 6.9%	9,627.16
Music and Entertainment 0.5%	697.62
Marketing 2.5%	3,488.10
Utilities 2.9%	4,046.20
Repairs and Maintenance 1.1%	1,534.76
General Administrative 3.0%	4,185.72

Non-controllable Expense:

Interest 5.5%	7,673.82
Occupation Cost	3,110.00
Depreciation	1,337.00

Income before Tax $ 11,737.78

14.   The Evergreen Country Club has established a budget for its Grill with 2,400 guests dining in the month of July. However, its Grill business depends heavily on the rounds of golf played. Knowing that the weather in July is very unpredictable, the manager would like to see the profit levels if only 2,000 guests or if there are 2,800 guests dine with the club. Given the 2,400 guest level budget, develop a flexible budget for the Grill at Evergreen for the month of July. Note: All controllable expenses are calculated as a percentage of sales while non-controllable expenses are fixed. The tax rate for Evergreen is 35%.

The Grill at the Evergreen

Revenues:	2,400 guests
Food Sales	$46,000
Controllable Expense:	
Cost of Food	16,200
Labor Cost	11,880
Administrative & General	1,440
Energy & Utilities	1,560
Marketing	900
Repair & Maintenance	870
Non-controllable Expense:	
Occupation Cost	2,000
Depreciation	1,560
Insurance	2,000
Property Tax	2,750
Income before Tax	4,840
Income Tax (35%)	1,694
Net Income	3,146

The Grill at the Evergreen

	Guest Counts		
Revenues:	2400	2000	2800
Food Sales	$ 46,000.00	$ 38,333.33	$ 53,666.67
Controllable Expense:			
Cost of Food	16,200.00	13,500.00	18,900.00
Labor Cost	11,880.00	9,900.00	13,860.00
Administrative & General	1,440.00	1,200.00	1,680.00
Energy & Utilities	1,560.00	1,300.00	1,820.00
Marketing	900.00	750.00	1,050.00
Repair & Maintenance	870.00	725.00	1,015.00
Non-controllable Expense:			
Occupation Cost	2,000.00	2,000.00	2,000.00
Depreciation	1,560.00	1,560.00	1,560.00
Insurance	2,000.00	2,000.00	2,000.00
Property Tax	2,750.00	2,750.00	2,750.00
Income Before Tax	4,840.00	2,648.33	7,031.67
Income Tax (35%)	1,694.00	926.92	2,461.08
Net Income	$3,146.00	$ 1,721.42	$ 4,570.58

Examination Type Problems

1.   The Blue Monkey Bar and Grill uses the 3-week moving average method in forecasting.

Given the following data, what will be its expected guest count for week 11?

Week	Actual Guest Count
6	340
7	260
8	382
9	323
10	299

To calculate the forecasted guest count for week 11, we will need to add the counts for the last 3 weeks and divide that total by three. Therefore, the expected guest count for week 11 will be:

$$= \frac{382 + 323 + 299}{3}$$

$$= 334.67 \text{ or } 335 \text{ guests}$$

2.   The White Horse, a 150-room inn, uses simple time series to forecast its guests and

thus occupancy percentages. The current month, September, records a guest count of

2,300. As the winter months approach, the hotel expects a decrease of 1% in guest

count per month for the next five months. What will the guest counts and occupancy percentages be for the months of October through February? (Assuming all single

occupancy and that it is not a leap year)

Month	Guest Count	Occupancy
September	2,300	$\dfrac{2{,}300 \text{ guests}}{150 \text{ rooms X 30 days}}$ = 51.11%
October	2,300 x 0.99 =2,277	$\dfrac{2{,}277 \text{ guests}}{150 \text{ rooms X 31 days}}$ = 48.97%
November	2,277 x 0.99 =2,254	$\dfrac{2{,}254 \text{ guests}}{150 \text{ rooms X 30 days}}$ = 50.09%
December	2,254 x 0.99 =2,232	$\dfrac{2{,}232 \text{ guests}}{150 \text{ rooms X 31 days}}$ = 48.00%
January	2,232 x 0.99 =2,209	$\dfrac{2{,}209 \text{ guests}}{150 \text{ rooms X 31 days}}$ = 47.51%
February	2,209 x 0.99 =2,187	$\dfrac{2{,}187 \text{ guests}}{150 \text{ rooms X 28 days}}$ = 52.07%

3.   Given the following information, prepare a budget for Restaurant Atlanta for the month of

September.

Average check $13.00
Customer count per day 258
There are 30 days in September
Food Cost 31.4%
Salaries and Wages 28.8%
Employee Benefits 4.0%
Direct Operating Expense 6.5%
Music and Entertainment 0.5%
Marketing 3.0%
Utilities 3.9%
Repairs and Maintenance 1.5%
General Administrative 3.0%
Interest 7.5%
Occupation Cost $2,110
Depreciation $1,637

A Budget for Atlanta for the month of September

Revenues:

Food Sales ($13 x 258 x 30days) $ 100,620.00

Controllable Expense:

Food Cost 31.4%	31,594.68
Salaries and Wages 28.8%	28,978.56
Employee Benefits 4.0%	4.024.80
Direct Operating Expense 6.5%	6,540.30
Music and Entertainment 0.5%	503.10
Marketing 3.0%	3,018.60
Utilities 3.9%	3,924.18
Repairs and Maintenance 1.5%	1,509.30
General Administrative 3.0%	3,018.60

Non-controllable Expense:

Interest 7.5%	7,546.50
Occupation Cost $2,110	2,110.00
Depreciation $1,637	1,637.00

Income before Tax	$ 6,214.38

4.   The Mountain Peak Ski Resort has established a budget for its Cafe with 1,300 guests dining in the month of January. However, its Cafe business depends heavily on the amount of skiers. Knowing that the weather in February is very unpredictable, the manager would like to see the profit levels if only 1,000 guests or if there are 1,800 guests dine with the resort. Given the 1,300 guest level budget, develop a flexible budget for the Cafe at Mountain Peak for the month of February. Note: All controllable expenses are calculated as a percentage of sales while non-controllable expenses are fixed. The tax rate for Mountain Peak is 35%.

The Cafe at Mountain Peak

Revenues:	1,300 guests
Food Sales	$28,000
Controllable Expense:	
Cost of Food	9,200
Labor Cost	5,880
Administrative & General	990
Energy & Utilities	1,050
Marketing	500
Repair & Maintenance	660

Non-controllable Expense:

Occupation Cost	1,000
Depreciation	1,110
Insurance	900
Property Tax	1,130
Income before Tax	5,580
Income Tax (35%)	1,953
Net Income	3,627

The Cafe at Mountain Peak

	Guest Counts		
Revenues:	1,300	1,000	1,800
Food Sales	$28,000.00	$21,538.46	$38,769.23
Controllable Expense:			
Cost of Food	9,200.00	7,076.92	12,738.46
Labor Cost	5,880.00	4,523.08	8,141.54
Administrative & General	990.00	761.54	1,370.77
Energy & Utilities	1,050.00	807.69	1,453.85
Marketing	500.00	384.62	692.31
Repair & Maintenance	660.00	507.69	913.85
Non-controllable Expense:			
Occupation Cost	1,000.00	2,000.00	2,000.00
Depreciation	1,110.00	1,560.00	1,560.00
Insurance	900.00	2,000.00	2,000.00
Property Tax	1,130.00	2,750.00	2,750.00
Income before Tax	5,580.00	(833.08)	5,148.46
Income Tax (35%)	1,953.00	(291.58)	1,801.96
Net Income	$3,627.00	$ (541.50)	$ 3,346.50

Case Study

The Case Study Hotel is contemplating opening another food and beverage outlet to complement the services offered by Model Restaurant. The General Manager would like you to develop a formal profit plan (budget) for the upcoming year. The budget will serve as a control document for you and the hotel. The hotel is in a 40% tax bracket. Also, as the new manager you will receive a bonus of 5% of income before occupation cost.

You are to develop an annual budget for the restaurant. The owner wants to review the budget in four weeks, and since managerial accounting was not your strongest suit in college, you decide to get busy immediately.

Being an educated graduate of Hotel & Restaurant Management, you have made a study of the external factors that may affect your business during the upcoming year. The following events may affect you:

★   The local economy has improved steadily since early last year and predictions are that it will continue to strengthen in the next year.

★   Because of adverse weather conditions, the Department of Agriculture and the Commerce Department predict beef prices will increase by 10%. Last year, the average food cost of similar restaurants was 35% of sales. You predict, with the increase in price of beef, that the food cost for this new venture will be 38%.

★   A new 100-seat Steak House will open in June of next year. The restaurant will be located two blocks from you. The local Chamber of Commerce predicts employment in the area to increase by 1500 jobs over the next year. There are 500 apartments, 200 single-family dwellings, and 100 condominiums under construction, or planned for completion before the end of the year. These facts may have certain effects on your restaurant. You do expect a net increase in the number of guests and check averages.

★   With all the above information, you have determined the following information about your restaurant:

-    100 seats in a 2,000-square-foot dining room with 2 times turnover for lunch and 1.5 times turnover for dinner.

-    Average food-check dinner $21.00

-    Average food-check lunch $12.00

For budgeting purposes you plan on being open 26 days each month.

Payroll:

Payroll runs 35% of sales, including benefits

Employee meals (30 meals per day) $12,355.20

Insurance (employee) 24 employees at $6.93 a week

Direct operating expenses include the following items:

Uniforms

It is estimated to be a fixed cost at $600 per month.

Laundry & Linens

Linen expense should be $6,200 per year.

China & Glassware

This account tends to be fixed; therefore, the budgeted expense for this account is $7,030 per year.

Advertising Expense:

Estimated to be 2% of sales

Utility Expenses:

Estimated to be 4% of sales.

Administrative & General Expenses:

Estimated to be 4% of sales.

Occupation Costs:

Occupation cost is expected to be $2,000 for the year while property taxes are at $2,780.

Insurance:

Insurance is 3% of sales.

Budget for the new proposed restaurant at the Case Study Hotel

Revenues:
Food Sales

Lunch *1	$ 748,800.00
Dinner *2	982,800.00
Total Sales	$1,731,600.00

Controllable Expense:

Cost of Food (38% of sales)	658,008.00
Labor Cost (35% of sales) *3	606,060.00
Direct Operating Expenses	13,830.00
Administrative & General (4% of sales)	69,264.00
Energy & Utilities (4% of sales)	69,264.00
Marketing (2% of sales)	34,632.00
Income before Occu. Cost	280,542.00
Manager's Bonus (5%)	14,027.10

Non-controllable Expense:

Occupation Cost	2,000.00
Insurance (3% of sales)	51,948.00
Property Tax	2,780.00
Income Before Tax	209,786.90
Income Tax (40%)	83,914.76
Net Income	$ 125,872.14

*1 = lunch sales = $12 x 100 seats x 2 turnover x 26 days/mo x 12 mos
*2 = dinner sales = $21 x 100 seats x 1.5 turnover x 26 days/mo x 12 mos
*3 = since the 35% includes employee benefits, employee meals and insurance
would have been included in the 35% and do not need to be added

CHAPTER 17

CAPITAL BUDGETING

I.   Purpose of the Chapter

Capital budgeting, capital expenditure analysis, or capital request is the process of analyzing potential projects and deciding whether they should be included or rejected in the operation's investment strategic plan. This process is most important since capital expenditures are of a larger magnitude and yield benefits for operations for years to come. In addition, since business operates on the economics of supply and demand, a hospitality operation needs to maximize its return by having the capital expenditure spent during the right time. As educators, we need to instill in our students that while one may think that graduates of a two-year or four-year program will not be making major capital investment decisions upon graduation, some companies or owners do expect college graduates to know these theories and apply them. Thus, knowledge of capital budgeting is pertinent.

II.   Overview of the Chapter

The hospitality industry is dynamic because it is a people industry. With the increase in technology, many equipment and gadgets are available for managers and owners to operate their units more effectively and for guests to have a better experience. Any update or purchase costs money. Even regular maintenance work can sometimes cost so much that it has to be capitalized. Thus, capital budgeting is important to the control function of any hospitality operation.

Once a capital budget is set, the control function takes over. There are three distinct stages. First, if there are any extensive installations, renovation or construction be done, the manager needs to oversee those projects so that there are no serious delays or cost overruns. The last thing owners or managers want is for the $100,000 per room construction cost has changed to $105,000 because of delays and other problems. A close eye needs to be kept on projects like these.

Once the construction or installation is finished and the hospitality entity has begun operation, the manager will then need to do a post-audit. These investigations help identify problem areas or challenges such as the accuracy of the original forecast or problems that might have occurred during the construction state, so that in the next turnaround, the management team will be able to handle similar projects better. This is much like debriefing after a laboratory session to discuss what went well and what went wrong.

Finally, the continuing control through performance measurement of the operation kicks in. Management will compare the actual figures that the project yielded to the budgeted figures shown in the forecast and capital budget analysis.

This chapter will discuss the time value of money concept and calculations of payback periods, net present values, and internal rate of return and how they can assist managers and owners to make sound financial decisions.

III.   Learning Objectives

1.   The importance of capital budgeting

Capital budgeting is also known as capital expenditure analysis or capital request. It is the entire process of analyzing potential projects and deciding whether they should be included or rejected in the operation's investment game plan. This process is very important because capital expenditure normally involves a substantial amount of money and the decision that is made will have an affect on the operation for a long period of time. The magnitude of the amount is so great that if a mistake is made in the decision, it does not only effect the operation negatively during that one accounting period, it will continue to hurt the business until the project is discarded. Second, the timing of the capital expenditure is also pertinent. For instance, if the hospitality industry is on an upward trend and all hotels and restaurants tend to expand at the same time, the demand for new equipment and products may be on back-orders.

2.   The differences between the various types of capital budgets

There are six main categories of capital budgets. The first type is replacement to improve revenues which includes investments in assets that will bring about more revenues through better efficiency. Second, replacement to reduce costs includes investments in assets that will lower the current level of expenses. Third, replacement for maintenance will be items that are needed to maintain the operation such as towels and sheets for the guest rooms and glassware for the food and beverage area. Fourth, expansion of existing concepts is another type where the company may wish to open up another unit, a new wing of rooms, or an additional nine holes of golf for a country club. Fifth, expansion into new concepts is similar to the last category except that the concept that an operation is considering is brand new. Finally, safety and environmental projects are important and cannot be ignored. Investment made here can be minimal or very substantial. The projects include anything from mandatory governmental regulations to compliance with insurance policies. In the hospitality industry, we work hand in hand with the Occupational Safety & Health Administration (OSHA) to ensure a safe environment for our employees.

3.   The relevancy of the different forms of cash flow in capital budgets

In preparing a capital budget, only the relevant cash flows will need to be considered. First, non-cash expenses such as depreciation and amortization should be calculated into the total cash flow. Since accounting income deducts these cash flows from the revenues, they will need to be added back to the accounting income to determine the net cash flow.

Second, interest expenses and dividends are not included in capital budget analysis since the return required by the investors will be accounted for in the cost of capital percentage rate, and hence including these cash flows would be double counting those cash flows.

Third, the incremental cash flow is most relevant. It is the difference between the operation's cash flow with the project and without the project.

Fourth, costs such as rehabilitation, brokerage fees etc. that were incurred in the past and have been expenses for tax purposes are counted as sunk costs and should not be included.

Fifth, any maintenance costs spent on the property that may incur during a new installation or replacement can be expensed as maintenance costs for the period and should not the added in the capital budgeting analysis.

Sixth, any opportunity cost incurred by foregoing an existing project to take on a new one is relevant to the project and needs to be included in the analysis.

4.   The worth of potential investment projects through the use of capital budget criteria

After the cash flows are obtained, an operation can employ one of the four ways to determine the feasibility of a proposal: the accounting rate of return method, payback, net present value, and internal rate of return. The accounting rates of return is a ratio of the average annual project income or cash flow and the average investment (ROI). The ARR is a criterion set by the company in question. If the company has a minimum acceptable ARR of 35%, then anything 35% and above would be acceptable to the company. Otherwise, the project should be rejected.

Two concerns need to be discussed with the students on using the ARR. First, this method concentrates on income and not cash flow so the sale price at the end is not included in the calculation at all. Second, since money from different time periods is simply added together, the time value of money is ignored.

The second method, payback, is also a ratio of two numbers. It has a set criterion, number of years, such as 2 years, so that any project that takes 2 years or more to recuperate its costs will be rejected. However, it differs from ARR because it uses cash flow rather than net income, which gives a much better and realistic picture of the investment return. Unlike ARR that results in a percentage, the calculation of payback yields a number. Payback is defined as the project cost divided by the annual cash flow. If a project yields uneven cash flows in its lifetime, then one subtracts the annual cash flow until one reaches the year in which the costs are totally recovered.

Net present value is a third method. It nets the present values of all future cash flows of a project with the initial investment amount of the project. A positive result signifies a gain and vice versa. A result of zero represents break-even.

Internal rate of return gives a percentage result rather than a dollar amount. It takes into consideration all cash flows and the time value of money. It is the interest rate that equates these cash flows and the cost of the project.

5.   The significance of capital rationing as it pertains to capital budgets

Capital rationing is important in capital budgeting. Most of the time, companies are faced with a very limited amount of resources and are not able to take on all proposals of investments. They are then forced to prioritize the results and choose the one that yields the highest NPV, then the next highest, until the budget cannot accommodate any more investments. Therefore, students need to know how to prioritize the results of the analyses and make the right decisions.

6.   The significance of the three stages of control in capital budgeting

As discussed in the overview of this chapter, with the hospitality industry being so dynamic and the influence of new technology, a substantial amount of resources are spent on upgrading or new investment. Once a capital budget is set, the control function takes over. The three distinct stages are installation, post-audit, and performance measurement of this new project or investment. In each stage, more resources might have to be spent if budgeting has not been performed properly or that there might be some cost overruns. Thus, during the installation or construction period, owners and managers need to keep a close eye on the process.

Once the construction or installation is finished and the hospitality entity has begun operation, owners and managers will then need to do a post-audit to help identify problem areas or challenges. Finally, the continuing control through performance measurement of the operation will give owners and managers data to compare the actual figures with the budgeted figures.

IV.   Definition of Key Terms

Accounting rates of return – are accounting ratios such as ROI, ROA, or ROE which measure the profitability of projects.

Capital rationing – is where a company does not have all the capital resources to take on all the profitable projects that are proposed. Thus, capital will have to be rationed out to the projects that can yield the most for the company.

Incremental cash flow – a project's incremental cash flow is the difference between the operation's cash flow with the project and without the project.

Independent projects – these are projects whose cash flows are independent and thus the acceptance or rejection of one project will not affect the decisions on the others.

Internal rate of return – is the percentage rate that equates the future cash flows of a project and its cost.

Mutually exclusive projects – these are a set of projects proposed for a company where only one project needs to be selected.

Net present value – is a method of ranking investing by deducting the initial investment from the future cash flows generated by a project, discounted at the rate of the cost of capital.

Operating cash flow – is the amount of cash that an operation earns during the life of the project.

Opportunity cost – is the cost to a company when it foregoes a choice and decides on another.

Payback – is defined as the project cost divided by the annual cash flow. It gives the amount of time needed for a project to recover its costs.

Post-audit – this is a process whereby owners and/or managers will evaluate the success of the installation or construction of a project.

Relevant cash flow – these are cash flows that have to be included in a capital budget analysis such as incremental cash flow, opportunity costs, all initial investments expenses, and non cash expenses. Sunk costs, finance costs, and maintenance costs should not be included in calculating relevant cash flows.

Replacement – replacement in capital budgets includes replacements to increase revenues, reduce costs, or simply for maintenance and upkeep.

Sunk cost – is a cost that was incurred in the past and has been expensed. It should not be included in a capital budget analysis.

Terminal cash flow – this is the total amount of cash that a project receives at the end of its life. It includes any gains or losses on the sale, any tax implications and also the return of any net working capital.

Time value of money – with inflation and other factors, the value of money changes as time passes by. With astute investments, the face value of a dollar may now become two dollars while the value of goods that the same dollar will be able to purchase will not be as much.

V.   Teaching Outline

A.   Classifications of Capital Budgets
     1.   Replacement to Improve Revenues
     2.   Replacement to Reduce Costs
     3.   Replacement for Maintenance
     4.   Expansion of Existing Concepts
     5.   Expansion into New Concepts
     6.   Safety and Environmental Projects
B.   Elements in a Capital Budget
     1.   Relevant and Incremental Cash Flows
     2.   Initial Cash Flow
     3.   Operating Cash Flow
     4.   Terminal Cash Flow
     5.   Total Project Cash Flow
C.   Time Value of Money
     1.   Compounding Your Dollars
     2.   Present and Future Values of a Lump Sum
     3.   Present and Future Values of an Annuity
     4.   Perpetuities
     5.   Uneven Cash Flows
     6.   Accounting Rates of Return (ARR)
     7.   Payback
     8.   Net Present Value (NPV)
     9.   Internal Rate of Return (IRR)
     10.   Comparison of the Net Present Value and Internal Rate of Return Methods

VI.   Questions and Answers

Review Exercises

1.   The present value of $500 after 3 years in an account paying 6% annual interest will

    become:

    a. $565.60
    b. $570.50
    c. $595.51
    d. $599.51

2.   If you need to save $200,000 to open a restaurant in 10 years, how much do you have to save per month if your investment will yield 14%?

   a. $771.99
   b. $799.71
   c. $817.63
   d. $871.67

3.   Which of the following is not a decision criterion for capital budgeting?

   a.   ARR
   b.   NPV
   c.   IRR
   d.   NRR

4.   Why is payback not the best decision criterion?

   a.   it is easy to compute
   b.   one does not need a computer for the computation
   c.   it does not take into consideration the time value of money
   d.   it takes into consideration all cash flows

5.   The formula for calculating the present value of a perpetuity is:

   a.   present value/interest
   b.   future value/interest
   c.   interest/payment
   d.   payment/interest

6.   To accept a project using the NPV criterion, the value of the NPV has to be:

   a.   0
   b.   larger than 0
   c.   less than 0
   d.   does not matter

7.   To accept a project using the IRR criterion, the value of the IRR has to be:

   a.   equal to the cost of capital
   b.   less than the cost of capital
   c.   more than the cost of capital
   d.   more than 10%

8.   Given the following cash flows, the payback of this project is:

Year	Cash Flow
0	<100>
1	70
2	50
3	20

a.   1.6 years
b.   2.0 years
c.   2.4 years
d.   3.0 years

9.   Using the cash flows in question 8, and a 10% cost of capital, the NPV of this project is:

a. $18.86
b. $18.95
c. $19.99
d. $21.25

10.   Using the cash flows in question 8, the IRR of this project is:

a.   20%
b.   21.54%
c.   22.46%
d.   23.56%

Review Exercises Answers
1. c
2. a
3. d
4. c
5. d
6. b
7. c
8. a
9. d
10. d

11.   What is the PV of $550 to be received in 6 years if the appropriate interest rate is 10%?

FV = 550
6 = N
10 = I/Y
Computer for PV = $310.46

12.   What is the FV of $500 after 5 years if it is in an account paying 11% annual interest?

PV = 500
N = 5
I/Y = 11
Compute FV = $842.53

13.   What is the FV of a 4-year annuity of $300 if the appropriate interest rate is 10%? What

is the PV of the annuity?

PMT = 300
N = 4
I/Y = 10
Compute FV = $1,392.30

PMT = 300
N = 4
I/Y = 10
Compute PV = $950.96

14.   An investor is considering the purchase of 1000 acres of land. His analysis is that if the

land is used for cattle grazing, it will produce a cash flow of $5,000 per year indefinitely.

If the investor requires a return of 10% on investment of this type, what is the most he

would be willing to pay for the land?

$$\frac{\$5,000}{0.10} = \$50,000$$

15.   The Roasting Company is evaluating the purchase of a new coffee cart for its outside

patio. The cost of capital for the cart is 8%, and the expected costs and cash flows are

shown below. Should the company take on this investment using the payback criterion if

the set limit is 1.5 years?

Year	Expected Cash Flows
0	($ 5,000)
1	1,000
2	4,000
3	3,000
4	2,000
5	4,000

Initial investment $5,000
1st year cash inflow = $1,000
($5,000 - $1,000 = $4,000, therefore $4,000 still needs to be recovered)

2nd year cash inflow = $4,000
($4,000 - $4,000 = $ 0, therefore, after 2 years, project cost was recovered)

Thus payback = 2 year

Since the criterion is set at 1.5 years, this project exceeds the set limit and thus The Roasting Company should not invest in this project.

16.   Restaurant Rosebud is considering buying a new stove which costs $4,900. In 6 years, the stove is deemed worthless and restaurant will not be able to sell it for anything. There is no change in net working capital. Estimated annual cash flow from this new stove will be as follows:

Year	Cash Flows
0	($ 4,900)
1	120
2	239
3	401
4	1,488
5	1,170
6	2,001

What is the estimated payback period for the stove?

Initial investment $4,900
1st year cash inflow = $120
($4,900 - $120 = $4,780, therefore $4,780 still needs to be recovered)

2nd year cash inflow = $239
($4,780 - $239 = $ 4,541, therefore, $4,541 still needs to be recovered)

3rd year cash inflow = $401
($4,541 - $401 = $ 4,140, therefore, $4,140 still needs to be recovered)

4th year cash inflow = $1,488
($4,140 - $1,488 = $ 2,652, therefore, $2,652 still needs to be recovered)

5th year cash inflow = $1,170
($2,652 - $1,170 = $ 1,482, therefore, $1,482 still needs to be recovered)

6th year cash inflow = $2,001 which is more than $1,482
Thus $\frac{1,482}{2.001} = 0.74$

It will take 5 + 0.74 or 5.74 years for the project cost to be recovered and thus the payback period will be 5.74 years.

17.   Hotel Wave is deciding whether or not it should open a Tea Room. The cost of capital is

12%. What is the project's NPV? Expected net cash inflows are as follows:

Year	Expected Net Cash Flows
0	($560,000)
1	230,000
2	290,000
3	180,000
4	150,000

Using a business calculator to enter the cash outflow of $560,000 and the inflows of the
4 years discounting them at 12%, the net present value is $99,991.52.

18.   What is Hotel Wave Tea Room project's IRR?

Using a business calculator to enter the cash outflow of $560,000 and the inflows of the
4 years, the internal rate of return is 20.97%.

Examination Type Problems

1.   What is the PV of $1,250 to be received in 6 years if the appropriate interest rate is 8%?

FV = $1,250
N = 6
I/Y = 8
Compute PV = $787.71

2.   What is the FV of $900 after 5 years if it is in an account paying 12% annual interest?

PV = $900
N = 5
I/Y = 12
Compute FV = $1,586.11

3.   What is the FV of a 5-year annuity of $220 if the appropriate interest rate is 6%? What is

the PV of the annuity?

PMT = $220
N = 5
I/Y = 6
Compute FV = $1,240.16

PMT = $220
N = 5
I/Y = 6
Compute PV = $926.72

4.   A farmer is considering the purchase of 5,000 acres of land. His analysis is that if the

land is used for growing avocados, it will produce a cash flow of $25,000 per year

indefinitely. If the investor requires a return of 10% on investment of this type, what is the

most he would be willing to pay for the land?

$$\frac{25,000}{0.10} = \$250,000$$

5.   The hotel is evaluating the purchase of an ice cream machine for upcoming summer.

The cost of capital for the machine is 11%, and the expected costs and cash flows are

shown below. What is the net present value of this investment and should the hotel

invest in this ice cream machine?

Year	Expected Cash Flows
0	($ 7,700)
1	1,200
2	4,000
3	3,900
4	2,000
5	4,000

Using a business calculator to enter the cash outflow of $7,700 and the inflows of the 5
years discounting them at 11%, the net present value is $3,170.48. Since this is a
positive value, the ice cream machine will be profitable for the hotel and thus this project
should be accepted.

6.   JJ's Pub is considering buying a new ice machine that costs $5,500. In 4 years, the ice

machine is deemed worthless and pub will not be able to sell it for anything. There is no

change in net working capital. Estimated annual cash flow from this new ice machine will

be as follows:

Year	Cash Flows
0	($ 5,500)
1	3,100
2	2,000
3	950
4	130

How long would it take until investment starts paying off?

Initial investment $5,500

1st year cash inflow = $3,100

($5,500 - $3,100 = $2,400, therefore $2,400 still needs to be recovered)

2nd year cash inflow = $2,000

($2,400 - $2,000 = $400, therefore, $400 still needs to be recovered)

3rd year cash inflow = $950, which is more than $400

Thus $\frac{400}{950} = 0.42$

It will take 2 + 0.42 or 2.42 years for the project cost to be recovered and thus the payback period will be 2.42 years.

7.   Hotel Star is deciding whether or not it should open an American Grill. The cost of capital is 12%. What is the project's NPV? Expected net cash flows are as follows:

Year	Expected Net Cash Flows
0	($ 960,000)
1	330,000
2	590,000
3	400,000
4	150,000

Using a business calculator to enter the cash outflow of $960,000 and the inflows of the 4 years discounting them at 12%, the net present value is $185,027.06. Since this is a positive value, Hotel Star should open the American Grill.

8.   What is Hotel Star American Grill project's IRR?

Using a business calculator to enter the cash outflow of $960,000 and the inflows of the 4 years, the internal rate of return is 21.69%.

Case Study

Model Restaurant has realized that brick-oven pizza is a new trend and the customers are asking for such items. Knowing that the guests are interested in this item, your General Manager asked you to decide whether Model should buy a pizza oven or sign a contract with a local pizza restaurant for them to deliver the pizzas.

Discounting all the expenses, you have calculated the net cash flows to be $5,580 per year for the next five years. By the end of this five-year period, you have the option to sell it for $500. The cost of the oven is $17,000.

If a contract is signed with a local pizza restaurant, there will be no initial investment. However, the cash flow that your restaurant will receive as part of the contract agreement will only be $2,260 per year.

If the cost of capital is 8% and a minimum time commitment to the contract is also 5 years, would you invest and buy the oven?

Purchase			**Local Pizza Restaurant**	
Year	Cash Flow		Year	Cash Flow
0	(17,000)		0	0
1	5,580		0	2,260
2	5,580		0	2,260
3	5,580		0	2,260
4	5,580		0	2,260
5	6,080		0	2,260

Entering the cash inflows and outflow for the purchase option with a cost of capital at 8%, the net present value is $5,619.61.

For the local pizza restaurant option, since there is not an initial investment, the cash flows resemble that of a regular annuity. Thus, with PMT = 2,260; N = 5, I/Y = 8, the PV = $9,023.52, which is clearly a better option for the Model Restaurant.

CHAPTER 18

THE WILD CARD IN HOSPITALITY COST CONTROL

I.   Purpose of the Chapter

This purpose of this chapter is to provide an overview of an internal control system in a casino operation. Thus, the topics are quite broad and general. To fully understand the intricacies of a good internal control system would take more than the scope of this text. Nonetheless, this will give the students a basic concept of the intricacies in managing cash flows in casinos.

II.   Overview of the Chapter

Casino and gaming are here to stay in the hospitality industry. The control function in casinos is much more imperative that that of a regular hotel because of the amount of cash that is transacted. While technology extends life's little pleasures in terms of new games and new control novelties, ultimately, it is still up to us, the management, to maintain an enjoyable yet temptation free environment for our employees and guests.

III.   Learning Objectives

1.   The role of a gaming control board

Establish regulations for casinos stating that casinos must establish and present a system of internal controls. This includes the organizational structure, the accounting procedures, authorization processes, record keeping, safeguarding of assets, and the accuracy and reliability of financial records.

2.   The issues that are addressed in the MICS

This system of internal controls will become the minimum internal control standards (MICS) which most jurisdictions require as part of the package for application for a casino license. The respective regulatory agencies will review the MICS presented to ensure that they conform to the jurisdiction requirements. After approval, gaming operations can start. Any subsequent changes will also need approvals. These regulatory agencies will then perform audits according to the MICS on the licensed casinos to determine the degree of compliance. If the MICS are not followed, the license can be revoked.

3.   Hold percentages

Hold percentage is the term that is widely used to measure the performance of the various games. The hold percentage is defined as the amount of win as related to the amount of wager that was placed. Thus if the total wager is $10, the casino pays out $8 and retains $2, then 20% is the hold percentage.
Hold percentage = Win / Drop

4.   The organization of an accounting department at a hotel and that of a casino hotel

Essentially, a typical accounting department of a casino hotel operation is very similar to that of a regular hotel. The chief financial officer, also known as the controller or comptroller, presides over all the events. Under this position, you will find the major positions such as the food and beverage controller or auditor, the hotel revenue controller, payroll, and general accounting that consists of payables, receivables, and cashiers. The one major difference is the presence of the casino revenue controller or auditor. This person will be in charge of the slot count (hard count—coins and tokens), the pit-game count (soft count—bills), and other duties. In addition, since cashiering under general accounting normally is responsible for all cashiers and cash banks, they will also be in charge of the cage cashiers, and thus the fills and credits.

5.   The flow of a casino revenue audit

The flow of a casino revenue audit is designed to divide the responsibilities of the department to the extent that it will minimize collusion fraud. Casino revenues accounting can be divided into three major areas, from the time the money comes into the casino through the front doors to when it ends up in the back office vault: casino operations, cage operations, and count rooms. In casino operations, the dealers at the various games, the pit clerks who record the game transactions and the drop teams to collect the drop boxes are the people who will take in the coins, tokens, and money from the players for the casino. In cage operations, the cage cashiers who change out chips and tokens for cash and the credit cashiers who give the players their chips and tokens once credit is approved are the main personnel. Finally in the count room, the hard and soft count personnel will count and verify the values of all coins, chips, tokens, and bills, all done according to the procedures set out in the MICS, and record the revenues for the casino.

6.   In evaluating the main cashiering activities at the cage the MICS state five areas that have to have control procedures as follows:

    a.   cashiers bank
    b.   daily deposit
    c.   credit
    d.   cash deposits and
    e.   cashing in

7.   Evaluation of revenue flows in the various table games and slots and a recommendation for at least three control procedures for each game are as follows:

The Control procedures for the flow of revenue for each game are usually established in writing to prevent any they of theft or collusion. However, the flow of revenue between each game and the cage can be controlled using the follow procedures:
    a.   First, the cage is a communication point between the vault and the floor, so that if money is running out at a game or, for the most time, there is an excess accumulation of money in the cage, the money and/or chips are transferred to the vault. In this case, the vault should not be opened and locked many times during the day.
    b.   The cage also takes care of the credits that are extended to the customers by receiving their approved markers or IOUs and giving them the chips to play. Thus, care should be given in exchanging markers and IOUs for chips.
    c.   The MICS for control purposes in the cage include cashiers bank, daily deposit, credit, cash deposits and cashing in. The cage itself may have several individual banks for fills, change and others. At the beginning of each day, the opening cage cashier will do a blind count to verify the amounts.   If the banks are not at

impress, the cage cashier will report that the cage supervisor who will investigate and reconcile the differences. During the change of shift, similar procedures apply where the incoming and outgoing cashiers agree on the inventory amounts and sign a two-part window count.

d.   The cage has to prepare settlement sheets for each bank. This does not only count what the inventory amounts are but also balances the beginning and ending inventories and the items that are included. The shift manager will then consolidate all the bank settlement sheets and reconcile all opening and ending inventories. The original documents will be sent to accounting where they will be audited and the copies kept in the cage.

e.   The cage also controls credit requests from players. The cage will take care of all the application forms and contact credit bureaus, banks, and other financial institutions to evaluate the worth of the application. Once the credit is approved, the player will be issued a marker through the cage. The cage, therefore, has control of issuing the marker.

IV.   Definition of Key Terms

Cage – is the official location for taking in money from players in exchange for chips and cash with the remaining chips or winnings of the players being taken in at the end of their stay.

Central Credit – is a casino credit bureau that may provide information on the player's past credit history with other casinos. Once the credit is approved, the player will be issued a marker through the cage. The cage, therefore, has the control of issuing the marker.

Drop – the wagers that players made are called drop. Drop is the measurement of the wagering activity in a casino. Drop in slot machine terminology is the amount of coins in the collection or overflow bucket at the bottom of the machine.

Drop boxes – are the boxes containing the wagers that players have made.

Fills and credits – if there is too much or not enough of some denomination of chips, the dealer can issue a fill or a credit to the main cage. A fill, as the word suggests, is to add to the table inventory and a credit is to take away from the inventory.

Gaming Control Boards – institute regulations that casinos must establish and present a system of internal controls.

Handle – the total wager in a slot machine is known as the handle. Therefore, the handle is the number of coins deposited. In the case of using modern technology where a card is swiped to record the wager and no coins are used, and then an electronic meter device measures the handle.

Hard count – is the initial counting of currency such as from slot machines and this count takes place in a hard count room equipped with surveillance cameras. When the individual buckets are emptied into the count machines, the team member normally holds the empty bucket to the camera to show that all the contents are removed from the bucket and that they are not pocketing any coins or tokens.

Internal audit – casino audit is designed to divide the responsibilities of the department to the extent that it will minimize collusion fraud and to ensure that no petty theft occurs.

Marker – a marker is an approval of credit for a specific amount.

Minimum standards for internal controls (MICS) – the regulatory agency for casinos.

Payouts – are funds that have been paid to guests when they win.

Pit podium – the area behind the games where there is access to chips.

Soft count – is the count of money from the drop boxes of the tables themselves.

Surveillance – is the close observation of activities within the casino and the majority is done by camera and the surveillance room is referred to as a sensitive area.

Table games – is one of six categories of games and is played with chips rather than with cash.

Win - in casino accounting and controls, win has just a slightly different bend. Win is the winnings of the casino and not the players. It is actually the winning of the operation; that means it is the net intake of the casino after all winning wages of the players have been made. These terms apply to all table games. To put it differently: Win = Drop - Payouts

V.   Teaching Outline

A.   Regulations Set by Gaming Control Boards
B.   Minimum Internal Control Standards (MICS)
C.   Accounting Control
    1.   Terminology
    2.   Organization
    3.   General Accounting
    4.   Casino Revenue
D.   Principal Revenue Flows and Cashiering
    1.   Main Cashiering and the Cage
    2.   Table Games
    3.   Poker
    4.   Keno, Bingo, Sports and Race Book
    5.   Slots-Electronic Gaming Devices
E.   Table Game Operations
    1.   Gaming Chips
    2.   Opening a Table
    3.   Drop
    4.   Fills and Credits
    5.   Closing a Game
    6.   Soft Count
F.   Slots Operations
    1.   Slot Machine Type
    2.   Primer
    3.   Profile
    4.   Slot Cashiering
    5.   Slot Drop Count Procedure and the Drop Team
    6.   Computerization in Slots

VI.   Questions and Answers

Review Exercises

1.   MICS stands for:

    a.   minimum international casino status
    b.   maximum international casino standards
    c.   maximum internal control standards
    d.   minimum internal control standards

2.   MICS include:

    a.   licensees identify the functions and responsibilities within the organization
    b.   licensees identify sensitive areas
    c.   licensees identify positions and individuals who have access to the sensitive areas
    d.   all of the above

3.   Win in casino terminology means:

    a.   win of the players
    b.   win of the casino
    c.   win of the rooms department
    d.   win of the food and beverage department

4.   Win can be defined as:

    a.   wager (drop) minus payouts
    b.   payouts minus wager (drop)
    c.   wager (drop) plus payouts
    d.   wager (drop) plus fills

5.   A win for slots can be defined as:

    a.   handle minus payouts
    b.   payouts plus handle
    c.   payouts minus handle
    d.   handle plus credits

6.   The hold percentage, given a $100 drop and $20 win, is:

    a.   5 times
    b.   500%
    c.   20%
    d.   5%

7.   Which of the following is not a major area in casino revenue audit?

    a.   food and beverage operations
    b.   casino operations

    c.   cage operations
    d.   count room

8.   Money flows into a casino through:

    a.   the cashier cage and the count room
    b.   the cashier cage and the play of games
    c.   the count room and the play of games
    d.   the count room and the players themselves

9.   MICS are set up for:

    a.   only table games
    b.   only slot games
    c.   a and b
    d.   a, b, and also main cashiering

10.   Computerized slot machines have not:

    a.   added more game choices
    b.   provided better control with updated information
    c.   caught all illegal activities in slot operations
    d.   recorded player information

Review Exercises Answers

1. d
2. d
3. b
4. a
5. c
6. a
7. b
8. d
9. c
10. a

11.   Calculate the game win with the following given data:

    Ending Table Inventory   5,560
    Beginning Table Inventory   250
    Fills   1,100
    Drop   900

    Game win   = drop (drop box amount) + ending table inventory + credits
                        – beginning table inventory – fills

                  = 900 + 5,560 – 250 – 1,100
                  = $5,110

12.   Ann is a new dealer at the Luxury Casino. In order to do her job correctly, she needs to learn how to calculate table win. If $5,000 is her game win and she also has the following information, what should her ending table inventory be?

Fills	1,000
Credit	800
Drop	2,000
Beginning Table Inventory	1,000
Game Win	5,000
Ending Table Inventory	?

Game win   = drop (drop box amount) + ending table inventory + credits
                    – beginning table inventory – fills

5,000   = 2,000 + ending + 800 – 1,000 – 1,000
ending   = 5,000 – 800
            = $4,200

13.   Describe the issues that are addressed in the MICS.

        A number of issues are addressed in the MICS. First, the licensee must clearly identify the functions and responsibilities within the organization and how they are segregated. This can be achieved through an organizational chart. Once these positions are in place, the detailed description of the duties and responsibilities for each of the positions has to be included.
        Second, the licensee also has to identify the sensitive areas and the positions or individuals that have access to such areas. The sensitive areas for access include drop boxes, cage, pit podium, surveillance, hard/soft count, credit information, and slot machines (and other electronic gaming device components). In addition, the positions or individuals that have signature authorities on various matters also need to be included.
        Then, the licensee also has to identify the administrative and accounting procedures that it will follow. These procedures can range from opening and closing a table, table inventories, fills and credits, transpiration of chips and tokens to and from game tables, shift changes, to the control of coupon redemption and other complimentary distribution programs for federal cash reporting purposes.

14.   What is the hold percentage for Magic Casino if the total wager is $150 and the casino

       pays out $105?

Hold percentage   = win/drop
                     = 150 –105
                       ⎯⎯⎯⎯
                          150
                     = 30%

Examination Type Problems

1.   Calculate the game win with the following given data:

      Ending Table Inventory   9,000

Beginning Table Inventory   300
Fills   5,060
Drop   500
Credit   100

Game win   = drop (drop box amount) + ending table inventory + credits
            – beginning table inventory – fills

            = 500 + 9,000 + 100 – 300 – 5,060
            = $4,240

2.   Casino Windmill has a new dealer who needs to learn how to calculate table win. If

$7,000 is game win and the following information is also given, what should the ending

table inventory be?

Fills   2,200
Credit   700
Drop   2,000
Beginning Table Inventory   450
Game Win   7,000

Game win   = drop (drop box amount) + ending table inventory + credits
            – beginning table inventory – fills

7,000   = 2,000 + ending + 700 – 450 – 2,200
ending   = 7,000 – 50
         = $6,950

3.   List at least five control procedures for the main cashiering activities at the cage.

Money flows into a casino through the cashier cage and the play of games. The main
cashier cage takes in money from players in exchange for chips and cash: the remaining chips
or winnings of the players at the end of their stay. The cage also takes care of fills and credits.
Thus, there are a number of control procedures for the main cashiering activities at the cage.
First, the cage is a communication point between the vault and the floor, so that if money
is running out at a game or, for the most time, there is an excess accumulation of money in the
cage, the money and/or chips are transferred to the vault. In this case, the vault will not need to
be opened and locked many times during the day.
Second, the cage also takes care of the credits that are extended to the customers by
receiving their approved markers or IOUs and giving them the chips to play.
Third, the MICS for control purposes in the cage include cashiers bank, daily deposit,
credit, cash deposits and cashing in. The cage itself may have several individual banks for fills,
change and others. At the beginning of each day, the opening cage cashier will do a blind count
to verify the amounts. If the banks are not at impress, the cage cashier will report that to the
cage supervisor who will investigate and reconcile the differences. During the change of shift,
similar procedures apply where the incoming and outgoing cashiers agree on the inventory
amounts and sign a two-part window count.
Fourth, the cage has to prepare settlement sheets for each bank. This does not only
count what the inventory amounts are but also balances the beginning and ending inventories

and the items that are included. The shift manager will then consolidate all the bank settlement sheets and reconcile all opening and ending inventories. The original documents will be sent to accounting where they will be audited and the copies kept in the cage.

Fifth, the cage also controls credit requests from players. The cage will take care of all the application forms and contact credit bureaus, banks, and other financial institutions to evaluate the worth of the application. Once the credit is approved, the player will be issued a marker through the cage. The cage, therefore, has control of issuing the marker.

[Other possible answers to this question include the issuance of the markers, safekeeping service for the players, and cashing-in procedures.]

4.   What is the hold percentage for Casino Thunderbird if the total wager is $1,150 and the casino pays out $700?

$$\text{Hold percentage} \quad = \text{win/drop}$$
$$= \frac{1,150 - 700}{1,150}$$
$$= 39.13\%$$

Case Study

In a casino/hotel operation, one of the most common but least publicized forms of theft is "theft of services." What is unique to a casino operation is that there is a built-in method of rewarding customers for their play. This method of reward is the issuing of complimentary or "comps."

There are two types of comps that a casino is able to offer the player. "Soft" comps require only a paper-transfer from one department budget to another department revenue budget line. Examples of soft comps are meals, lodging, and in-house transportation. Generally speaking, any in-house service that is offered may be issued to a player as a soft comp. The other type of comp is known as a "hard" comp. This comp involves the actual transfer of moneys to a vendor. Examples of hard comps are airline tickets, specialty restaurants, off-site shows or boxing matches. The casino operator will be more likely to grant a soft comp request, while requiring greater justification for issuance of a hard comp. Justification for all comps is generally found in the casino operations player rating computer files.

When a comp is requested, the issuer, usually the Casino Marketing department or the Pit boss, will go to the computer and look up the requester's account. This account is a lot like a bank account. Frequent, lengthy play helps to build up the theoretical win, while the granting of comp requests lowers the theoretical win. The issuer will grant a comp of up to 30% of theoretical win for soft comps and 15% for hard comps. One of the increasingly more common types of comp theft is the barter system.

Smith is a floor person at the local casino. His neighbor, Jones, is a salesman at the local car dealership. They strike a deal. In return for Jones' assistance in getting Smith the lowest price on his new car and preferred repair service time, Smith agrees to submit false player ratings in Jones' name. Jones agrees not to go to the casino for a number of months, so that the casino "savings" account can build. A few months later, on some special occasion (birthday, anniversary) Jones will call the Casino Marketing department and request dinner and a show for two. The marketing department will review the account. If there is an adequate amount available, it will make the reservations and issue the comp. The casino is then down a few hundred dollars in stolen services. This type of theft is very difficult to detect. The primary reason for the difficulty is that there are multiple departments involved. Without the complete cooperation of the Internal Audit, Casino Games, Casino Marketing, Food and Beverage, Surveillance, Comp Accounting and Security Departments, this form of relatively petty theft will go undetected and unpunished. What are some of the measures that you can recommend to deter such thefts?

Case Study Answers

This is a delicate situation since at times it is difficult to track all the activities that took place to ensure that procedures are followed. Recently, there have also been instances where employees of airline companies colluded with travel agencies in stealing frequent flyer miles, converting them into tickets, and selling such tickets for cash. However, the following measures can be carried out to deter such thefts:

1. Have internal meetings will all personnel involved in the process and let them know that management is aware of some illegal procedures that exist and will not tolerate such practices. This will serve as a warning to those personnel and they may stop these practices.
2. Use more electronic or automatic systems to record the players' rating. This will cut the unnecessary step of having a floor person and the possibility of collusion.

3. If floor persons are still used as a service to the guests, monitor all players' ratings submitted by these personnel. An unusual pattern may alert management to fraudulent activities.
4. Send player rating statements to the players so they can monitor their status. Educate the players so that they can help protect their own assets.

GLOSSARY

A la carte – is being used when each item on the menu has a separate price.

ABCD classification – is a method for prioritizing the importance for placing security and control methods on products.

Absenteeism – is referred to as being habitually absent from work.

Accounting rates of return – are accounting ratios such as ROI, ROA, orROE which measure the profitability of projects.

Administration and general expense – this category of expense encompasses items that are related to the administrative functions of the business. Examples include credit card collection expenses, information systems and general office supplies, from photocopies to pencil sharpeners.

As Purchased (AP) – describes how an item is purchased and delivered to the hospitality facility. Most products must undergo some type of additional preparation that may include trimming or cooking. Because of this process additional portions or weight may have to be purchased.

Attainable – standards must be attainable or managers and employees are apt to become discouraged and productivity and quality may decrease.

Bank check card – prevents the guest from having to write a check and allows those facilities that do not accept checks to have the backing of a credit card. The amount of payment owed to the hospitality operation is deducted immediately from the cardholder's checking account. In the case of hotel stays, a hold is placed on the account for the number of anticipated days plus an additional amount to cover other incidental expenses such as telephone, movies, etc.

Bar codes – is a method for tracking products through an operation. It was invented with the idea that uniform symbols on items would facilitate control and tracking measures, reduce labor costs and increase inventory precision. Bar codes are printed on bundles of products, labels on products or the packaging itself. With the bar code method, a company assigns a number to every asset to be tracked and uses software to generate bar code asset tags encoded with the particular item's asset identification number. The number then links each item to its electronic file, which contains information such as the purchase date and cost, the person the equipment is assigned to, its location, the vendor, and any warranties, upgrades or license agreements. When the manufacturer provides bar codes, dealerships adapt them to their particular internal system. In this manner, all inventories that come in and out of their facilities is uniformly scanned, tracked and stored.

Beverage control – applies to the controls that are necessary to ensure efficient and effective operational procedures of service and security of beverage operations.

Blind receiving – is a method of receiving in which the areas on the receiving report that would contain quantity and evaluation comments are blacked out. This requires receiving personal to count, weigh, and give their own evaluation of products. The price can also be blackened out so that receiving personnel will have to ensure prices are correct for the products received. This would be a more effective way of ensuring that receiving personnel checked products and prices.

Bonding employees – is accomplished to provide additional security to the hospitality operation because some employees may have access to large sums of money. If events are dependent upon subcontractors to supply equipment or services, bonding can eliminate some of the liability in these situations.

Break-even – occurs when sales cover all variable costs and all fixed costs; the amount remaining is profit or at the point wherein fixed costs are covered is break-even. Therefore, break-even is fixed cost over 1 minus the variable cost percent.

Budgeting – is a "formal" plan; normally expressed in terms of dollars, the revenues and expenses of an operation over a period of time.

Business failure – when revenues being generated by a business operation do not meet the expenses or the financial expectations of the owners which results in the closing or selling of the business.

Business plan – provides information concerning the business mission, goals, objectives, and a method of strategies to reach the anticipated outcome.

Cage – is the official location for taking in money from players in exchange for chips and cash with the remaining chips or winnings of the players being taken in at the end of their stay

Capital rationing – is where a company does not have all the capital resources to take on all the profitable projects that are proposed. Thus, capital will have to be rationed out to the projects that can yield the most for the company.

Cash bank – is the amount of change fund that employees would have access to start their business day.

Central Credit – is a casino credit bureau that may provide information on the player's past credit history with other casinos. Once the credit is approved, the player will be issued a marker through the cage. The cage, therefore, has the control of issuing the marker.

Cold storage – is the temperature from 30°F to 45°F and is the preferred temperature for numerous perishable products.

Commercial purchasing – can influence the price, the method of marketing, and the manufacturer chosen by the supplier's management. This is because the commercial purchases can be very large. The purchases of most hospitality operations are large in volume, and in many cases, very specialized. Due to such volume purchases, large sums of money are involved, and therefore commercial buyers may have more bargaining power than an individual, basic consumer may have.

Competitive advantage – is to be able to accomplish some type of business activity more effectively and efficiently than the methods being used by competitors.

Compromise – can occur once a manager exposes himself/herself to suspicion or disrepute. Therefore, a manager must always conduct himself or herself in such away to avoid suspicious conduct.

Computerized systems – are electronic systems used to strengthen the control system so a larger volume of data and information can be maintained and accessed faster.

Consumer purchasing – is on such a small scale that the consumer cannot have a great influence on price, method of marketing, or the manufacturer chosen by the supplier.

Contingency menu – is a menu that is designed for major fluctuations in sales. There could be a vast increase or decrease but without being able to adjust the hospitality facility could incur a loss.

Contingency plan – is simply a plan in place when a particular event that expected to have a possibility of happening did in fact happen.

Contracts and services – these are contracts and services that the operation uses. They may include maintenance contracts, contracts for cleaning vents and hoods or even a contract with a credit card company.

Contribution margin – is the dollar amount remaining after variable costs have been subtracted from the sales dollar.

Control – the managerial function of ensuring that all operational procedures are in accordance with established standards.

Controllable expense – this is an expense that a manager should have influence over and the authority to make decisions. Examples of this category are utilities and marketing.

Cost – is the price paid by the operation for products. Cost represents the expense of operating a business and can be fixed, variable, total costs, or semi-variable.

Credit cards – are given to customers to use and with the card is a line of credit that the customer can pay on a revolving basis.

Credit memo – if there is a rejection of a product during receiving or if an order is incomplete the delivery personnel to account for this shortage should issue a credit memos.

Cyclical – is a menu wherein items are regularly repeated and is normally written for a week or more. There are several benefits including control factors, which are associated with this type of menu.

Debit cards – are issued by a financial institution that maintains cash holdings of the card user. When the card is used the amount is automatically deducted from the card user account.

Decomposition – this is a time series that is broken down into trends, cyclical, seasonal, and randomness to offer the user more in-depth information.

Delphi method – when performing a forecast for the entire industry, the Delphi method used is a formal process conducted with a group of experts to achieve consensus.

Demographics – are the characteristics of the population segment for identifying the consumer market.

Direct operating expense - direct operating expenses include items such as uniform and laundry, china, glasses, silver, linen, kitchen fuel, cleaning supplies, paper supplies, bar supplies, menus, dry cleaning, and the like.

Directs – are usually inexpensive perishable products that are frequently purchased for immediate use, e.g., fresh produce, baked goods, and dairy products. For record keeping purposes, directs are treated as issued the moment they are received, and no further record is kept by receiving or storeroom personnel of these particular items.

Drop – the wagers that players make are called drop. Drop is the measurement of the wagering activity in a casino. Drop in slot machine terminology is the amount of coins in the collection or overflow bucket at the bottom of the machine.

Drop boxes – are the boxes containing the wagers that players have made.

Dry storage – is usually maintained at a temperature of 50°F to 70°F.

Effective discount rate – is the rate associated with using a credit card. The effective discount rate must be known before making a decision as to whether to use or accept a particular card.

Empowerment – is to provide employees with the decision making power over activities in their functional area.

Evaluation frequency – refers to how often business operational activities are being evaluated to compare operational activities against budgetary standards.

Expense category – expenses can be monitored more easily and effectively if like items are grouped together. In so doing, if one category is very high, management can take action and see if there are some issues that need to be resolved.

Feedback – is the informing of employees and upper management concerning operational activities and procedures. Feedback is important to an operation if positive conduct is to be continued or if negative conduct is to be changed.

Fills and credits – if there is too much or not enough of some denomination of chips, the dealer can issue a fill or a credit to the main cage. A fill, as the word suggests, is to add to the table inventory and a credit is to take away from the inventory.

Fixed costs – remain constant despite increases or decreases in sales volume.

Flexible budget – is an operations budget with more than one level of sales, thus the adjective flexible. This is a more preferred method for an operations budget as management can ascertain the effect on costs and income if the projected sales level change.

Forecasting – is similar to budgeting in that it is also used to predict some future outcomes. However, it normally is used to predict the outcomes of future events such as sales level or the number of room nights but not the expenses.

Formal communication – within an organization is usually information that comes from the top down through the chain of command and may or may not be in writing.

Four-step control cycle – a four-step process in which control objectives are established, employees are made aware, operational procedures are then evaluated, and feedback is given and corrective action is taken if necessary.

Freezer storage – is kept at a temperature of $0°C$ or lower.

Fringe benefits – are employee benefits that are given to employees in addition to their wages or salary.

Gaming Control Boards – institute regulations that casinos must establish and present a system of internal controls.

Guest checks – are the documentation that is used to record orders from guests to have the orders prepared by the hospitality facility.

Guest comments – should be solicited as guests will often inform management of service or quality as meeting, exceeding, below expectations. These comments can also assist in identifying possible flaws in the control system.

Guest count – is the number of guests that enter or order from an establishment. If the hospitality operation does a large amount of takeout and a large amount of in-house business management may want to maintain separate counts.

Guest expectations – are the expectations of guests based on their perception of value of the level of service and quality that would be anticipated as a guest in that facility.

Hand held server terminal – is a device that has been designed for efficiency in placing orders to prevent mistakes in reading orders and reduce the utilization of additional time and motion of having to walk to a POS system to place and order.

Handle – the total wager in a slot machine is known as the handle. Therefore, the handle is the number of coins deposited. Using modern technology where a card is swiped to record the wager and no coins are used, an electronic meter device measures the handle.

Hard count – is the initial counting of currency such as from slot machines and this count takes place in a hard count room equipped with surveillance cameras. When the individual buckets are emptied into the count machines, the team member normally holds the empty bucket to the camera to show that all the contents are removed from the bucket and that they are not pocketing any coins or tokens.

Hidden costs – those incidental expenditures that were not given sufficient accountability in funding during budget development.

Hiring – is to engage someone for their services and to pay them for such.

Incentives – some type of reward or punishment that induces a certain type of action and incentives are usually used to motivate employees to take some type of positive action.

Incremental cash flow – a project's incremental cash flow is the difference between the operation's cash flow with the project and without the project.

Independent projects – these are projects whose cash flows are independent and thus the acceptance or rejection of one project will not affect the decisions on the others.

Informal communication – is communication that is basically horizontal in nature with the best known source being the grapevine.

Insurance expense – as the name suggests, any type of insurance for the business excluding employee health insurance as that will be part of the employees' benefits package) will be included. Examples can be general business insurance or flood insurance.

Internal audit – casino audit is designed to divide the responsibilities of the department to the extent that it will minimize collusion fraud and to ensure that no petty theft occurs.

Internal rate of return – is the percentage rate that equates the future cash flows of a project and its cost.

Inter-unit transfer – is used to transfer items within the same organization or that have the same owners.

Issuing – the process of passing or giving products or services to eligible individuals with proper documentation of authority to receive the products or service.

Juries of executive opinion – this is where the opinions of top executives jointly serve as the basis to prepare forecasts.

Labor intensive – is a major problem for the hospitality industry as machines have not been developed to provide the majority of work to replace employees.

Labor legislation – is any type of law that is enacted that can affect labor laws.

Labor skills – refer to the knowledge, skills, and ability of the available employees.

Labor sources – the labor sources normally consist of the labor market within the demographic area surrounding the hospitality operation.

Leftovers – are products that are remaining because the total amount forecasted on the production sheet was not requested by the guest.

Life cycle curve – is a means of illustrating how a business or products will normally go through the four stages of starting, growing, maturing, and declining

Limited menu – is more closely associated with the quick service industry and is used to reduce waste and target a specific market.

Major events – are events of such magnitude that they can have a major significance in increasing or decreasing sales.

Marker – a marker is an approval of credit for a specific amount.

Marketing expense – this is an expense that will help market or promote the operation to the guests. Examples include direct mailings, radio spots, and newspaper advertisements.

Marketing research – entails establishing the possible success of a business by defining whether the external environment is willing and able to support the possible success of the business.

Markup – is often referred to as gross profit or margin, is the difference between the cost of the products and the selling price. The percent of markup can be based on the cost percentage of selling price. The markup for products must be large enough to cover operating expenses and have an amount left over for net profit.

Measuring efficiency – in the area of labor, is a means of determining how efficiency the hospitality operation is in spending it labor dollars. Methods of measuring efficiency of labor dollars spent is sales per labor dollar, sales per man-hour worked or sales per employee and the use of those standards for comparison.

Menu – a list of products or services provided by an organization and all business activities concerning the utilization of resources such as location, facilities, equipment; personnel must be designed to support the menu.

Menu mix – alludes to the different products that are on the menu and their amount of contribution margin.

Minimum Standards for Internal Controls (MICS) – the regulations that casinos have to follow.

Missing checks – are guest checks that have been misplaced or stolen. This creates a very complicated situation because management may not have any real means of determining the amount, honesty, or method for having a misplaced check.

Mission statement – informs as to what type of business the operation is conducting and may include the method in which the operation conducts business and the anticipated market.

Moving averages – are compiled based upon average past values of a time series. This method is also very popular due to its simple and quick calculation.

Music and entertainment expense – this will include royalties paid to music associations to for playing certain music in the establishment or hiring an entertainer to perform in the operation.

Mutually exclusive projects – these are a set of projects proposed for a company where only one project needs to be selected.

National standards – are those percentages, especially in the area of prime costs, that are used by industry to gauge how efficient and successful comparative operations are.

Net present value – is a method of ranking investing by deducting the initial investment from the future cash flows generated by a project, discounted at rate of the cost of capital.

Net profit – is the amount of money that remains after operating expenses have been paid and the percent of net profit is based on the selling price.

Non-controllable expense – this is an expense which management has no control over. The owner normally is the party that negotiates all these expenses. For instance, rent is negotiated by the owner and although it is an expense under the income statement, management can also do its best to best to utilize the space rented but will not decrease the amount of rent that the owners need to pay.

Objectives – are the measurable standards that must be attained for an organization to reach its goals and mission.

Off-hour menu – an excellent tool for increasing sales and for assisting managers in controlling the utilization of labor. Special menus and special prices during slow periods can be an excellent way to market to a different market segment. Off-hour menus could also provide managers with a means of utilizing leftovers from lunch and utilizing employees that must remain on duty.

Operating cash flow – is the amount of cash that an operation earns during the life of the project.

Operating expenses – are expenditures such as rent and utilities and other types of expenses that are involved in the daily cost of running an operation

Operational cost – is the cost involved in paying for the expenses to run the operational activities.

Operations budget – is also known as the revenues and expense budget. It mirrors the income statement by providing the operator an estimate of the income or loss potential before the actual accounting period. It serves as a benchmark for the company for comparison to past efforts and also as a realistic and yet attainable goal.

Opportunity cost – is the cost to a company when it foregoes a choice and decides on another.

Orientation – is an important part of having employees adjust to the new working environment and all new employees should have an orientation.

Overages/shortages – the amount of different between the cash bank that was given an employee and the amount of cash that should have been tendered. The difference in the amount could be more or less.

Par stock – or "par" is the amount of product that should be on hand between one delivery and the next.

Payback – is defined as the project cost divided by the annual cash flow. It gives the amount of time needed for a project to recover its costs.

Payouts – are funds that have been paid to guests when they win.

Payroll analysis – is the evaluation of the sum of wages as to how successful the operation is utilizing these wages.

Payroll budgeting - is a blueprint that lets management know the monetary resources that will be needed in order to achieve the estimated sales level with the proper and appropriate service standards.

Percent of markup – is the desired percentage that management would like to add to the selling price of an item. A desired percentage for marking up items and the price for a product can be obtained by dividing the dollar cost of the product by the desired percent.

Perpetual inventory - is accomplished by recording the amount of products purchased, and as items are issued for use, the amounts issued are also recorded. The amounts recorded must reflect the movement of items into and out of storage. By following this procedure it is possible to examine the perpetual inventory records to determine how much of an item is in stock at any given time.

Physical inventory – is a process that requires that a physical count be made of each product on hand.

Pilferage – is to take or consume resources without permission.

Pit podium – the area behind the games where there is access to chips.

Point-Of-Sales (POS) – is an electronic computerized system that aids in accounting for cash and other resources and can be programmed for numerous functions. The system can easily maintain sales and inventory records and can be linked to any sales outlet in the facility.

Popularity of items – defines the number of times that an item is chosen as compared to other items on the menu.

Post-audit – this is a process whereby owners and/or managers will evaluate the success of the installation or construction of a project.

Preparation and production – entails the process of preparing products for further production procedures or for direct service to the customer. It is during this process that internal controls must be implemented to ensure that quality is maintained.

Price analysis – must be obtained whenever possible because we live in a world of over-choice and a particular item can have numerous different prices.

Pricing – deals with the balancing of costs to the organization and the perception of value to guests. An operation must spend a great deal of time in establishing price because of the perception of value and the difficulty of changing prices.

Prime costs – are those primary cost associated with hospitality operations which are labor, food, and beverage costs.

Production errors – occur when mistakes are made in not following standard recipes.

Production schedule – is a worksheet designed to inform production personnel with the who, what, and when, amount, and the standard recipe number of how to prepare products.

Productivity scheduling – is a method wherein management looks into each job category to see how the estimated sales will affect each job category and during what hours. Then, managers will plan the payroll by scheduling the full, part-time, and other personnel accordingly. In certain restaurants, specific operating hours are busier while others are slower.

Professionalism – is conducting oneself in a manner that would be in keeping with organizational procedures and standards without jeopardizing, fraternizing, or compromising one's position and would set standards for employees to emulate.

Profit – is the difference between costs, revenue, and sales that are generated after break-even is reached.

Publicity – is information that is disseminated to attract public notice and differs from advertisement in that it is free.

Purchase Order – informs receiving personnel of the quantity, quality, and price thatwas negotiated. Purchase orders (POs) should be on hand to indicate what deliveries are expected. This form is used to record the products ordered and to standardize the information about those products. The quantity and quality delivered should be compared against the purchase order and receiving report to see if there are any discrepancies.

Purchasing – is the initial spending of resources to establish and operate a facility. Efforts must be made to ensure that quality and consistency are maintained at the most cost-effective price.

Purchasing cards – are credit cards that are issued to individuals within an organization who will be performing purchasing functions. Corporate purchasing cards are used to reduce the administrative costs for low-dollar direct items.

Purchasing directs – present a problem for owner and managers of largefacilities as these items are usually inexpensive and do not go into storage. Because directs do not go into storage the accountability for such items can become losses very quickly.

Purchasing strategies – will allow all personnel who are performing the purchasing task at any level to know what is expected by the organization. Staying within the framework of the strategies will allow the hospitality organization to control and reduce costs.

Quality service – is the perception of service to the quest Management can establish a standard for service but it will always be the guests perception as to whether the service is regarded as quality. The standard of service should be designed to meet or exceed guests' expectations.

Ratio analysis – is essentially a mathematical calculation of one value divided by another, expressed in the form of times or percentages. It is the presentation of such relationships that ratios generate new information, making the numbers and values more meaningful, informative, and useful. Primarily, financial ratios are used to assess the performance of businesses. Through financial ratios, absolute numbers are transformed into meaningful relative terms where owners and managers can then extract more invaluable information.

Receiving – is the process of accepting products that have been purchased by the organization and every effort must be made to ensure that the required purchase specifications are met.

Receiving report – is completed once everything checks out during the receiving process. The receiving report provides the accounting department with a detailed breakdown of what has been received on a daily basis.

Receiving tools –that equipment that should be available to open containers and to be used to verify the specifications of the order that is being received. At a minimum, receiving personnel should have the following equipment: thermometers, scales, rulers, knives, chippers, and chipboards.

Recipe conversion – is the method used to increase or decrease the yield amount of a standard recipe.

Recipe yield – is the formula amount that is developed for a standard recipe; therefore, the recipe when properly prepared will yield that amount.

Regression – regression is a statistical method to determine the effect independent variables have on dependent variables using the least squares method. The R^2 statistic, derived from regression, will have a value of 0 to 1 and it indicates the percentage of how much the independent variable can explain the changes that occurred in the dependent variable. Thus a higher R^2 value indicates that the independent variable is a better predictor of the dependent variable. For example, rooms sold can be a predictor of labor costs in the rooms department.

Relevant cash flow – these are cash flows that have to be included in a capital budget analysis such as incremental cash flow, opportunity costs, all initial investments expenses, and non-cash expenses. Sunk costs, finance costs, and maintenance costs should not be included in calculating relevant cash flows.

Reorder point – is the number of units to which the supply on hand should decrease before additional orders are placed.

Replacement – replacement in capital budgets includes replacements to increase revenues, reduce costs, or simply for maintenance and upkeep.

Requisition – is a form that is used to request supplies from storage.

Revenue centers – are those components of an operation that are actually in the business of generating revenue for as opposed to providing support services.

Sales and cash control – must be implemented to protect guest checks and cash, as cash is the most important resource that is generated by the business operation.

Sales force estimates – this is a bottom-up approach to forecasting by aggregating unit managers' forecasts to compile one for the entire organization. At a unit or departmental level, this will be done by gathering data from the first-line employees.

Sales history – is the important data concerning previous sales. It may include any sales information that management prepares to retain.

Seat turnover – is the number of times a seat or table is used by customers in a hospitality facility during a specific business time or period.

Selection – is the process of trying to choose the right person for the job.

Servable portion – or usable portion (UP) price can be completely different from the AP; and this can significantly change the overall costs to the operation.

Service – provides an opportunity to satisfy or exceed customers expectations. If service is perceived to be unsatisfactory the facility can lose sales and customers.

Simple time series – simple rules such as forecast equals last period's actual activity, or adding/subtracting a certain percentage from last period's data are called simple time series. They are especially useful for smaller scale hospitality operations where time, technology or expertise is lacking.

Site selection – can often determine the success of a business operation. Management must ensure that products can be developed, prepared, and are acceptable to the demographics of the location. Since a return on investment in a business venture is usually based on an operation succeeding in the long run, it is important to discover if there are plans for rezoning or reconstructing the area in which the facility will be constructed. Accessibility, safety and security of employees and guests are of the utmost importance to the long-range success of an operation.

Smoothing – smoothing is similar to moving average except that it gives more weight to the more recent past values of a time series, thereby discounting the older data that may not have as much impact on the forecast.

Soft count – is the count of money from the drop boxes of the gaming tables themselves.

Specifications – are descriptions written for the purchasing of a particular product and they should be written for every item that the operation intends to purchase as a direct means of carrying out its day-to-day functions.

Standard yield – is the amount remaining after a product has gone through the production process. The As Purchased (AP) weight of products can be totally different from the Usable Portion (UP).

Standardized recipe – is a formula for preparing a prescribed amount of a product and it provides all of the necessary information for preparing the product.

Standards – is a model or method that serves as a basis for comparison.

Statement analysis formula – allows a business to evaluate the true cost of accepting a credit card.

Static budget – when an operations budget reflects only one level of sales, it is known as a static budget.

Staying power – the ability to sustain business operations through the decline phase of the life cycle curve.

Stock out – this is when an operation does not have enough inventory to fill the orders.

Stores – are products that will be placed into storage as they have a long shelf life and will not be used for the delivery day's function.

Storing – entails the protection of products from deterioration and theft for future utilization.

Substitution – is the replacing in a recipe of an item of similar texture and origin so as not to distort the recipe itself.

Suggestive selling – is a process of making suggestions or recommendations to help guests recognize true needs rather than to sell them unwanted products. In this process suggestive selling can be very beneficial to the guest and the hospitality facility.

Sunk cost – is a cost that was incurred in the past and has been expensed. It should not be included in a capital budget analysis.

Support centers – are those components of an operation that are not directly involved in generating income such as housekeeping in hotels.

Surveillance – is the close observation of activities within the casino and the majority is done by camera and the surveillance room is referred to as a sensitive area.

Table d'hote – a full-course meal served at a fixed price.

Table games – are one of six categories of games and is played with chips rather than with cash.

Tagging – is accomplished during the receiving process to aid in first in first out (FIFO) procedures, which will help in preventing food from becoming deteriorated. Tagging will also assist in maintaining sanitary procedures and will help to reduce theft. If prices are placed on products during tagging, prices will be readily available during the inventory process.

Terminal cash flow – this is the total amount of cash that a project receives at the end of its life. It includes any gains or losses on the sale, any tax implications and also the return of any net working capital.

Termination – is to bring to an end the employment of an employee.

The magic number – refers to what should be the number of items on a menu. The magic number is the number of menu items that can be safely controlled and will still maximize the profit of the organization. Items should not be carried by an operation if they cannot be safely prepared, safely held and safely served. A manager will have to balance guest satisfaction, sanitation, labor skills, service required, and profit in determining the magic number.

Time and labor saving devices – any procedure that management or employees can develop to reduce labor time; these procedures can be found through the utilization of equipment, or other forms of time and motion.

Time value of money – with inflation and other factors, the value of money changes as time passes by. With astute investments, the face value of a dollar may now become two dollars while the value of goods that the same dollar will be able to purchase will not be as much.

Tolerable variance – is the amount of overage or shortage that management is willing to accept. Thus, variances on either side may occur. Management will need to decide what percentage variance is acceptable. Normally, any amount with plus or minus 1% is deemed acceptable.

Total costs – is fixed cost plus variable costs.

Training – is the process of making employees proficient with specialized instruction and training; essential in successfully accomplishing organizational goals and objectives.

Truth in advertising - is a responsibility of management to ensure that items stated on the menu are in fact what they are advertised to be. Control the mistake of misspelling and ensure that products are of the correct specifications and correct origin.

Turnover – is referred to as the number of time a goods, customers or employees are rotated during a given period.

Unethical conduct – is the practice of deviating from the principles, policies, and procedures of the organization and may or may not be for personal gain.

Uniform systems of accounts – are standard account procedures that are used within a certain industry to allow for easy comparison of operational activities and allow for the smoother transition of managerial personnel throughout the industry.

Unionism – is the principle of forming a union and once a union is formed employee cost may increase; therefore the best way of preventing unionization is to treat employees fairly.

Unit pricing – is used when evaluating product brands. From one container to another, you may pay one or two cents more per ounce for the same product. The amount of daily utilization also plays a part in the decision making process. It is important to use a convenient size of a product even if it is more expensive. The amount of labor saved by using a convenient size can warrant the utilization of a more expensive product.

Usable Portion (UP) – refers to that portion of a product that is actually of quality to sell to a customer.

Utilities expense – this included all kinds of utilities from electricity to gas, and from water usage to sewage charges.

Variable costs – are costs that usually increase as sales volume increases and decreases as sales volume decreases.

Variance analysis – The difference between the budgeted figures and the actual performance of the hospitality operation is the variance. Depending on whether it is a revenue variance or cost variance, a positive or negative difference may be favorable or unfavorable.

Variety and appeal – can be accomplished by pairing and placing foods together that will give good eye appeal and perception of value. Eye appeal can have a great deal to do with whether a meal is perceived to be outstanding or unacceptable.

Voids or over rings – occur when employees entering sales into a system enter the incorrect amount. Because an over ring or void is a cash transaction, management should ensure the correctness of the occurrence and the amount.

Win – in casino accounting and controls, win has just a slightly different bend. Win is the winnings of the casino and not the players. It is actually the winning of the operation, that means, it is the net intake of the casino after all winning wages of the players have been made. These terms apply to all table games. To put it differently: Win = Drop – Payouts

Working factor – is a fraction that can be used to convert the yield of a standard recipe. If the amount required is less than the amount yielded by the standard recipe place the amount desired over the amount yielded by the standard recipe to form a fraction. Simplify the fractions to the lowest terms to find the working factor and multiply the quantity of each ingredient in the recipe by the fraction to get the desired amounts.

Work production standards – are measurements of work performance that may be expressed in different ways. They can be expressed in terms of rooms sold, sales dollars generated, guests served, net profit level and the infamous labor cost percentage. Different departments in a hospitality operation will have their own standards.